How to Grow Herbs
for Gourmet Cooking

HOW TO GROW HERBS
FOR GOURMET COOKING

Including 100 Recipes
from 25 Countries

by

FREDERICK O. ANDERSON

HAWTHORN BOOKS, INC.

Publishers

New York

To *Lois*

HOW TO GROW HERBS FOR GOURMET COOKING

2 3 4 5 6 7 8 9 10

Contents

I

GROWING HERBS

1

"Just Lucky, I Guess"

Many visitors to Anderson Farm have asked me, "How in the world did a New York advertising executive ever get into the herb business?" This is a reasonable question, and the classic answer, "Just lucky, I guess," is true but too cursory. Therefore I should explain.

When I bought my farm here in Bucks County thirty years ago, I got the thrill only a city man can get when he owns land—lots of land—for the very first time. So I sent for every nurseryman's catalog I could hear about. And I ordered with a passion: fruit trees, shrubs, flower seeds and plants, vegetable seeds—all there was room for near the house. One catalog listed a few herb seeds—sage, thyme, marjoram, and not a great many more. I had heard of herbs in a vague way as something to improve the taste of food. I enjoyed eating. So, of course, I planted herb seeds.

Now thirty years ago "herbs" was a very esoteric subject, and very few people knew anything about it. There were almost no newspaper or magazine articles on the subject. America had very few pertinent books (although, had I but known it, there were plenty of English herb books). And what books there were seemed long on lore but short on practical instructions. In other words, I had to learn by trial and error—and the errors were

3

many. For instance, my first little herb bed had very poor drainage. By rights I shouldn't have had any herbs at all.

But, fortunately, in spite of my bungling, some of the seeds came up and grew. I tried some of the leaves on my food, and it *did* taste better—so I was off and running! The next year I planted more seeds in a better location, with much better results. After several years I heard about drying herbs to use during the winter, so I knocked together several screens and a rack to hold them, and tried it. It worked. I kept increasing the size of the herb bed and planting more kinds, until one day inspiration struck. Why not combine herbs having a strong, heavy taste (such as sage) with those having a light, flowery taste (such as basil) to get a kind of "chord" of taste which would be good on anything? After much trial and error, I arrived at a blend of nine different kinds which I called, laconically, Mixed Herbs. And I was very proud of it: You could use it on anything. Indeed, I was so proud of it that one Christmas I sent little jars of it to friends as a sort of Christmas card. A few months later several friends told me they had run out of Mixed Herbs and asked, shyly, whether they could possibly buy more from me— it was a terrible thing to ask, they knew, but they had enjoyed them so much, and so forth. They could, and did—and Anderson Farm was in the herb business!

Later I added five or six kinds of herb vinegars to "the line." (Vinegars are easy to make; I explain how to do it in Chapter 8.) Then a friend handed me a jar of mustard sauce with herbs in it and suggested I might make something like it. I decided I could do better, and finally, after long experimenting, I arrived at an Anderson Farm Herb Mustard which satisfied my palate.

After this, ideas for new products came more easily. But never the products themselves—this was always infinite, and often discouraging, trial and error. One product, a meat sauce, I recall, was my Formula Number 46 (forty-five failures ahead of it).

Another was Formula Number 74. And so on. Until I was, and am now, selling between twenty-five and thirty different herb products by mail order—herb blends, mustards, salad dressings, meat sauces, etc.—and had reached the heady eminence of, as I like to put it, "the smallest specialty-food business in the United States"!

I have included this capsule history simply to qualify the author as someone who has been working enthusiastically with herbs for thirty years. In that time I have eaten delicious herb-flavored food, have had an engrossing hobby and a small business paying a modest income. In short, it is true enough—I've been "just lucky, I guess."

In mentioning Mixed Herbs above, I said I had tried to arrive at "a chord of taste which would be good on anything." This touches on a very important subject which needs explaining: the tyranny of rules. After I had started to grow herbs, I read as much about them as I could find to read, and I began to be struck by the awe the authors seemed to have for them. I kept running across such phrases as "these magic things," "these precious little plants," and such. This seemed terribly out of focus; they were, after all, only plants—and didn't have to be "precious" if you had enough of them. Sometimes I was tempted to write an author and say, "Don't be so afraid of herbs—you're bigger than they are!"

Concurrently, I noticed a rise of rigid instructions for the use of herbs in cooking, as exemplified by a flood of herb charts. One chart from twenty to twenty-five years ago had this entry: "Savory—vegetables: in string beans, limas, peas, lentils, savory rice." Now I *knew* you could use savory with profit on many other things, and I began to resent this dictatorial attitude. It reminded me of the hanky-panky about wines in the years just after the repeal of prohibition. In case you have forgotten—or slept blissfully through it in your baby carriage—I'll give you an example.

The book, *Wines,* by Julian Street, a respected gourmet of the time, was published in 1933. It contains this litany for the use of wines with dinner:

With oysters: Chablis or a Rhine or even an Alsace
With soup: dry sherry or Madeira
With fish: a dry white wine: Alsace, Moselle, Rhine, dry Graves
With entrees: ... a not too important Claret or a Beaujolais
With red meat or game: Medoc of a good year and Cru; better, Saint-Emilion
With salad: none, if vinegar is in the dressing
With dessert: Château Yquem or some other honey-sweet Sauternes
With coffee: fine old Cognac served in balloon glasses.

This is an excellent example of the early *mystique* of wines. It is technically impeccable, but such pronouncements succeeded in frightening hostesses half to death and driving people away from wines by the millions. The reaction of most people to such elaborate rules was, "It's so complicated that, rather than make a mistake, I'll just skip the whole thing." Fortunately I had had occasion to deal with old-time wine merchants, so I knew that to people who really understood wines there was, and is, only one simple rule: The "right" wine is the one you like best.

I knew that over-ritualism had effectively discouraged many people from the use of wines, and therefore I deplored seeing herbs blighted in the same way. There is even less excuse for a mystique in herbs than in wines. That is why I sought a herb blend which would allow one to enjoy the taste of herbs without bothering to look at rules or charts. That's one way to beat the ritualistic approach. Another is to adapt the primary rule for wines: *The "right" herb is the one you like best.* If you prefer tarragon on chicken, use it! Or basil, or whatever. The main thing is: *You're* the boss!

It is pleasant to note that this early awe of herbs and diffidence about using them has, in large part, evaporated. But not entirely; even in the last few years I have heard many times, "I'd like to use herbs, but I don't know anything about them, and they seem so complicated." This book will try to make herbs seem uncomplicated—but not by the use of charts; there is no chart in the book. I feel strongly that any of the familiar seasoning herbs helps the flavor of virtually any food except dessert. Therefore, if I did draw up a chart, it would begin this way:

	Soups	Stews	Roasts	Poultry	Vegetables	Eggs	Fish	Salads
Basil	any	any	any	any	any	any	any	any
Thyme	any	any	any	any	any	any	any	any

But, you say, "If I don't know anything about cooking with herbs, how am I ever going to know which herbs to use with what?" Fair enough.

For each individual herb I will give a consensus of the outstandingly best uses. Not all the uses; just some of the best. Try some of these, and you'll soon develop preferences.

Then, of primary importance, do learn the taste of each herb as quickly as possible. The first step is to smell and chew a leaf. But this isn't nearly enough; you have to use it in food. A very good proving ground, in my experience, is to add about ½ teaspoon of chopped leaves to soft boiled eggs. You'll quickly know whether—and how well—you like the herb. An even better proving ground is a bland cheese. Mix a 3-ounce package of cream cheese with 1 tablespoon of sour cream and 1 tablespoon of whiskey. Separate this mixture into three little dishes to test three herbs, and to each, add 2 teaspoons or more of the herb you want to test, chopped finely. Make sure you use enough of the herb so that the taste comes through. Or you can use a mild Cheddar, if you wish, in the same proportions. You will end up with three interesting cracker spreads. This is also a good way to test combinations of herbs, fresh or dried. After you know thoroughly the taste of each herb, you won't need herb charts.

This is one of the small things I have tried to convey in this book. The major things are these:

First, I have tried to provide the kind of simple, explicit, detailed instructions for raising herbs which I was so eager for, years ago, but couldn't find.

Second, to give you some idea of the power herbs have to make food taste delicious, I am sharing with you some of the best recipes my wife and I have collected in traveling over the world for the past years. Many are not in their original form; we have added herbs and otherwise changed them, again by trial and error. But to our palates they are now superb.

Third, I have tried to condense some of the most interesting recipes and lore I have collected over the years, on the assumption that you, too, are interested in the subject—or will become so. Some are recipes currently useful, such as a sauce for roast wild boar from the time of the Roman Empire (you can use it on any roasted meat). Some of the ideas are superstitious and childlike. And some are remarkably perceptive for people who lacked the benefits of scientific medicine. In any case, they represent the days when herbs were—literally—a matter of life or death. Thus, as a herb student, you will want to know about them.

And, finally, I have tried to convey a point of view which, I feel most earnestly, can contribute vastly to your enjoyment of herbs. It is to do your own experimenting—and thus become self-reliant. No one will ever know your tastes in food as well as you know them yourself, and therefore no one has a right to dictate to you. It can be summarized this way: *Learn the basic principles; learn the taste of each herb; then throw away the rule book.*

Actually, there are three ways to read this book:

1. If you simply want to grow herbs and cook with them, then you can skip Chapters 7 through 10 and skip the background material given for each herb.

2. If you now grow herbs and want simply to get more good herb recipes (and why be modest—these are truly great), then you can read only Section II.

3. However, if you find yourself really interested in herbs, then I hope you'll enjoy the whole book.

Whichever way you read it—*Bon appétit!*

2

Fifteen Questions You'll Be Asked Once *You* Become a Herb Expert

After you have started to grow herbs and to flavor your food with them, a lot of your guests will quickly come to consider you an authority—and ask you questions. So you really should have your answers ready. As a starter, here are some of the questions most often asked by people who come to visit Anderson Farm and the answers I've given.

The first one is personal:

1. *Question:* Mr. Anderson, I notice that you pronounce the *h* in "herb." I've always said "erb." Which is correct?

Answer: They're both correct in Webster—so it's dealer's choice. "Urb" prevails in best United States usage, although "hurb" is also used. In England "hurb" now prevails in best usage; if you say "urb" in England you are considered a cockney. I say "hurb" as a personal nod of respect to the English who are the deans of the herb world, you might say. (And, parenthetically, that is why this book will speak of "a herb," etc.) But, I repeat, it's your choice.

10

2. *Question:* Just exactly what is a herb, anyway?

Answer: For our purposes, it is any plant whose leaves or seeds or even roots give a flavor which improves the taste of food. If you want to be technical, Webster's third definition (after "a seed plant which does not develop woody stems" and "grass or herbage collectively") is: "A plant of economic value; specif. one used for medicinal purposes, or for its sweet scent or flavor." Or, if you want to be poetic, Charlemagne is supposed to have given this definition (and he probably did): "The friend of physicians and the praise of cooks."

Both definitions are interesting as showing that herbs are now, and for many centuries have been, used for medicines and cosmetics as well as food flavorings. But this book has no intention of invading the fields of Elizabeth Arden or the American Medical Association. Our serious concern here is only with food, and any references to medicines or cosmetics will be those of folklore.

3. *Question:* What is the difference between herbs and spices, or are they the same?

Answer: No, they are not the same. Spices are defined as "the buds, leaves, seeds, roots or bark of aromatic, pungent tropical or subtropical plants." A simple rule-of-thumb difference between them is that spices, virtually always, are hot on the tongue—and herbs are not. I don't mean only the obvious hot ones such as pepper and ginger; the staples—cloves, cinnamon, nutmeg, and the like—all are hot on the tongue. In other words, to whatever slight degree, they irritate the inside of the mouth. Herbs do not.

4. *Question:* If you're on a special diet, do you have to stop using herbs?

Answer: Naturally that depends on the diet, and only a doctor could give the answer. If you're on a salt-free diet, for instance, you certainly can use herbs. In fact, for years we've sold our dried herbs to hospitals all across the United States specifically to flavor the food of patients on salt-free diets.

5. *Question:* What would you say were the very most essential four or five herbs?

Answer: The "big four" are usually considered to be basil, thyme, savory, oregano—and I certainly agree. For the fifth, you could toss a coin between sage and dill.

6. *Question:* If you could only grow one single herb, which would you select?

Answer: Basil.

7. *Question:* What is the relation between fresh and dried herbs as to the amount used in a recipe?

Answer: A teaspoon of dried herbs should have the same flavor strength as 2 teaspoons of fresh herbs.

8. *Question:* How long can you keep dried herbs?

Answer: If you keep them in an airtight jar, they'll still have a lot of flavor after a year. They'll even have *some* flavor for a long time after that—but why bother with something inferior?

9. *Question:* What is the difference in taste between fresh herbs and dried herbs?

Answer: In the finished recipe there should be no difference.

10. *Question:* Are herbs hard to grow?

Answer: No. Fortunately they are among the easiest to grow of all plants. Insects don't bother them; they seem to repel insects. They're virtually immune to plant diseases. And they don't have to be pampered as to soil and care. (Of course, you'll get better results if you do pamper them a little bit, as is explained later on.)

11. *Question:* What is the correct role of herbs in flavoring food? That is, how strong should the herb flavor be in relation to the food flavor?

Answer: Herbs should *enhance* the natural flavor of the food, not *cover* it. Indeed, if you taste the herbs clearly, you've used too much. For example, two good pinches of a dried herb blend in soft-boiled eggs should make you feel you are eating perfectly wonderful eggs; you taste egg, not herbs. (And I do mean "pinches"—as much as you can pick up by pinching your thumb and forefinger together.) You might describe the taste as "like eggs but better!" For another example, the superb Italian dish, Saltimbocca Romana: You put a few leaves (three) of fresh sage between a slice of veal and a slice of ham before cooking. The taste you get is that of a perfectly marvelous meat. Sage is a very strong herb, but you don't taste the sage as such at all (if you do, you've used too much). In other words, the function of the sage is to make the meat taste better; but it is indispensable in this dish to give the full potential flavor. (And, incidentally, if a restaurant serves you Saltimbocca Romana without the sage leaves between the slices, send it back; the kitchen doesn't know Italian cooking.)

12. *Question:* What are the herbs used in *fines herbes* and *bouquet garni?*

Answer: Fines herbes has almost as many variations as there are cooks, but there is general agreement on parsley, chives, chervil, tarragon, basil, and thyme. Rosemary is also sometimes used. You don't have to use all of them at once; for instance, basil, thyme, chives, and parsley is an excellent combination. In southern France and Italy, oregano, sage, and fennel are often used. In all cases the leaves are chopped very finely.

Bouquet garni also has many variants, but there is general agreement on parsley, a bay leaf, thyme, basil, and savory; rosemary, celery, or lovage are often added. You tie the stems together to make a little bouquet if the herbs are fresh. If you use dried herbs, tie them up in a little square of cheesecloth. Add it to the soup or stew as you start to cook, and remove it before serving.

13. *Question:* When you cut herbs, how much of the plant do you cut?

Answer: For fresh herbs, cut only what you'll need at

the moment, which is just a few sprigs. If you're going to dry the leaves, you can cut as much as two thirds of the plant, leaving the rest to start growing again.

14. *Question:* Should you put herbs in every dish in a meal? Do you have to flavor everything with them to epitomize "gourmet" cooking?

Answer: In the first place, you don't *have* to do anything about herb flavors—and I urge you not to become a slave to customs unless you're a very willing one. An old friend, Tom Warrington, simply hates the taste of herbs—or thinks he does, which is the same thing—and likes his steak and mashed potatoes plain. I, on the other hand, think steak tastes better with herb butter and that mashed potatoes, as well as baked potatoes, are much better off with a little sour cream and chives. Neither of us could ever budge the other—and it would be foolish to try, because we're both happy. In other words: No, you certainly shouldn't put herbs in every dish in a meal, unless you prefer the taste that way. Upon reviewing the menus here at Anderson Farm —I mean the day-to-day, non-guest ones—I find we use herbs in *nearly* every dish. The exceptions are those things which have such a superb and complete flavor in themselves that it seems a pity to change them with anything at all. Lamb chops is one of these; prime ribs of beef is another. Lobster qualifies, and asparagus just might—although the decision between plain butter and herb butter for asparagus is a delicate one. However, the lamb chops would be accompanied by new potatoes with chives and parsley, zucchini-and-tomato casserole with mixed herbs and garlic, and a Greek salad with herb French dressing—so there's no herb starvation here. In short, don't let anyone tell you how many dishes to put herbs in, except yourself and your family.

15. *Question:* How long does it take from planting the seeds to using the herbs I've grown?

Answer: Germination (for the seed to sprout and appear above the surface) takes six to fifteen days for most of the plants we will want to grow. If the plants are kept moist, as they should be from the time they appear above the surface, they should reach a height of 1½ inches in about twelve days. By the time they reach 2 inches—in about a week more—you can start to thin out the row (as explained in the next chapter), and you can use the discards in your food. So "seeds to food" should take roughly twenty-five to thirty-four days depending on the kind of plant.

3

A Small Kitchen Garden
for Fresh Herbs

To make it as clear and simple as possible, let's divide this chapter into four sections:

1. Which herbs should you start with?
2. Where should you plant them?
3. How should you plant them?
4. How should you take care of them?

So now let's plant our first herb garden.

WHICH HERBS SHOULD YOU START WITH?

If you read the chapter headings and saw that Chapter 9 was about a garden of 234 herbs, you may have had the sinking feeling that growing herbs was so complicated it would be better not to start. Well, take heart; that is a garden of six hundred years ago, and most of the herbs were for medicines. The cooking herbs are much simpler. Actually, people who know herbs will quickly narrow the list down to twenty—or even a dozen— basic herbs which can fill all cooking requirements except the very exotic.

If this is going to be your first herb garden, there is a great advantage, I think, in limiting yourself to only six or eight for purposes of ease and simplicity—and mastering the growth and cultivation of these to see whether you really enjoy it. This way your investment in time and trouble is cut to a minimum. Then, later, you can branch out to others.

In a selection of six or eight, we might touch base by starting with what the French think are most useful and therefore use in their classic combinations, *fines herbes* and *bouquet garni*. As we saw in Chapter 2, the exact combination of each varies from cook to cook, but those most often used are included in this list of thirteen:

basil	parsley
bay	rosemary
chervil	sage
chives	savory
fennel	tarragon
lovage	thyme
oregano	

Now these are *very* fine herbs indeed! However, what we should seek in a first garden is a combination of the very most useful and those which are fairly easy to grow, and which are reasonably "beginner-proof." On this basis, some on the above list don't qualify. Rosemary winter-kills north of Virginia, and bay north of Georgia. Chervil, frankly, does not always come up from seed and by rights should have partial shade. And parsley is sometimes very stubborn about coming up. So let's save these for a later garden.

From my own experience, I would say that the eight herbs which qualify best—and which are the eight most indispensable —are these:

basil	sage
chives	summer savory
dill	tarragon
oregano	thyme

But if even a planting of eight scares you, don't hesitate to cut it down to whatever number you would feel comfortable with— start with two or three or four. Basil, thyme, savory and oregano are usually considered to be the "big four." Let's find out something about these herbs.

BASIL (*Ocimum basilicum*)

Sweet basil rhymes with "dazzle." This is one of the very most useful herbs. It's an annual and grows eighteen to twenty-four inches high. The flowers are small and white, on spikes. (But, of course, you don't want them to come to full bloom; that weakens the plant and dries up the aromatic oils. Pinch off the flower buds before they open.) It needs a sunny spot and is very hardy. You can grow from seed; germination takes about six days. There are two other species of basil: dwarf basil (*O. minimum*) which has either green or purple leaves (the latter is sometimes known as "sacred basil"), and curly or Italian basil (*O. crispum*) which has curly leaves considerably larger than those of sweet basil. Sweet or curly are the varieties to grow.

Uses. Add the chopped leaves to soups—tomato, bean, turtle. Put in chopped meats and sausages. In stews. Add to a butter sauce for fish. In any egg dish. Sprinkle on peas, eggplant, cucumbers. Sprinkle on lamb chops before broiling. Add to veal, beef, liver. Good on poultry. Basil seems to have a natural affinity for any tomato dish—as Italians know very well. Indeed in Italy— and in Spain, too, for that matter—basil is virtually always in any tomato sauce. You'll find this herb a pleasure to work with; it's so aromatic, with a clovelike smell and taste.

Background. Basil has a long and honorable history. It has been in use for thousands of years. The word derives from *basileus,* the Greek word for king. This may have a connection with French chefs sometimes calling it *l'herbe royale.* At any rate, the old herbalist, Parkinson, wrote, "The smell of Basil is so excellent that it is fit for a king's house." It was in the kitchen gardens in Roman times. In Italy it signified love—and in the countryside probably still does. At any rate, it is called colloquially "Kiss me, Nicholas" (*Baccia Nicolo*), and in the countryside a boy calling on his girl friend sometimes has a sprig of *basilico* behind his ear—to show *fidelity!* In India it has signified sanctity and has been a sacred plant for many centuries. In Elizabethan England it was one of the many "strewing herbs." (In the mid-1500's aromatic herbs took the place of rushes to put on the floors; after they got too filthy they were swept out and replaced.) In Tudor England basil was sniffed for "nervous headaches"— that is, the dried herb was used as snuff. And an old folk belief was that pots of basil in the house would drive away flies. They also kept witches away. Basil made its way from the Middle East to Greece, Italy, Spain, France, and England. It reached North America early in the seventeenth century and was a favorite kitchen herb of the American colonists. In other words, when you enjoy basil you can be sure you're part of a very large company.

THYME (*Thymus vulgaris*)

There are many species of thyme (pronounced "time")—I'm looking at this moment at a selected list of thirty, and there are some sixty altogether—but the best for a kitchen garden is the English, broad-leaved version of *Thymus vulgaris*. It is a perennial and grows to a height of about 12 inches. You can grow it from seed, and germination takes about ten days. It needs a sunny location.

At some time in the future you may want to grow other varieties, especially *Thymus serpyllum*, creeping thyme, which is fine in rock gardens and simply great growing between flagstones, because when you step on it you release the delightful pungent thyme aroma. The two most useful creeping thymes are *T. ser-*

pyllum album—white flowers—and *T. serpyllum coccineum*—crimson flowers. However, our interest now is in thyme for cooking.

Uses. Thyme has a very strong, pungent flavor, and too much of it can overpower a food. But if you use it with restraint, which you will quickly learn to do, you can achieve real subtlety in taste. Sprinkle the fresh leaves in meat sauces; put it in soups as they cook—onion, tomato, pea, vegetable. Mix it with chopped meat and meat loaf. In stuffed eggs and omelets. In poultry stuffing. It's fine with lamb, mutton, veal, and pork. Cook it with rice, peas, carrots, onions, and asparagus. Sprinkle it on sliced tomatoes and on shirred eggs. Thyme has a natural affinity for fish and shellfish. It will liven nearly any fish dish, and it's excellent in chowders and oyster stews. (*Note*: Some people add a pinch of thyme to their tea.)

Background. It is believed that thyme (and a few other herbs) was used by the ancient Greeks to burn before their gods, in temples, before they started to use it in cooking. In any case, it is an ancient herb with a long history of use. In past centuries it was a symbol of strength and bravery. Apparently the origin of this was that in medieval times an infusion of thyme was added to the bath water, and the aromatic bath gave a tired soldier renewed strength, which made him feel brave! It is still used to a slight extent as an aromatic bath, and I daresay it would be very refreshing. An infusion of thyme—thyme tea—was considered a sure cure for "that troublesome complaint, the nightmare." It was also thought good for nervous headaches—and hangovers. Thyme, also, was a strewing herb, and the floors of castles and monasteries and churches were strewn with it. In the last century in America it was used in clothes chests to keep out moths. The word "thyme" is connected with the Greek word to fumigate, because it was long ago recognized as having antiseptic qualities. The Elizabethans believed that, made into an ointment, it "took away swelling and helped sciatica." Nicholas Culpeper, writing in 1684, says, "It is a noble strengthener of the lungs, as notable a one as grown . . . it purges the body of phlegm and is an excellent remedy for shortness of breath." This seems very perceptive of him when we reflect that thyme is a principal ingredient— probably the "magic" one—of the contemporary cough medicine, Pertussin.

Thyme is another herb which originated in the Middle East and spread to the shores of the Mediterranean. It still flourishes there; one of the most exotic kinds of honey in the world is the Mount Hymettus, Greece, honey from the millions of thyme plants which carpet its slopes. And in Italy, Sicily, Greece, and southern Spain you see thyme plants growing all around you as a weed. *What a weed!*

SAVORY (*Satureia hortensis*)

Savory is an annual which grows 16 to 18 inches high. You can grow it from seed, and germination takes about ten days. It has small narrow leaves and tiny purple flowers. There are many species of savory—about 130 in all, including the well-known winter savory (*S. montana*), a perennial. But the most satisfactory is *Satureia hortensis,* summer savory. It is probably called "summer" savory because it gives the best flavor when harvested first in early summer. (You can get a second harvest later.) It needs a sunny spot and very little fertilizer.

Uses. Boil it with cabbage, Brussels sprouts, turnips, and peas; a sprig in the boiling water will keep down the heavy cabbage smell. Good with boiled ham or any other boiled meat. Excellent in soups—potato, bean, pea, lentil. Use it in stuffings. Use it in the cooking water for asparagus and artichokes. Delicious when added to scrambled eggs. Excellent in lamb and other stews and chicken fricassee. Use it in salads. It's especially good on fish. And above all, it has a natural affinity for string beans. Indeed, in Germany and Switzerland, summer savory is known as *Bohnenkraut,* which means "the string bean herb." This affinity is recognized here, too. For example, a Pennsylvania Dutch neighbor, when she cans string beans, will always ask me for a cup or so of fresh savory, so she can put a few leaves in each jar. This is a very useful herb—and subtly delicious.

Background. Savory is another herb whose use goes back for more than two thousand years. It originated in the eastern Mediterranean and was used for centuries by the Greeks and Romans. The latter took it to England, and it eventually became popular with the Saxons who used it in their soups and meats. Charlemagne included savory in a list he wrote in A.D. 812 of the plants he wanted in the royal garden—kitchen garden, that is (which also included onions, garlic, leeks, shallots, celery, parsley, chervil, coriander, dill, lettuce, poppy, radishes, parsnips, carrots, cabbage, beets, etc.). It was also included in his "physic" or medicine garden (along with kidney bean, rose, watercress, cumin, lovage, fennel, tansy, sage, rue, pennyroyal, peppermint, rosemary, etc.). In the sixteenth century it was recommended that the fresh leaves be laid on bee stings to relieve the pain. (I've never tried this, because, fortunately, I've only been stung once by a bee. And then, I confess, I forgot all about savory.) It was thought excellent for the colic. The juice was recommended as an eye lotion, to "clear a dull sight." Made into a poultice with flour it was held to "give ease to the sciatica."

Savory was brought to America by the early colonists and has always been one of our favorite seasonings.

OREGANO (*Origanum vulgare*)

Oregano—"wild marjoram"—is a perennial which grows to about 2 feet. The tiny flowers are rose-purple or white. It is best planted from cuttings or root divisions, which means, naturally, if you are starting from scratch, you should buy plants. It needs a sunny location and fairly good soil, well drained. It will continue growing for years if it is cared for, because it is very hardy. There are more than thirty species of marjoram, of which this and sweet marjoram (Marjorana hortensis) are the most used. Hereafter we will use oregano and marjoram interchangeably.

Uses. Sprinkle chopped leaves on roast beef, lamb, or pork. Use it in salads, especially shrimp. In stuffings. Use it on peas, beans, spinach, and tomatoes. In soups—tomato, lentil, onion. Excellent on chicken. Add it to scrambled eggs, omelets, and sprinkle on boiled eggs. Good in most Italian dishes and a *must* for spaghetti sauces. Use in chopped meats and stews. Excellent on squash and eggplant. Add a pinch to cheese spreads. Especially good with veal and calves liver. It adds a new flavor to potato salad and creamed potatoes. You can see from this wide range what a useful herb oregano is, and as you work with it, you will discover many more uses.

Background. Origanum comes from two Greek words—*oros,* meaning "mountain" and *ganos,* meaning "brightness, beauty." They refer to the plant's native home, the mountains ringing the Mediterranean. Actually it started in Syria and Palestine and was spread around Europe by the Greeks and Romans. The ancient Greeks valued marjoram as a food flavoring and also as a tonic. Vergil is only one of many Roman writers who wrote the praises of its delightful aroma. In Greece and Rome it was the custom to crown newly married couples with wreaths of marjoram as a symbol of happiness hoped for. Because marjoram was a symbol of happiness, the ancient Greeks planted it on graves, and thought that it had to be there so that their dear ones could rest in peace.

The old herbalists thought highly of it also. Gerard said in 1597 that it "easeth the tooth ache being chewed in the mouth. The leaves dried and mingled with honey put away black and blew markes after stripes and bruises, being applied thereto." He also advised a tea made of the leaves for "those that are given over to much sighing," and added "oregany is very good against the wambling of the stomacke." (I wonder whether we should not bring this expressive word "wambling" back into the language?) Culpeper thought that "it restores the appetite being lost" and that "the juice dropped into the ears, helps deafness."

As a Mediterranean native, oregano is extensively used by the Spanish (who took it to Mexico where it is much used) and the Italians. Indeed, a pizza without oregano is like a cup without a saucer.

SAGE (*Salvia officinalis*)

Sage is a shrubby perennial which grows to about 2 feet. It may well be the best known of all herbs. It grows readily from seed, and germination takes about fifteen days. The flowers are bluish-purple and very handsome (but, of course, if you're growing sage for flavor, you won't let them come to full bloom). It likes a light, well-drained soil in a sunny location. The soil doesn't have to be rich if it is not a heavy and clayey soil. After a sage plant is established, you can usually get at least two cuttings in a season, but the last one must not be later than September or the plant will be seriously weakened. There are more than five hundred species of salvia. The three other common ones are *S. sclarea,* clary sage; *S. rutilans,* pineapple sage (the leaf has the smell of pineapple when bruised); and *S. splendens,* the common red salvia used in flower gardens. But *S. officinalis* is the "eating" kind.

Uses. Sage has a remarkably strong and pungent flavor, so it must be used very gently. Incidentally, a little chopped parsley mixed with the chopped sage leaves will help to tone down the flavor. Add it to cottage cheese, cream cheese, and cheese omelets. Sprinkle over poultry and veal. Use in stewed tomatoes, string beans, lima beans, eggplant. It's used in most poultry stuffings. Add it to sharp cheese spreads and to melted butter before basting fish. Good in stews. Excellent with game. It has a natural affinity for pork, and probably it helps one digest it. The English drink sage tea and state, "It is said to be very good for the stomach."

Background. The name of sage, *Salvia,* comes from the Latin *salveo,* "I am well." The Romans borrowed from the Greeks and

put sage in many dishes—and were probably the ones who originated sage stuffings for rich meats such as pork and duck. The
Romans took it to England where the use of it has flourished
since. "Eat sage in May, and you'll live for aye," is an old English
jingle. Old people in rural England take it seriously and attribute
their long life to sage tea in spring and fall, to sage sandwiches
for supper, and to chopped sage in their porridge. Before
the introduction of tea from China, the English drank sage tea
entirely—and the Chinese came to like sage so well they would
trade two pounds of China tea for one pound of sage. In the ninth
century, Walafrid Strabo in *The Little Garden* says, "Amongst
my herbs, sage holds the place of honor; of good scent it is and
full of virtue for many ills." John Gerard in the sixteenth century
said that it "is singular good for the head and braine, quickeneth
the sences and memory, strengtheneth the sinews, restoreth health
to those that have the palsie." In short, an all-purpose drug. He
also wrote of putting it "up into the nostrils" for clearing the head
—a sixteenth-century version of snuff. Sage originated on the
shores of the Mediterranean, and nowadays it, as well as thyme,
grows as a weed in Greece, Italy, and Spain.

TARRAGON (*Artemisia dracunculus*)

Tarragon, or French tarragon, is a bushy perennial which
grows to about 18 inches. It bears tiny yellowish flowers and
very narrow leaves about an inch long with an anise or licorice
taste. The plants almost never form seed, so you must start with
plants. Thereafter you can propagate by root divisions—and this
should be done about every two years anyway to keep the plant
healthy. Tarragon will grow in sun or in partial shade if the soil is
well-drained and light, preferably sandy. There is another variety,
Russian tarragon, an annual grown from seed, but it's vastly inferior to the French variety.

Uses. In vinegar, of course. Very good in mixed salads. Use it
in ravigote, cream, bearnaise, and tartar sauces. In chicken dishes.

In butter sauce for fish. Add it to cheese spreads. Excellent in seafood cocktails, with shrimp, crab, salmon. Use it in seafood salads and green salads. Add it to scrambled eggs and omelets. Very good with lamb, veal, sweetbreads. Use it in chicken and tomato soups. It adds a new flavor to cauliflower, tomatoes, peas, spinach. Try to think what food would be livened up by an anise flavor—and let yourself go!

Background. Tarragon, like so many other herbs, originated in western Asia and the Middle East. We know it was used by the Greeks as early as the fifth century B.C. because it was one of the simples of Hippocrates, a contemporary of Pericles and Plato. (I might explain in passing that centuries ago a "simple" was a medicine—which meant a herb—thought to be a remedy for one particular ailment. Of course, sometimes several simples were combined into a single remedy—a sort of buckshot treatment.) More than half of some four hundred simples used by Hippocrates are in use today, and tarragon is one of them. (Others, interestingly enough, are basil, sage, thyme, rosemary.) Tarragon was included in the garden of the Benedictine monastery of St. Gall, near Lake Constance, Switzerland, during the ninth century. In France, the peasants called it *esdragon* or *estragon,* meaning *l'herbe au dragon,* and it was known in olden times as a specific for healing the bite of wild beasts and mad dogs. On a lighter note, it was recommended by botanists in the thirteenth century for sweetening the breath. In short, tarragon is a venerable herb as well as a very delicious one. It has been called the king of herbs—but then, so has basil.

DILL (*Anethum graveolens*)

Dill is an annual which grows to a height of about 3 feet. It is easily grown from seed, and germination takes ten or twelve days. The leaves are blue-green and feathery, resembling fennel (indeed, Culpeper says "so like fennel that it deceives many"). The tiny yellow flowers grow in umbels so they look something like small umbrellas. It needs a sunny location and light, well-drained soil which need not be rich but should be fairly good. It does not transplant easily, so you should sow it where you want it and then thin out so the plants are about 6 to 8 inches apart. When it reaches a height of about 18 inches, it will need to be staked so it won't be blown over by the wind. The dried seeds are the primary crop, but the green leaves, chopped, have many uses. To keep a continuous supply of young leaves, you can resow every three weeks.

Uses. Use the *seeds,* whole or ground, in soups, such as bean and beet. Use in spiced beets. Excellent with cucumbers. In sauerkraut. In fish sauces. Sprinkle on seafood salads, on potato salad. Sprinkle on shirred eggs and add to scrambled eggs. Excellent in gravies. For pickling, of course.

Use the fresh *leaves,* chopped—rather sparingly, since the taste of dill is somewhat sour and bitter—in cottage cheese, cream cheese, and potato salad. Sprinkle over steaks and chops when they're almost broiled. In soups and stews. Fine with new potatoes. Add to the cooking water for squash, cauliflower, green beans. Good in creamed chicken. Use dill butter on broiled or fried fish. Add to the water when boiling shrimp—it seems to reduce the strong fish smell as well as giving a piquant taste.

Background. The name comes from the Norse word *dilla,* "to lull," and it used to be thought a remedy for sleeplessness. It was also used to sharpen the appetite. It originated in Mediterranean lands and in southern Russia; it grows wild, currently, in parts of Africa and Asia. The Romans spread it across Europe and were very fond of it. They used it as garlands for state occasions and in decorating banquet halls, where its pungency might have helped clear the heavy air. Their poets praised it; Vergil called it "this pleasant and fragrant plant." There is mention of it in an early Anglo-Saxon herbal. It is also mentioned in the Bible as one of the tithes paid by the pharisees. Dill was another of the herbs in the garden of the St. Gall monastery in the ninth century. Culpeper wrote, "The Dill, being boiled and drank, is good to ease swellings and pains. . . . It stays the hiccough, being boiled in wine, and but smelled unto, being tied in cloth." Parkinson agreed about its value for hiccoughs: "Some use to eate the seed of Dill to stay the hiccough." And as early as the first century A.D. Dioscorides claimed that "ye decoction of ye dried leaves and seeds of Dill, being drank, stayeth ye hickets." Generations ago, when Sunday sermons were very long, women carried dill seeds to church to nibble on as a diversion so they and their children wouldn't go to sleep. This was done so generally that dill seeds were called meetin' house seeds.

CHIVES (*Allium schoenoprasum*)

Chives, a member of the onion family, are perennials which grow 8 to 10 inches high. The flowers are lavender-colored pompoms, the leaves slender, dark green, and grasslike. Planting can be done from seed, but it is very chancy, and the sensible thing to do is buy plants. Chives want a good soil, well drained, in a sunny location. They are very hardy and will grow very well indoors. This is fortunate, because they cannot be dried; a dried chive stalk has no more smell or taste than dried hay. The bulbs multiply very rapidly and should be dug up every two or three years and divided; otherwise they become overcrowded. You can divide each clump into several smaller clumps and set each division 4 to 6 inches from the others; or you can set each bulb out in the same way as onion sets. The flowers are attractive enough to qualify for rock gardens. But if you grow them for flavoring, be sure to keep the flowers picked, or the stems will lose their flavor.

Uses. Add the chopped fresh leaves to soups. Mix with cottage cheese and cream cheese. Excellent in green salads. Add to sour cream for a sauce for baked potatoes. Use as a garnish for boiled potatoes. Fine in omelets and scrambled eggs. Excellent in stews and casseroles. Sprinkle on vichysoisse, of course, and also on bean and asparagus soups. In short, use chives anywhere you think a little onion flavor belongs.

Background. Chives are a form of onion, even though they are the most delicately flavored member of the family. And the onion family has magic and superstition in its background. For example, it seems that when Satan fled the Garden of Eden, garlic shot up from the spot where he put his right foot, and onion from where he put his left foot. Perhaps chives sprang from a spot he touched with a finger? Like other forms of onion, chives were used all over Asia millennia ago and were known in China before 3000 B.C. As with other important herbs, the Romans spread chives all over Europe, including England. It is said—although I haven't myself seen them—that many of the Roman importations, chives, chervil, parsley, coriander, rosemary, and such, may still be seen growing lavishly in the neighborhood of old Roman camps. Chives were another herb in Charlemagne's garden. And to suggest the versatility of the *Allium* group, this is what Culpeper has to say of the onion: "They do somewhat provoke appetite, increase thirst, ease the belly . . . help the biting of a mad dog and of other venemous creatures. They much conduce to help an inveterate cough. It hath been held by divers country people a great preservative against infection, to eat Onions fasting with bread and salt. The juice of Onions is good for either scalding or burning by fire, water, or gunpowder, and used with vinegar, takes away all blemishes, spots and marks in the skin." Now who could ask for more than that? Currently, chives are believed to help the digestion of fatty foods.

WHERE SHOULD YOU PLANT THEM?

The answer to this question is governed by the space you have available. If, for instance, your back yard is mostly shady, but you *have* got a sunny space for a vegetable garden, then by all means plant your herbs in the vegetable garden. Plant the annuals in rows with the other crops, and plant the perennials together in one corner or along one edge, so they can be undisturbed when your garden is dug up or plowed up each spring. If your back yard is shady, and you have no space for a vegetable garden, you're still not beaten. You can plant your herbs in fourteen-inch or sixteen-inch wooden tubs, which you can put in whatever sunny spots there may be on your property, even lining the front walk, if necessary.

If, on the other hand, you have plenty of space, you're in clover. Then you can put all your herbs together in one bed, which is much more fun than having them separated, particularly when one is learning about them and is interested in comparing their growing habits. You can locate the bed in any spot which

1. has full sun;
2. is well drained;
3. is as close to the kitchen door as possible.

The first point is of paramount importance. You can't grow most herbs successfully without plenty of sun, and you can't grow any in the list above.

The second point is important also but somewhat less so: While natural drainage can be simulated, as we will see in the next section, there is no good way to duplicate sunlight. Naturally, though, you mustn't select a site where water stands after a rain. The best place is on a gentle slope.

The third point is merely a convenience. It's nice to be able to dash out of the kitchen for a few basil leaves, or chives, as the spirit moves, but walking fifty feet is not really much more of a struggle than walking fifteen feet.

So, having decided on the site, what shape should you make the bed? Well, what about a plain rectangle? But that's too simple, you say? Perhaps it is. I have seen small herb beds in the shape of circles—and triangles and crescents. I have even seen herbs planted between the spokes of an old wagon wheel. But it seems to me that this contradicts the purpose of "a small kitchen garden for fresh herbs," which is not for show but simply to produce as easily as possible the herbs needed in cooking. In another chapter we will look at some of the really fancy shapes used by gardeners of several centuries ago—and I urge you to try them if you feel ambitious, because the fancy formal gardens now in this country are really beautiful. But for the growing of only six or eight plants each of eight kinds of herbs, the most practical shape is the rectangle. I might say that this shape is not only "the one that comes naturally" to the ignorant beginner, as I was when I started, but it is dignified by a long tradition. Medieval-castle herb gardens, old English farmhouse gardens, the early colonists' gardens —all had the rectangular shape. Not that we care too much about that. What we do care about is that this is the simplest, easiest-to-work-with shape.

Now that we have a rectangle, how big should it be? Where we want to come out is with forty-eight to sixty-four plants, so the distance between each plant is important. Most books say, "Plant 12 inches apart in rows 15 inches apart, etc." Frankly, all that space is just not necessary for most herbs. If you have a large plantation, you will normally want to plant in rows, and the rows must be far enough apart to allow a cultivator to go between them. But a plant—except gross plants such as lovage or angelica —simply does not have to have a whole square foot in which to flourish. For example, I plant basil in 100-foot rows, and the rows are 20 inches apart so that a power cultivator or the old, but excellent, man-powered wheel hoe can go down them. But I don't thin out the plants in the row; they grow spang next each other but still reach 2 feet or more in height. Now, I'm not asking you to crowd your plants. The reason I don't thin out is just to save man hours in caring for hundreds and hundreds of feet of row. But I *am* saying that about 8 inches between plants will give each one all the space it needs. Actually, a good practical gauge is the width of a garden hoe—if you can hoe between two plants, they're far enough apart. The blade of my garden hoe is 6¼ inches wide; therefore 8 inches is ample for *most* plants. Thus a plot 18 inches square would hold four plants, and obviously, one 18 by 36 inches would hold eight, as in Fig. 1.

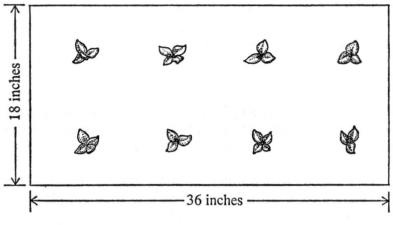

Figure 1

This is just about where we want to arrive, so let's make the bed 36 inches wide. Then 18 inches—the other dimension—times 8 plants equals 12 feet.

You can save space by giving only 1 foot to chives; a plot 1 by 3 feet is an awful lot of chives. And if you want only fresh sage leaves, which is what this bed is for, you simply don't need as many as 8 sage plants. Some books say one is enough, but I think this is cheating the plant and oneself. At any rate, four plants will be ample; then we can limit the sage plot to 1 foot wide. The space saved from chives and sage can be added to savory and basil. Thus, we arrive at a herb bed as shown in Fig. 2.

You will see that the perennials are grouped together. This is so that they will not be disturbed when you spade up the annual section the following spring.

Ideally, the length of the bed should run north and south, so that all plants will get both morning and afternoon sun without the risk of shade from the taller plants adjoining. However, if your land doesn't permit this, don't be disturbed. None of these plants grows tall enough to do any real harm to its neighbor.

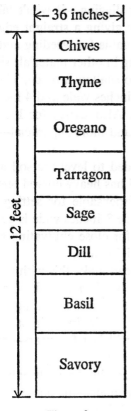

Figure 2

HOW SHOULD YOU PLANT THEM?

The simple and necessary tools for making a small herb bed are described below. If you have a vegetable garden or a flower border, you doubtless already have them all. But please don't be impatient; they are given for people less fortunate than you, who are planting a garden for the first time.

Shovel. This is for heavy digging and turning over the sod; thus it is basic. Make sure the one you buy is sturdy and amply large. The blade on mine is 11 inches long.

Spade. For lighter digging—it won't take as much resistance as a shovel—and for giving a straight edge to the bed you dig.

Garden hoe. Invaluable for weeding and loosening crusty soil. Also useful for mixing in other materials such as sand. Therefore it should not have too shallow a blade. The blade of mine—very satisfactory—is 6¼ inches wide and 4 inches deep.

Speedy cultivator. Also useful for loosening caked soil. It's somewhat quicker—and more superficial—for this than the garden hoe.

Garden rake. Needed to level the soil and to break up clods. The most useful kind has heavy curved teeth.

Hand trowel. Indispensable for setting out small plants and such. One with a blade 3 inches wide is generally useful.

Scratcher. Useful for close cultivating around plants where a long-handled tool might miss.

Garden line. You can make this with two solid sticks (such as sections of a broom handle) and fifty feet of stout twine. It's needed to make sure the edges are straight.

With these in hand, you're in business for any reasonably sized garden bed. And they'll last for years—my garden hoe is over twenty years old.

Fertilizers? The herb books of twenty-five years ago said—unanimously as I remember—the poorer the soil the better; if you add fertilizer, you get bigger plants and bigger leaves but lose a lot of the flavor. Nowadays, some herb experts favor the extensive use of fertilizers and suggest that herbs be treated like any other plant you try to grow. My own view is somewhere between the two. I don't use commercial fertilizers, but I do use compost from our compost piles. This is a mild form of fertilizer, and certainly the herb flavors are not weakened in the slightest. For example, at this moment I happen to have two catnip plants growing wild on one of the compost piles. They are at least one third taller and bushier than catnip plants usually get. And I have been at pains to take a "blind test" between leaves of these and leaves of catnip grown in rocky soil. Answer: absolutely no difference in smell. If compost is not available to you, then you can substitute dehydrated cow manure, but used very sparingly. However, if you can possibly find the space for it, I do urge you to start a compost pile or pit right after you've planted your herb bed. If you do, by the next spring you'll be able to use it on your herbs, a very desirable thing to do, I think. In the next section I'll give the simple directions for making one.

Preparing the soil. As we have noted, good drainage is an absolute essential to success in growing herbs. If you're not sure the site you have picked has good drainage, then by all means pick a better site. If there is no other site, then you should build in the drainage for your bed. It's the hard way, I'm afraid, but it's much better than losing herb plants because their roots are too wet. Stake out the 3-foot-by-12-foot bed, using four stakes, a folding ruler, and the garden line. Then—

1. Dig out all the soil to a depth of 20 inches and pile it beside the hole. When you get down to subsoil—which is light yellow clay in Bucks County—put that in separate piles.

2. Fill the hole with gravel to a depth of 3 inches.

3. Put back half the subsoil, using a hoe and rake to get it level.

4. Cover the subsoil with a layer of sand a generous inch thick, and mix the sand into the subsoil.

5. Fill in half the balance of the subsoil and half the good dark earth, the topsoil. Use the half that has sods in it—and be sure the sods are upside down.

6. Add a 1-inch layer of sand and mix in thoroughly.

7. Add the rest of the good earth and rake the bed level; throw away what's left of the subsoil.

At this point you should have a bed as shown in Fig. 3. The surface will be a little above ground level—and it will have good drainage.

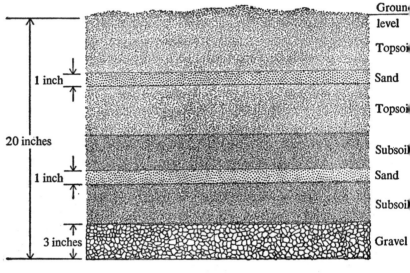

Figure 3

If you don't find it necessary to dig out the bed and put in a drainage base—and I hope you don't—then, using a shovel, simply spade up the bed you have laid out. This means pushing the top of the shovel blade all the way down to the surface of the ground—and as far as your heel can pound it—turning the shovelful of dirt upside down. This is important in any case, but it's especially important if you're digging into sod. If you don't get the grass plants on the bottom, and some of them show on the surface—as they will if you put back the shovelful sideways—they'll start to grow again, and you'll really have a nuisance on your hands. After you have turned over six or eight shovelfuls, then pound the dirt with the back of the shovel so you get a roughly level surface. And so on until the bed has been turned over.

At this point, whether you've put in a drainage base or not, you're ready for the next step:

1. Cover the bare earth with a layer of ground limestone (it's a better leavener than dehydrated lime and lasts longer) to a depth of about ⅛ inch—or so you see only limestone and no bare earth.
2. Cover the limestone with a 1-inch layer of sand.
3. Cover the sand with a layer of peat moss 1½ inch thick.
4. Add a layer of compost, if you have it, ½ to 1 inch thick; if you haven't compost, use a very little dehydrated cow manure —eight to ten cupfuls sprinkled over the bed.
5. Finally, using the garden hoe and the rake, mix all these things thoroughly into the soil. Don't dig down so deeply with the hoe that you pull up any of the sods at the bottom, but do mix so well that the bed is all one even shade of brown.

You're now ready for planting, except for one thing—straightening the edges. The shovel will have left curved marks in the earth where it has dug down, and a proper herb garden should look neat. So, following the straight edge of the garden line, even up all four edges with the spade. Dig down 2 to 3 inches and chop what the spade brings up into the middle of the bed, so no small cuts of sod are visible.

Before planting, the bed must have a chance to settle, and this means plenty of rain. So you should make your bed at least two weeks before you want to plant. And when you plant is, of course, in the spring "when all danger of frost has passed."

Planting. As said earlier, chives, tarragon, and oregano should be started from plants. Chives you can surely buy locally. Get two boxes of them (they're often sold in the thin fruit boxes about 6 by 8 inches). Divide them, by pulling clumps of the roots apart, into six sections, to be set out, with equal spaces between the clumps, in the 1-foot-wide strip reserved for chives. This way they have room to expand, and there will be space for them when you divide again a couple of years hence. Dig holes with your trowel, large enough for the clump to fit in easily and deep enough so the surface earth of the chive clump is slightly below the surface of the bed. Pull a little soil around the clump and press down firmly on all sides so that air cannot get to the roots. Water at once and profusely—*and be sure to water again the next day.*

Oregano and tarragon plants are usually hard to find nearby, but you can certainly get them by mail. When the plants arrive, be sure to set them out as quickly as possible, because they may have been some days in the mail and on the way to drying out. If there is some earth around the roots of each plant, it is best to set them out as is; but if the roots are mostly bare, it is helpful to set them in a bucket of water for half an hour before planting. Dig a hole for each plant, wide and deep enough so you can spread out the roots in it; they should not be jammed into the hole in a lump, if the roots are bare. Again, make sure the hole is deep enough so that the plant's previous surface level is below the surface of your bed—in other words, the plant should be slightly deeper in the ground in your bed than it grew before. Gather the soil around each plant and press down hard all around so that a little saucer is formed around each to hold the water longer. Water very thoroughly—long enough so there is water standing in each little saucer. And be sure to water just as thoroughly the second day. Then water them every other day until they start to put out shoots.

The other five plants you can start from seed, as we have seen, and all can be treated in much the same way, except thyme. Thyme has a special need for a light soil, so even though your soil should now be in very good shape, as an extra precaution I would sprinkle about a quart of sand where you want your rows and mix it in well with the scratcher.

In the future, you will certainly want to transplant seedlings. But if you've never done it before, the easiest thing is to plant the seeds in a row and thin out after they are up. Therefore, for thyme, dill, basil, and savory, I suggest you plant in two rows running across the bed so that the plants remaining after you have thinned out will be in the positions shown in Fig. 1.

The first thing is to make sure that the soil where your row will be is pulverized very finely. The flat side and the edge of a board—and your fingers—can do this. Then make a shallow furrow, about ½-inch deep, with the edge of a board. Water the furrow with a very fine spray and let drain off. Now sprinkle the seeds carefully in the furrow, trying to space them out a little. Some seeds, such as savory, are so tiny it is useful to mix them with sand when you sow, so that the seeds won't drop right next to each other. Cover the larger seeds, such as sage, with ⅛ inch of finely pulverized soil. The tiny seeds need not be covered at all. Now use the edge of a board to press down the earth over the larger seeds and the tiny seeds as they lie there (the pressing will put a very slight covering over them). Then water with a very fine spray so that the seeds and the earth are not washed around. Water freely the first two days—and don't let the soil get completely dry during the germination.

The seeds you have planted should be covered while they are germinating to keep out the light. Use paper (naturally weighted down at the edges with stones)—or, better still, burlap.

When the plants are about 2 inches high, you should start to thin out, making sure you hold down the plants you want to keep so they won't be uprooted. Thin out the first time so that you will have strong-looking plants 4 inches apart. And you don't have to throw away the seedlings you have pulled out—use them in cooking. (You're already growing herbs!) Later, when the plants are about 3 inches high, thin out finally, to get 8 inches between them. And eat these throwaways too!

HOW SHOULD YOU TAKE CARE OF THEM?

Once you have your herb garden growing, you can just about sit back and clip your coupons—which, in this case, are herb leaves. Herbs take care of themselves to a remarkable and happy degree.

Insects don't bother them. Apparently the fragrances, so delightful to us, smell just awful to bugs; at any rate they let herb plants alone. (The solitary exception to this I have found in all these years was with my sage plants a number of years ago. A lot of them seemed to be dying. This was easy to deal with—I called in my county agent. He sent a plant, earth and all, to the state agricultural laboratory. They reported that the trouble was nematodes—very tiny white worms which were eating the roots—and that the answer was to pour a very dilute solution of bichloride of mercury around the roots of each plant. Done. The plants recovered, and there has been no trouble since.)

Plant diseases don't bother herbs. The only exception I have found to this is that some of my mints develop rust spots in late summer. This seems to be caused by too much water—rainfall, that is. Of course, it is most fortunate herbs have this immunity; you simply could not spray them with arsenate of lead or such.

All you need bother about are watering, keeping down the weeds, keeping the soil loose, and giving them a little food. The watering is simplicity itself. After a plant has gotten well started, don't water it—unless it actually starts to droop from a long drought, such as the summers of 1964, 1965, and 1966.

Weeds, of course, must be kept down, but this takes almost no time in a small bed. Just chop them down with the garden hoe or pull them up. You can save even this time by covering the whole bed around each plant with a little mulch. The ideal mulch is grass cuttings, but failing this, peat moss will do very well. Not only does a mulch keep down weeds, it also helps preserve the moisture in the soil which the sun would otherwise lift up. If your bed is surrounded by grass, this will tend to sneak in around the edges. You can keep cutting it back with the spade, or you may want to sink a three-inch metal strip around the edges of the bed so the grass roots can't push in.

About every two weeks the soil should be loosened up. This can be done with the speedy cultivator, through the mulch. The scratcher is good for working closely around the plants, but use it very delicately so you won't tear the roots. A small bit of mulch will be worked into the earth by this operation (and that's good for it), so add a little more mulch.

As I have said, herb plants need a little food once in a while—at the beginning of the season and in mid-summer. To me, the ideal "little food" is compost, and this is so important that I think we should now address ourselves to:

Making a compost pile. Compost is decayed vegetation, and its usefulness increases in proportion to the completeness of decay. You can make a compost pile of sorts simply by dumping leaves, grass cuttings, pulled-up weeds, and such in one spot. However, decay takes longer this way, and to get any reasonable quantity of compost the pile will spread over a large and untidy area. It is best to pile compost in depth.

My first compost pile, years ago, followed instructions I had read somewhere: Find four stout saplings, cut them to 5 feet in length, sharpen an end of each, and pound them into the ground 2 feet deep to outline a rectangle 3 feet wide and 5 feet long. Then nail slats along the sides, leaving ½-inch spaces between them, and fill up with leaves, etc. This plan proved to be very unsatisfactory. As the vegetable material rotted, so did the wooden frame, so that it was useless after a couple of years—and lumber is too expensive for that sort of life.

The next step was a compost pit, dug 30 inches deep to whatever size your digging ambition prompted you to go. This was considerably better. However, in very rainy seasons the pit sometimes filled with water—which meant that a lot of the nutrients in the compost were leached away.

My present compost arrangements consist of two large boxes made of concrete 6 inches thick (cinder blocks cemented together would also do very well), the walls 3 feet high. The reason for two pits is so that there will be a continuous supply: You fill up the first during one growing season, and by the following spring it will be ready for use. And while you're using it, you proceed to fill up the second, and so on—the "ever-normal" compost pile. If your local ordinances allow it, you can throw in garbage as well; we do. The classic structure of a compost pile is alternating layers of vegetation and earth, but this is not necessary. However, it is useful to put in a thin layer of good earth (not clay) about every foot of depth. By keeping out light and air, it speeds decay. You can buy in hardware stores a preparation which accelerates decay, but if you maintain two compost piles, you don't need it —nature does the work. Two concrete boxes, each 3 feet by 4 feet and 3 feet high, will supply you with plenty of compost for a small herb garden—and for the larger one described in a later chapter.

4

A Larger Garden for Fresh and Preserved Herbs

I may have sounded somewhat didactic in the last chapter about what herbs to grow. If I did, it was in an effort to give you the kind of help—the definite, detailed instructions—I wished for but couldn't find twenty-five years ago on how to get started with the most basic herbs.

This chapter tries to take you a few steps further. If you followed Chapter 3—even though you only planted four or six herbs —and you used the herbs you grew on your food, and the food tasted better—and you want to keep on doing it, only more so— then let's go on to what we might call the high-school course. This includes:

1. what other herbs to plant;
2. a more professional form for the garden;
3. how to preserve herbs by drying, salting, or freezing;
4. how to propagate.

WHAT OTHER HERBS TO PLANT

From the chapter title we're talking about cooking herbs only. We are not considering herbs for ornament, such as hyssop, or santolina which many people grow because they like its feathery gray foliage; nor the medicinal herbs such as St.-John's-wort or yarrow which the old folk used to grow. Just herbs for food.

This time instead of specifying a group of, say, eight, I'll give you a "shopping list" from which you can choose the ones that appeal to you most after you have read about them. In my experience the fourteen next most useful herbs are these:

anise	lemon balm
bay	mint: spearmint and
bergamot	peppermint
borage	parsley
caraway	rosemary
chervil	sweet marjoram
coriander	winter savory
fennel	

Let's find out about them:

ROSEMARY (*Rosmarinus officinalis*)

A tender perennial, looking like a miniature pine tree, rosemary grows to about 3 feet but can reach 5 or 6 feet in warmer places such as Arizona. Leaves needlelike and dark green to gray-green. Flowers are pale lavender or pale blue. It grows best in a light, dry, and alkaline soil, and it is well to add pulverized limestone to the soil where it is to grow. It is easy to propagate by layering or by cuttings. Use 6-inch pieces of new growth and let them stand with two thirds of their length in wet sand until they take root. It will winter-kill north of Virginia and therefore must spend the winter indoors.

Uses. Rosemary has a resinous and rather pungent taste and adds a subtle flavor to many foods. Sprinkle over lamb or beef roasts. Add to deep fat for frying potatoes. Add to pea, chicken, turtle soups; minestrone. Use as a marinade for such fish as halibut or salmon. Good in beef stew and ragout of veal. In stuffings and sauces. Good in scrambled eggs. Add to cauliflower, peas or green beans, potatoes. On broiled veal. On chicken or duck. It makes an interesting jelly, using an apple base. Also a good tea: 1 teaspoon of leaves per cup of water.

Background. Rosemary originated on the shores of the Mediterranean. *Rosmarinus,* its Latin name, means "dew of the sea," and it was called this because it grew on the coast in the salt spray. It was known in ancient Greece and was believed to strengthen the brain and the memory, and from this it became the symbol of remembrance. Pliny recommended it for failing eyesight and for jaundice, and the juice of the root for healing wounds. It was taken to England by the Romans and has flourished there ever since because of the prevailing dampness of the climate. It was one of the best-loved herbs in medieval gardens and was one of the herbs on Charlemagne's royal farm. At Christmas, the boar's head was garlanded with rosemary, and it was used in recipes for salads and for fish. But its greatest value was medicinal. In *Banckes' Herbal,* sixteenth century, we find: "If thou have a cough, drink the water of the leaves boyled in white wine and ye shall be whole." William Langham, also sixteenth century, goes even further: "Seethe much Rosemary and bathe therein to make thee lusty, lively, joyfull, likeing and youngly." *Banckes' Herbal* also refers to this fountain-of-youth quality: "Also make thee a box of the wood and smell to it and it shall preserve thy youth." But it had a wide variety of uses: "Take the flowers and put them in a chest among your clothes or among books, the moths shall not hurt them. . . . Also, boil the leaves in white wine and wash thy face therewith . . . and thou shall have a fair face. Also, put the leaves under thy bed's head and thou shalt be delivered of all evil dreams." Another herbalist, Gerard, advises it to clean the breath: "The distilled water of the flowers of Rosemary being drunke at morning and evening first and last, taketh away the stench of the mouth and breath and maketh it very sweet, if there be added thereto, to steep or infuse for certaine daies, a few Cloves, Mace, Cinnamon, and a little Annise seed." Rosemary came to play many parts in England. It was believed to bring good luck and to break magic spells; it was burned in place of frankincense in religious rites, used as a fumigant in hospitals, used to decorate banquet halls and churches, to symbolize remembrance at weddings and funerals, and to cure headache and heartache.

But we can't really understand how rosemary was admired by the ancients unless we see what the fabulous Physicians of Myddrai said about it. These were Welsh doctors who had a sort of hereditary guild. Their book of remedies was compiled in the thirteenth century and contains material which may well have gone back to the sixth century. These doctors did actually exist until the nineteenth century. And here, as quoted by Mrs. Leyel,* are just a few of their rosemary remedies:

Take the flowers of rosemary, mix with honey and eat them daily fasting. You will not suffer from nausea or any other noxious condition as long as you use this remedy.

Also put these flowers or leaves under your head in bed, and you will not be troubled with disagreeable dreams or oppressed with anxiety of mind.

Also if you carry a stick or fragment or this shrub, no evil spirit can come near you or anyone do you any harm.

It is useful as a lotion for the head when affected with a headache from cold or fever, or when a man is threatened with insanity.

A spoonful of this liquid with a spoonful of honey and a spoonful of melted butter, or thick fresh cream, is useful for a cough. . . .

Also a decoction thereof is helpful to an insane person, or one threatened with delirium; indeed it is good for every disorder which can exist in the human body.

It is also well to boil the flowers and leaves in water and to wash yourself therewith every morning, omitting to dry it with a cloth but leaving it to do so naturally. By washing thus with perseverance, the aged will retain a youthful look as long as they live.

Also rosemary and betony pounded and mixed with pure water is

* Hilda W. Leyel, *The Magic of Herbs,* New York, Harcourt, Brace & Company, 1926. Copyright Hilda Leyel. Used by permission.

a good wash for all venomous bites, whether animal or reptile. It will cure them without the help of any other ointment.

As you can see, rosemary is a truly remarkable herb!

CHERVIL (*Anthriscus cerefolium*)

Chervil is sometimes called French parsley, since it is so widely used in France. It is an annual which reaches 1 to 2 feet and somewhat resembles parsley, but the foliage is more feathery. The tiny white flowers grow in umbels. You can grow it from seed and germination takes about fourteen days. It should be planted in a rather moist, partly shaded spot where you want the plants to stay since it does not transplant easily. But it will not thrive in a heavy soil which is badly drained. If you are able to find the right spot for it, it will self-sow year after year. As soon as these seedlings are 2 to 3 inches high, they should be thinned to stand 5 inches apart. In six to eight weeks after sowing, you can begin to cut it for use.

Uses. The delicate anise flavor of chervil is pleasant in many dishes—all kinds of fish and most chicken recipes, for example. Since its flavor is mild, you can use it generously. Try it in sorrel or spinach soup. In tossed salads and on potato salad. Sprinkle on spinach, peas, green beans, tomatoes. Use in any egg dish; chervil omelet is delicious. In cream cheese. Sprinkle generously on lamb, roast beef, veal steaks, broiled chicken, just before serving. *Note:* The flavor of chervil is at its best if it is not cooked, so add it at the last. Chervil has the remarkable characteristic of enhancing the flavor of other herbs. This explains why it is such an important component in the French *fines herbes.*

Background. Chervil is a native of southwest Asia. The old Greeks and Romans used it as a vegetable; they boiled the leaves, as we do spinach, and also ate the roots, as we do parsnips. Chervil was one of the herbs in the St. Gall monastery garden in the ninth century. It was taken to England by the Romans and in

Saxon times was a favorite potherb as well as a salad herb and a flavoring for soups. It was also used as a simple in medieval times. Pliny said that vinegar in which chervil seeds had been soaked was a remedy for hiccoughs. Culpeper recorded that chervil "bruised and applied dissolves swellings in any part, or the marks of congealed blood by bruises or blows, in a little space." And Parkinson wrote that the candied roots comforted a "cold phlegmaticke stomach and [were] a good preservative in time of plague."

ANISE (*Pimpinella anisum*)

Anise is an annual, growing to 1½ feet. It grows easily from seed, and germination takes about ten days. Leaves are gray-green, lacy, and deeply notched. Small white flowers grow in 2-inch umbels. The seeds are a crescent-shaped, greenish gray, and the ends are rather blunt, not pointed like caraway. Seed should be planted in early spring in fairly rich, well-drained soil in full sun. It is difficult to transplant, so seed should be sown where the plants are wanted and seedlings thinned out to stand about 5 inches apart. The plant matures and blossoms in about ten weeks, and the leaves can be used from this point on. The umbels begin to turn a grayish green in early fall. When the tips of the seeds turn slightly brown, it is time to cut the seed heads and place them on a screen to dry. When thoroughly dry, the seed can be separated from the chaff by rubbing between your hands.

Uses. Anise *leaves,* chopped, add a delicate flavor to stews, vegetable soups, fruit salads, or green salads. The French add it to young carrots and to salads and soups. Add it to beet salad, as they do in Sweden. Sprinkle it on canapes. Sprinkle on sausages. Anise *seed,* pulverized, can be added to cakes, cookies, applesauce, and apple pie. Try adding anise leaves to the water in which you cook shellfish. Anise tea is thought by some to be good for a headache (and a stomachache); partly crush a teaspoonful of seed and boil in a cup of water for five minutes. If you soak 3 tablespoons of anise seed in a pint of brandy for six weeks, you will have made anisette, one of the most delicious of liqueurs. It is thought by some to be good for asthma. In any case, it's good for drinking.

Background. Anise has had a long history. It originated in the Middle East. The Egyptians used it as a medicinal herb as early as 1500 B.C., and mention of it is found in the clay tablets of the Assyrians. In the sixth century B.C. Pythagoras stated that a sprig of it held in the hand would prevent "the falling sickness" (epilepsy) and that it was an antidote for scorpion bites. Hippocrates praised it for coughs. The Romans used it as a spice for their food. One particular use was in the cakes they called *mustacea* which were made of meal, cumin, anise, and other spices and served after rich banquets as a *digestif*. Pliny, of the first century A.D., said that "anise has the effect of sweetening the breath and removing all bad odours from the mouth if chewed in the morning"; you were then to rinse your mouth with wine. He also said, "This plant imparts a youthful look to the features, and if suspended to the pillow, so as to be smelt by a person when asleep, it will prevent disagreeable dreams." Anise was also thought able to avert the evil eye. Altogether Pliny gave more than sixty remedies which included it. Anise was considered so important in Biblical times it was used to pay taxes, and in fourteenth century England it was heavily taxed as an imported spice. It was still considered important in colonial America; the first assembly of the Virginia colony decreed that every man was obliged to plant a few seeds of anise. Hippocrates' thought that it was good for coughs is borne out today—its essential oil, anethole, is used in contemporary cough mixtures.

MINT

Spearmint (*Mentha spicata*) and Peppermint (*M. piperita*)

There are many species of mint—apple mint, woolly mint, orange mint, pineapple mint are just a few. Indeed, a ninth-century writer said there are as many varieties of mint "as there are sparks from Vulcan's furnace." But spearmint and peppermint are the best. Plant them both or take your pick, always remembering that peppermint is very much stronger. The mints are hardy perennials, and you will need to start with plants or slips. Once started, they will propagate themselves by underground stems or runners; indeed, unless you curb them, they can spread so rapidly as to be a nuisance. The best procedure is to sink aluminum strips 4 to 6 inches wide around the border of the mint section. Spearmint grows to about 18 inches and produces tiny white flowers. Peppermint grows somewhat taller and produces tiny red flowers. Both prefer a moist but well-drained soil, fairly rich, where there is partial shade; they need a lot of moisture to thrive. Peppermint has a curious characteristic you should keep in mind—it tends to die out if grown in the same location. Therefore you should find a new bed for it every third year. Mint takes a lot of nourishment from the soil and so should be fed with compost at least twice a year.

Uses. Mint is excellent in fruit salad and, used sparingly, in green salad. Mix it with cream cheese. Add it to fruit juice. A spearmint omelet is an adventure in eating. Excellent in pea soup and lentil soup. Sprinkle it on carrots, peas, green beans, spinach, cabbage, new potatoes. Mint is traditional with roast lamb, either in a sauce or in a jelly. Also excellent with roast beef, baked fish. Rub it on chicken before roasting. Good in applesauce and with stewed pears. Spearmint is the traditional mint-julep mint—and a stalk of it is excellent in iced tea. A tea made of mint leaves, fresh or dried, has been used time out of mind as a digestive aid. Mint is an important ingredient in three liqueurs, crème de menthe, chartreuse, and Benedictine—which recalls that liqueurs were originally meant to aid digestion. Fresh mint leaves scattered about have been used to repel mice and, dried, to repel moths.

Background. Mint has been helping men's food and health for more than three thousand years. It was an important herb as long ago as the early Egyptians. It originated in western Asia and the Middle East, and was much used by the Greeks and Romans in their food. They also used it to flavor their wine. Mint was used in paying tithes in Biblical times; in other words, it was considered a valuable commodity. The Greeks discovered the value of rubbing their dining tables with mint before meals—the oil preserved the wood and the fragrance increased the appetite. At one period in ancient Rome, drinking wine was forbidden to women, and the penalty was death. The women responded by mixing mint with honey to cover up their wine breaths.

The strong but pleasant smell of mint inspired its use as a strewing herb, to overcome the bad smells in medieval buildings. As Gerard says: "The smell rejoiceth the heart of man, for which cause they used to strew it in chambers of places of recreation, pleasure and repose where feasts and banquets are made. . . . The smell of Minte does stir up the minde and the taste to a greedy desire of meate." He felt it was "marvelous wholesome for the stomacke." Culpeper gives many medicinal uses for mints, such as: "It is safe medecine for the biting of a mad dog, being bruised with salt and laid thereon. The powder of it being dried and taken after meat, helps digestion, and those that are splenetic. Being smelled unto, it is comfortable for the head and memory. The decoction hereof gargled in the mouth, cures the gums and mouth that are sore, and mends an ill-savoured breath." *Banckes's Herbal* agrees as to its value as a mouthwash and says that if rubbed on the teeth it will give "a sweet-smelling mouth." It will also "make thee to have a talent [appetite] to thy meat" if it is made into a sauce. It is good for toothache, and a poultice of it will cure "botches on the face." Parkinson wrote that "mintes are sometimes used in baths with balm and other herbs as a help to comfort and strengthen the nerves and sinews. It is much used either outwardly applied or inwardly drunk to strengthen and comfort weak stomackes." Peppermint tea was used to cure colds as well as stomachaches, and leaves laid on the forehead were thought to cure headache and sleeplessness. The moral seems to be: grow plenty of mint!

FENNEL (*Foeniculum vulgare*)

A hardy perennial, often grown as an annual, fennel reaches 4 to 5 feet. Sicilian fennel, or carosella (*F. vulgare* var. *piperitum*), grows to only about 2 feet as does Florence fennel or finocchio (var. *dulce*). All the varieties have a feathery foliage of a handsome bright green and bear umbels of tiny yellow flowers. They can be grown from seed, and germination takes about ten days. Fennel will do well in any soil except a heavy, clayey one, and needs full sun and plenty of moisture. Both the carosella and and finocchio can be cultivated like celery—as the base of the stalk becomes wide and thick, compost should be added to the soil, and when it reaches the size of an egg, earth should be hilled up around it to blanch the stalk. After about ten days it can be harvested, to use as celery or as a boiled vegetable. Of course, the leaves can be cut and used at any time after the plant has become established. If you are growing a plant for seed, be sure to cut the umbels for drying before the tops turn brown and release the seed.

Uses. Leaves: Fennel has a natural affinity for fish and this has been recognized for many centuries. One of the great local dishes of the French Riviera is *loup de mer* (bass) *au fenouil*, which is a grilled fish stuffed with fennel leaves. Add to green salads and potato salad. Good as a potherb, cooked with spinach. Excellent in soups, especially fish soup. Good in omelets. On cauliflower, peas, green beans, cabbage, tomatoes. Add before serving to roast chicken and roast lamb; also creamed chicken. *Seeds:* Add to sauerkraut, to spiced beets. Excellent in shellfish casseroles. In scrambled eggs. Good in beef and lamb stews. Add to water for boiling fish, and to fish soups and stews. Good on cakes and cookies and in puddings. Excellent in apple pie. *Note:* The large stalk of Florence fennel is often cooked as a vegetable, and the stalks of carosella are eaten like celery—quite aside from these varieties being used for their leaves and seeds.

Background. Fennel originated on the shores of the Mediterranean and has been used for more than three thousand years, starting with the Egyptians. With the Greeks, it was a symbol of victory and was used to crown heroes. The Romans used it for this too but also ate the stalks raw and cooked, just as Italians do today. The Romans also took it to England, and Saxon herbals mention it both as a food and a medicine—it was one of their principal healing herbs. Sometimes cooked with beet tops and parsley, it was a favorite potherb in medieval England. One widely held belief about fennel was that it benefited the eyes. Both Gerard and Parkinson recommended it for this, and Gerard says, "The powder of the seed of Fennell drunke for certaine daies together fasting preserveth the eyesight." They probably got this from Dioscorides, who also recommended it for fever and nausea. Another attribute was thought to be that of a reducing agent. William Coles in 1657 recommended its use in broths "for those that are grown fat, to abate their unwieldiness and cause them to grow more gaunt and lank." This idea was derived from the fact that chewing fennel seed dulls the appetite. For this reason in past centuries fennel seeds were chewed on fasting days. Culpeper recognizes both benefits: "Both leaves, seeds, and roots thereof are much used in drink or broth, to make people more lean that are too fat. The distilled water of the whole herb . . . dropped into the eyes, cleanses them from mists and films that hinder the sight." He also says, "The seeds, boiled in water, stays the hiccough"—but this is scarcely news, because it was said about nearly every herb we've looked at so far. Culpeper begins his essay on fennel with its importance to fish: "One good old fashion is not yet left off, viz. to boil Fennel with fish." And on the same gastronomical note Parkinson said, "The seeds is much used to be put into Pippin pies and divers other such baked fruits, as also into bread, to give it the better rellish." A most versatile herb, fennel.

BERGAMOT (*Monarda didyma*)

Bergamot is a hardy perennial reaching 2 to 3 feet. Leaves are dark green, 4 to 5 inches long, and fragrant. Flowers are whorls at the top of a square stem and may be scarlet, lavender, white, or pink depending on the variety, but the scarlet flowers are the most familiar, and some feel these make the best tea. Bergamot prefers a moist, fairly rich soil and partial shade. Plants can be grown from seeds which, preferably, should be planted in November. They will germinate the following spring. Propagation thereafter is by root division. The roots spread quickly, and the plants should be set 18 inches apart. For best results, a plant should be dug up every two or three years, the center should be thrown away, and the younger outside shoots used. Don't forget that it must be watered well in dry weather, or it will die out.

Uses. The most familiar use is as a tea; 1 teaspoon of dried flowers or dried leaves to a cup of boiling water, allowed to steep for five minutes. But it has other uses. Try some shredded fresh flowers in a green salad; they add a subtle and delicious taste and look very handsome. The young leaves are also very good in a green salad. Try sprinkling chopped leaves on poultry, veal, and pork. Add some chopped leaves to a chopped ham omelet. In cottage cheese and cream cheese. Excellent sprinkled on green beans, stewed tomatoes, and spinach. Also very good in cream soups and fish chowders.

Background. Bergamot is one of the very few native American herbs in our gardens. It gets its name from a Spanish physician, Niccolo Monardes, who discovered it in the sixteenth century. Virtually all our herbs have come to us from Europe. But as a kind of "man bites dog," bergamot was taken from here to France in the eighteenth century. It has since become extremely useful there, because the French use oil of bergamot in some of their most valuable perfumes. Because the flowers have a delightful fragrance which bees love, bergamot has long been called also bee balm. And it has long been called Oswego tea. The reason for this is that long ago the Oswego Indians in New York State used it extensively as a tea, and this use was taken up by the colonists. At the time of the Boston Tea Party, when Americans were boycotting tea from England, it was Oswego tea they used instead. Bergamot tea, incidentally, is said to relax people and induce sleep.

PARSLEY (*Petroselinum crispum*)

Parsley is a hardy biennial but is usually grown as an annual because the leaves are crisper the first year. However, it is possible to establish a parsley bed, let it alone, and it will become, in effect, a self-sown perennial. Parsley is often considered difficult to grow, probably because of its remarkably long germination period, which is three to six weeks. This is one herb which resents a sandy soil, and if your soil is light and sandy, you will do well to mix in loam or clay—plus plenty of compost—where you want your parsley to grow. Partial shade is safer than full sun. Because of the long germination period, it is wise to mix a few radish seeds in with the parsley seeds to mark the row. Also, germination will be hastened if the parsley seed is soaked in water for twenty-four hours before planting. Plant in early spring in drills 1 inch deep and cover lightly with soil. After the parsley seedlings have come up, the radish seedlings should be removed. Make sure the planting gets plenty of water during the germination period. When the seedlings are 1 inch high, they should be thinned out so they stand at least 6 inches apart. Some people believe that one secret of growing parsley successfully is to make sure that the leaves of a plant do not touch another plant, even as seedlings. This means that the seedlings should not stand crowded together even when tiny. If you cut your parsley often, it is advisable to add compost to the rows at least twice during the summer. For growing indoors during the winter, it is a good idea to sow a few seeds again in midsummer so you can start the indoor season with small, vigorous plants. And don't forget to water plentifully, though not to the point of stagnant dampness. There is an Italian variety of parsley with plain, uncurled leaves which has an excellent flavor. It is a good idea to plant some of both kinds so you can find out which you prefer. Parsley is one herb which does not dry satisfactorily. The only way to preserve it is to freeze it.

Uses. Culpeper often said in his herbal, "This herbe is so well known it needs no description," and this must be true of the uses of parsley. Perhaps we can get a better perspective on this herb if we reflect that it is very valuable in the diet. Nutrition chemists have found it is an excellent source of iron, calcium, and Vitamins A, B, and C. Indeed it is said to be four times as rich in Vitamin C as oranges (one assumes on a volume-for-volume basis). To remind you of some of the uses of parsley: In soups and stews, chopped. In creamed vegetables. On egg dishes. On boiled potatoes. It adds a delicate touch to a green salad. Excellent sprinkled over sliced tomatoes. Sprinkle on fish and shellfish. On chicken. It is an ingredient of the French *fines herbes* and *bouquet garni*. To boil it down, parsley can be used in any dish. Parenthetically, in England parsley is highly regarded as a daily supplement to the food of dogs, as a kind of tonic.

Background. Parsley had a Mediterranean origin, and some even pinpoint it to the island of Sardinia. It was one of the first plants used for making wreaths. These varied from those used to crown Greek athletes to those given to loved ones as a token of affection. The Romans added another use—one wore a crown of it at banquets because it was believed to absorb the fumes of wine, and this would prevent the wearer from getting drunk! But the Romans also used it to flavor their food, and it was eaten after meals to take away a garlic breath. According to Pliny, the name was derived from a Greek word meaning "stone breaker," perhaps because it often grew on rocky soil. *Banckes' Herbal* says that "it is good for the side and the dropsy. It comforteth the heart and the stomach. . . . It multiplieth greatly a man's blood." It was also believed to cure baldness if the ground seed were sprinkled on a man's head three nights every year, and ground seed would also cure the ague. William Turner said in the sixteenth century that, if parsley were scattered on a fish pond, the sick fish would get well. The bruised leaves were used to cure insect stings. In England, parsley tea was believed to be a remedy for rheumatism. Also in England the country folk used to strew parsley on the floor to keep out insects. Culpeper ascribed many virtues to parsley: "... is very comfortable to the stomach" (which is fair enough—it is now believed to stimulate the digestive glands). "The distilled water of Parsley is a familiar medicine with nurses to give their children when they are troubled with wind in the stomach or belly, which they call the frets. . . ." Galen commended it against the falling sickness "and to provoke urine mightily" (again fair enough for the latter use—it is now known to have a mildly diuretic action). "It is also effectual against the venom of any poisonous creature . . . and also takes away black and blue marks coming of bruises or falls." Who would guess that this modest little garnish was so full of character?

CORIANDER (*Coriandrum sativum*)

Coriander is an annual growing from 1 to 2 feet. The leaves are lacy and fernlike, the lower leaves broad and lobed, the upper very narrow. Flowers are pale pink or white and grow in umbels. The seeds when ripe are a yellow-brown, globular, and about ⅛ inch in diameter. When dried and ground, they have a sweetish, appealing flavor which some people claim is like a mixture of lemon peel and sage. I don't get this taste myself, but in any case the flavor is delicate and pleasant. Coriander is easy to grow from seed and will grow almost anywhere, but it is at its best in full sun and a well-drained, fairly rich soil. Germination takes about fourteen days. The seeds should be planted ½ inch deep where you want them to grow because they can't be transplanted successfully. When the seedlings are 2 inches high, they should be thinned to about 6 inches apart, by pinching off at the surface the ones you don't want. A May planting will bloom in about eight weeks, and the seed will mature about three weeks later. Be sure to harvest the brown umbels before they get so dry as to release the seed, and place them on a screen for thorough drying. After they are completely dry, it is easy to separate the seed from the chaff. Store the seed in airtight containers.

Uses. The *seed* must be crushed or ground for use, the only exception being to sugarcoat the whole seed (and, frankly, I don't see why anyone should bother to). Sprinkle the ground seed on baked apples. On cookies. Good in poultry stuffing. Add to beet salad and pickled beets. It adds a subtle note to soups and casseroles. Use in chopped meat and sausage. Good in beef stew. Very good in gingerbread. Coriander is an ingredient of curry powder, so you can add it to curries if you care to tone down the heat. Sprinkle on stewed fruit and fruit salads. Add to sauces for meats. In Rome, I have seen people add several crushed seeds to a demitasse—apparently the Roman equivalent of the Arab custom of adding cardamom seeds. As to the green *leaves* of coriander, I have met in my life exactly one American who uses them —a well-known New York food editor, who adds the green leaves to chops and steaks. This speaks well for the editor's sophistication, because, while Americans are instructed that coriander leaves are unfit to eat, they are relished as *cilantro* in Mexico and by various names in the Middle East, China, and India. If you're really adventurous, you just might like to try it.

Background. Coriander must be one of the very first seasoning herbs. Seeds have been found in Egyptian tombs, and there is mention of it in a papyrus found in the tomb of Cheops near Cairo. The Chinese were using it by 3000 B.C. to flavor beverages and cakes. They also ate the boiled roots. It is a Biblical herb, mentioned in Exodus: "And the house of Israel called the name thereof Manna: and it was like coriander-seed, white; and the taste of it was like wafers made with honey." Pliny called the plant "coriandrum" from the Greek word *koris,* which means bug, because of the strong and unpleasant smell of the green seed and green leaves. (Gerard wrote, "Coriander is a very stinking

herbe.") The old Romans used coriander on meat as a preservative—specifically, ground cumin and coriander seed mixed with
vinegar. It was also much used as a medicine long ago. It was
one of Hippocrates' simples in the fifth century B.C., and in
the sixteenth century William Turner wrote, "Coriandre layd to
wyth breade or barly mele is good for Saint Antonyes fyre"
(erysipelas). *Banckes' Herbal* says that coriander seeds are
"good to do away with the fevers that come the third day."
Curiously enough, if a large amount of coriander is eaten, it acts
as a narcotic. Dioscorides noted this eighteen hundred years ago:
"But being taken too much it disturbs ye understanding dangerously." So did Turner when he wrote four hundred years ago
that if coriander is "taken out of measure" it "taketh men's
wyttes." On the other hand, it was thought that normal amounts
were "sovereign goode for the stomacke."

BORAGE (*Borago officinalis*)

Also called bee-plant, borage is a hardy annual of luxuriant
growth, reaching 2 to 3 feet. The leaves are oval, about 6 inches
long, covered with gray hairs which look like a fuzz and make
them look gray-green. Flowers are pale blue, star-shaped, and
really lovely. Borage grows easily from seed, and germination
takes about fourteen days. It needs full sun but will grow readily
in a poor, dry soil. Sow in the spring and thin out the seedlings
to stand 12 inches apart, since the mature plant becomes large
and bushy. Transplanting can be done when the seedlings are
very small, but after that there will be trouble. Both the leaves
and the flowers are used, but don't try to get both from the same
plant—once it starts to flower the leaves are apt to become tough.
Borage grows so luxuriantly that it must be cut often to get the
tastiest leaves. But let a few plants flower. A dozen or so plants
will provide all the leaves and flowers an average family will need.

Uses. The most familiar uses are to add the leaves to salad, to
float the flowers in cool drinks such as a claret cup, or to candy
them (dip them first in beaten egg whites, then in sugar, and let

them dry). The salad use for the leaves is a good and valid one; they have a pronounced cucumber taste which is a splendid addition to a salad. But don't stop there. Cook the leaves as you would cook spinach—as people have been doing for centuries. Try adding borage to spinach. Use the chopped leaves instead of parsley to flavor soups and stews. Excellent when chopped and added to bean, pea, and tomato soups. Very good added to cabbage. Incidentally, the flowers are very good in salads too. The old folk used to add the flowers to soup.

Background. Since the Greeks, borage has been thought to have the power to drive away melancholy. Pliny said that borage, crushed in wine, would drive away sorrow and bring courage: "I, borage, bring always courage." This is an old English saying, brought to England by the Romans, who in turn got it from the Greeks. Gerard said, "Those of our time do use the flour in sallads, to exhilerate and make the minde glad. There be also many things made of them used for the comfort of the heart, to drive away sorrow." By "them" he meant "the gallant blew floures" of borage. He also said, "A sirup concocted of the floures quieteth the lunatick person and leaves eaten raw do engender good blood." John Evelyn (1699) "Borrage . . . purifying the blood, is an exhilerating cordial, of a pleasant Flavour: the tender Leaves, and Flowers especially, may be eaten in Composition; but above all, the Sprigs in Wine like those of Baum, are of known Vertue to revive the Hypochondriac and chear the hard Student." Sir John Hill (1756) added, "Borage procureth gladsomness, it helpeth the giddiness and swimming of the head, the trembling and heating of the heart, it increaseth memorie and removeth melancholy." Clearly a happy herb to have around. Borage had cosmetic uses too; it was believed to beautify the skin. In *The Toilet of Flora,* published in London in 1779, we find this recipe for "A Cosmetic Bath: take two pounds of Barley or Beanmeal, eight pounds of Bran and a few handfuls of Borrage Leaves. Boil these ingredients in a sufficient quantity of spring water. Nothing cleanses and softens the skin like this bath."

BAY (*Laurus nobilis*)

Bay is an evergreen shrub or tree growing to 30 feet—or even 60 feet in Greece. But for our purposes, growing in a 16-inch wooden tub, it reaches no more than 4 to 6 feet. It is a tender perennial and winter-kills in most of the U.S.—say, north of Georgia. Even in the south of England, where it grows readily and is considered hardy, the severe winter of 1963 was fatal to most bay trees. This means that if you want to grow it north of Georgia, you must plant it in a wooden tub, to sit majestically— in pairs or fours—in your herb garden. Or, if you like, for aesthetic reasons, plant it in very large clay pots and bury the pots— for the summer only—in your garden. Start your bay by buying one or more plants (and only one plant will really grow in a 16-inch tub). Although for most of us the bay must be brought indoors for the winter, it cannot stand the dry heat of an ordinary room and must winter in a temperature between 36 and 50 degrees, which means a greenhouse or a partially heated sun porch or garage or a cool basement. It needs as much sun as possible. The potting mixture should consist of equal parts of loam, peat moss, and sand, with a little dehydrated cow manure added. The tub should be filled at least ⅘ full, but of course don't fill to the top because there must be plenty of room for water. Bay can be propagated by cuttings of new shoots, placed in a mixture of two sand to one peat moss, and kept moist. The leaves can be harvested all year and should be dried out of the sun (like all herbs) in a warm place. The dried leaves should be kept in airtight containers, because the oil which gives the flavor is very volatile. In other words, bay is difficult to grow because of the wintering problem, but if you can succeed with a plant, it is most rewarding.

Uses. The dried leaves (not the fresh ones) add a subtle note to sauces, stews, casseroles, and stuffings. Be very careful not to use too much since the flavor can be overpowering. The French are particularly fond of bay and feel it is indispensable in their classic *bouquet garni*. Bay gives an excellent flavor when boiled with beets, carrots, eggplant, potatoes, peas, artichokes. Place in the roasting pan with lamb or chicken. Excellent in marinades. Good in seafood dishes. Put half a leaf in the water for boiling fish or smoked tongue. Be sure to remove bay leaves from pot or pan before serving.

Background. Note that bay is the true laurel and must not be confused with the native American laurel, *Kalmia latifolia,* which is poisonous. Bay is a native of the Middle East and the Mediterranean countries, and has been used for more than two thousand years. The Greeks and Romans made wreaths of it, as they did with a number of aromatic herbs, to honor kings and important people. But it was apparently the herb most favored for this purpose, since such phrases as "crowned with laurel" are frequent in Greek and Roman literature. Our expressions "look to your laurels" and "poet laureate" have the same ancient origin. It was used for cooking too, of course, and the Roman cookbook *Apicius* gives bay as an ingredient in sauces for seafood, suckling pig, and boiled boar. In the Middle Ages bay leaves were used to flavor soups, meat stews, and cooked fruits. They were also used for tea—which is interesting, since they have a narcotic effect. And, as you would expect, it was much used in medicine. Culpeper gives a full page to the wonders of bay as a remedy, of which these are a few: "The berries are very effectual against all poison of venomous creatures, and the sting of wasps and bees; as also against the pestilence or other infectious diseases. . . . They wonderfully help all cold and rheumatic distillations from the brain to the eyes, lungs or other parts. . . . The oil made of the berries is very comfortable in all cold griefs of the joints, nerves, arteries, stomach, belly or womb, and helpeth palsies, convulsions, cramps, aches, tremblings and numbness in any part, weariness also, and pains that come by sore travelling." He also quotes a folk belief of the day (1684): ". . . neither witch nor devil, thunder nor lightening, will hurt a man in the place where a Bay-tree is." John Parkinson (1629) gives the final encomium:

"The Bay leaves are of as necessary use as any other in Garden or Orchard, for they serve both for pleasure and profit, both for ornament and for use, both for honest civill uses, and for Physicke. . . . It serveth to adorne the house of God as well as of man: to procure warmth, comfort and strength to the limmes of men and women, by bathings and annoyntings outwards and by drinkes etc. inward to the stomacke and other parts: to season vessels etc. wherein are preserved our meates, as well as our drinkes: to crown or encircle as with a garland the heads of the living, and to sticke and decke forth the bodies of the dead: so that from the cradle to the grave we have still use of it, we have still neede of it. The berries likewise serve for stiches inward and for paines outward, that come of cold eyther in the joynts, sinewes, or other places." As I said, growing bay is rewarding!

LEMON BALM (*Melissa officinalis*)

Balm is a fragrant perennial 1½ to 2 feet tall. Leaves are 2 to 3 inches long, about 1 inch wide, becoming much smaller toward the tips. When crushed, the leaves have a strong lemon smell and taste. Flowers are white or pale yellow and very small. Lemon balm will grow almost anywhere but does best in a light, well-drained soil which gets shade part of the day. You can grow it from seed, and germination takes about fourteen days. You can propagate by cuttings thereafter. It can become rather bushy if it thrives, so the plants should be set 12 inches apart. If they are well cultivated and kept free of weeds, the tops will spread up to each other and keep down the weeds thereafter, especially if the first top leaves are pinched back. If you grow lemon balm in an exposed location, it is well to give it a frost cover in November, such as a 4-inch to 6-inch thickness of autumn leaves, using chicken wire or branches or burlap to keep the leaves from blowing away. With even a reasonable amount of care, the plants will last for years.

Uses. It has been used as a tea for many centuries, because the mint-lemon taste is so pleasant and because it was thought to have medicinal properties. Even today in Europe, it is used as a home remedy for dizziness and feverish colds; and a modern English herbal (Harold Ward's *Herbal Manual*) recommends it for "influenza and feverish colds, to induce perspiration. Aids digestion." But it has plenty of cooking uses. Sprinkle the chopped leaves on fruit salad and add sparingly to a green salad. Try it in fish soup, asparagus soup, vegetable soup. Good with roast lamb. Add to stuffing for chicken and pork. Excellent with fish. In short, use it anywhere you feel a little mint-lemon flavor would improve things. Be adventurous!

Background. Lemon balm was written about as early as the Old Testament. It originated in the Middle East, as have so many herbs, and found its way around the shores of the Mediterranean. Its name, *melissa,* is the Greek word for honeybee, and for more than two thousand years the two have been connected. The old Roman naturalist Pliny said, "When bees have strayed away, they do find their way home by it"; and English beekeepers for centuries have grown it near their hives. Indeed, there was an old folk belief that if balm were growing nearby, bees wouldn't leave the hive. Aside from its importance to bees, it was thought to have valuable properties, as, for example, a seventeenth century claim that "an essence of Balm drunk every morning will renew youth, strengthen the brain, relieve languishing nature, and prevent baldness." There was a famous elixir called Carmelite Water several centuries ago which was made of lemon balm, lemon peel, angelica, nutmeg, and honey, which was thought to be good for nervous headache, dizziness, and neuralgia—and also to give you a long life! (Incidentally, the "balm of Gilead" referred to in the Bible is a Middle Eastern tree and has no relation to balm.) It was thought to have an astringent quality and thus be useful for treating wounds. Dioscorides thought that the leaves "assuage ye paines of ye goutie." Gerard said, "Bawne drunke in wine is good against the bitings of venemous beasts, comforts the heart, and driveth away all melancholy and sadnesse." This belief, that it raised the spirits, was widely held—there is an old Arab saying that balm tea "makes the heart merry and joyful." and John Evelyn adds, "Baum, Cordial and exhilerating, sovereign for the Brain, strengthening the Memory, and powerfully chasing away Melancholy."

CARAWAY (*Carum carvi*)

A hardy biennial, caraway reaches about 2 feet in height. The leaves are feathery and handsome, somewhat resembling carrot leaves. The flowers are white and grow in average-light soil and full sun. Seeds are best planted in September, so that the plant will flower and seed the following summer. Seeds should be sown where you want the plants to grow since it is difficult to transplant due to its long root. Germination takes about fourteen days. When the seedlings are 3 inches tall, thin to 4 inches apart. The plants grow slowly at first, and therefore careful cultivation is necessary to keep back the weeds. Caraway can be grown as a perennial if you let every second plant go to seed, because it will self-sow year after year.

Uses. The leaves are delicious chopped into soup and sprinkled on vegetables. Try a few in a green salad. Sprinkle chopped leaves on meat loaf and in stews. Add to new potatoes. The *seeds* are often used in rye bread and on cookies. Add them to apple sauce, baked apple, and apple pie. Add to sauerkraut. Good in cabbage soup. Good in goulash. Mix with cream cheese and cottage cheese. It is an old Pennsylvania Dutch custom to cook caraway seeds with cabbage, in order to prevent the bloating effect which cabbage has on some people. In England it has been a custom for centuries to serve apples and caraway seeds after a heavy banquet to "settle the stomach." Add to potato salad. Add to the vinegar used to pickle beets. The *root* is still much used as a boiled vegetable in Europe, as it has been for four hundred years.

Background. This is one of the first herbs used by civilized man. Caraway seeds have been found in the remains of the Swiss lake dwellers who flourished about 5000 B.C. And there is a record of it as a medicine in an Egyptian papyrus of 2500 B.C. It originated in the Middle East, and Pliny pinpoints it to Caria in Asia Minor. The ancient Greek physician Galen wrote of its efficacy in digestive troubles. The Romans grew caraway in their gardens, as did Charlemagne. Dioscorides reported that caraway was good for the stomach and was "warming." Parkinson says, "The seede is much used to be put among baked fruit, or into bread cakes, etc., to give them a relish, and to helpe digest winde in them that are subject thereto." *Banckes' Herbal* said that it destroys "wicked winds and the cough. Also it restoreth hair where it has fallen away." And Culpeper goes even further: "The root is better food than the parsnips; it [the seed] is pleasant and comfortable to the stomach, and helps digestion. The seed is conducing to all cold griefs of the head, stomach and bowels . . . and helps to sharpen the eyesight. The powder of the seed put into a poultice takes away black and blue spots of blows and bruises. Carraway confects, once only dipped in sugar, and half a teaspoonful of them eaten in the morning fasting, and as many after each meal, is a most admirable remedy, for those that are troubled with wind."

WINTER SAVORY (*Satureia montana*)

This is the perennial form of summer savory (*Satureia hortensis*), which we looked at in Chapter 3. It is a hardy, bushy evergreen sub-shrub, reaching 6 to 12 inches. The leaves are gray-green and needlelike, and the flowers are white, pink, or purple. It prefers a thin, light, well-drained soil; indeed, it may die out in a soil which is too rich or too damp. Sow the seeds in September for a crop the following summer, but don't cover the seeds in the drills because this is one seed which germinates by light. Germination takes about twelve days. Although the plant is hardy, a light frost cover is good insurance. It can be grown easily indoors and should be potted for this purpose in late August. Winter savory is a rewarding herb to grow, and your plants will do well in the same location year after year. Incidentally, it is considered an excellent border plant.

Uses. Both savories were much used in medieval times when a peppery, spicy flavor was wanted in a dish, and, in fact, they are the closest thing to a spice in the whole herb garden. You can use winter savory in all the dishes given for summer savory— but use less of it. The flavor is stronger and less delicate.

Background. This is the same for both savories. Additionally, it might be noted that the name *Satureia* is thought to derive from "satyr," and the plant used to be considered an aphrodisiac. *Banckes' Herbal* says, "It is forbidden to use it much in meats, because it stirreth him that useth to lechery." Culpeper has this to say of both savories: ". . . it quickens the dull spirits in the lethargy, the juice thereof being snuffed up into the nostrils. The juice dropped into the eyes, clears a dull sight. . . . The juice heated with oil of Roses, and dropped into the ears, eases them of the noise and singing in them, and of deafness also. Outwardly applied with wheat flour, in the manner of a poultice, it gives ease to the sciatica and palsied members, heating and warming them, and takes away their pains."

SWEET MARJORAM (*Majorana hortensis*)

This is the annual form of *Origanum*. We looked at wild marjoram, usually called oregano (*Origanum vulgare*), in Chapter 3. There are some thirty varieties, of which the third most important is pot marjoram (*M. onites*), but it has less flavor than sweet marjoram and need not concern us. Sweet marjoram is an attractive bushy plant, growing 8 to 12 inches. The leaves are small, gray-green, and rounded at the ends. Flowers are small and white or pink, growing in clusters. Sweet marjoram prefers full sun in a dry, well-drained neutral soil. You can grow it from seeds, but germination is slow, about fourteen days, and during this time they should be covered with a little peat moss and kept moist. Transplant when the seedlings are 2 inches high, and keep shaded until their growth is established. They must also be kept free of weeds. The plants should stand 8 to 10 inches apart. Ideally, to lengthen the period of use, the seed should be sown in a cold frame in early March and transplanted to the garden in the middle of May. Since the seeds are very tiny, it is useful to mix them with sand so they will not be sown so thickly. Keep in mind that the young plants grow very slowly and need careful nurturing.

Uses. All the uses given for oregano apply also to marjoram. In addition, you might try it in pea, tomato, onion, turtle, and potato soups, and in clam chowder. Sprinkle the chopped leaves on carrots, mushrooms. Excellent on broiled fish. Good in chicken salad and chicken potpie. Especially good in sausage; indeed, in Germany the name for marjoram is *Wurstkraut* or "sausage herb." It is also much used in sausage in England.

Background. What was said about oregano applies also to marjoram. Additionally, it might be noted that marjoram, because of its fragrance, was much used as a strewing herb in medieval times. It was also used then to flavor meats, soups, salads, and egg dishes. Before someone discovered that hops added to the flavor of beer in brewing, marjoram was used as "hops." Culpeper wrote, "Our common Sweet Marjoram is warming and comfortable in cold diseases of the head, stomach, sinews, and other parts taken inwardly or outwardly applied. . . . The powder thereof snuffed up into the nose provokes sneezing, and thereby purges the brain. . . . Marjoram is much used in all odoriferous waters, powders, etc., that are for ornament or delight." Fair enough, this last—the oil distilled from the leaves is still an important ingredient in perfumes.

And so we have had a brief look at the fourteen herbs next most important to the basic eight in Chapter 3. Does this list include all the top-ranking herbs for seasoning food? No; lovage and salad burnet are not included, and they can be classed as top ranking. But they are discussed in the next chapter on a Salad Garden. Because lovage leaves taste like celery and burnet leaves taste like cucumber, they are fine additions to a green salad. However, it is fair to say that you just won't need any seasoning herbs beyond these twenty-two.

But should you plant them all? And, if not, which should you select? Well, how big a garden do you want and how do you want it to grow? It's time we had a look at—

A MORE PROFESSIONAL FORM FOR THE GARDEN

In the last chapter we arrived at a bed 3 feet by 12 feet as being the simplest and most functional way of growing eight herbs in sufficient quantity to provide fresh leaves for the kitchen during the summer. Such a bed is ample and efficient, and in a plantation this small, one can overlook a somewhat Spartan appearance. But if you intend to preserve a fair quantity, you will need a considerably larger space for these eight herbs, and if you intend to grow even half the new herbs in this chapter, you will need still more. In other words, you will have a good-sized herb garden, so we should add a little aesthetics to our efficiency.

First, the space for the basic eight. How ambitious are you as to the amount you will want to dry or freeze? If your thought is "to preserve a few herbs to try it out," then I suggest you just arbitrarily double the size of each herb plot. If you are pretty enthusiastic about the idea—and perhaps would like to give away some of your crop to friends—then I suggest you triple each herb plot. Now, the idea of a herb plot 3 feet wide is not an idle whim; it is about the greatest width which allows you to reach every herb from the two sides of the bed. Therefore, the width should stay the same, and if you want to double your crop, you will have a bed 3 feet by 24 feet. Let's call this Bed A.

Now suppose for a moment (we'll come back to it later) you

decide to plant eight of the new fourteen in this chapter. Where will you put them? You could, of course, simply add them to the length of Bed A and arrive at a bed 48 feet long. If you have a 50-foot walk going from the kitchen to the vegetable garden— or the flower garden, or the kitchen to the tennis court, or the kitchen to *someplace*—this could be a perfectly good and interesting plantation, as the border of a walk. But I don't think it would be very attractive simply to have a 48-foot bed marching across the middle of the back lawn. The usual way to handle the new herbs—which we'll call Bed B—is to have it match Bed A, with a walk between them. The walk can be anywhere from 18 inches to 36 inches wide.

From the standpoint of ease of preparation, the simplest material for the walk is grass. However, the grass will spread into the herb plots and become a real nuisance. It is worth the trouble to dig the dirt out of the walk to a depth of 5 or 6 inches and fill in with gravel. If you can get the kind which is tiny white pebbles, so much the better; this gives a very handsome effect. An even better idea, if you're willing to take the trouble, is to surface the walk with old bricks or pieces of flagstone, being sure to leave enough spaces between the bricks or stones to set in plants of creeping thyme. The two best varieties for this purpose are *T. serpyllum album,* white flowers, and *T. serpyllum coccineum,* red flowers. If you set out a dozen or two plants, every step you take on the walk will be a pleasure, because up will float the wonderful fragrance of thyme as you bruise some of the leaves.

With beds as long as 24 feet, you will find it useful to have a little walk crossing them about midway of their length, so you won't have to jump over a 3-foot bed when you're weeding or cutting.

What I have described so far is a series of neat herb plots joined together, with the herbs in neat rows in each one. I rush to tell you that there is no law which says they must be planted in neat rows. You can plant them in clumps of whatever shape you wish—triangles, circles, you name it. You will notice that the Pennsbury Manor herb garden (see Chapter 7) uses clumps of symmetrical shapes, and Mrs. Richardson's garden uses clumps of irregular shapes. The advantage of clumps is that the total effect is more decorative, more like a flower garden, and this way of planting is hallowed by tradition. The disadvantage is that clumps are harder to keep weeded—and somewhat harder for harvesting. So it all comes down to which your primary purpose is—to grow herbs for beauty or for use in the kitchen. If your first interest is herbs for use, you will find the "neat row" pattern is the most satisfactory.

A word about the location of this herb garden. Ideally the main walk should run north and south. This way you can place the tallest plants on the north so they won't shade the smaller ones. Also ideally, the main walk should end near some natural division of your property—a fence or a stone wall or a shrub border. It could even end near the wall of a building if this wall faces south (otherwise the building would give too much shade). The reason for this is to make the garden look like an integral part of the total rather than a unit of greenery dropped on your lawn at random. This is purely an aesthetic consideration; it's just more satisfactory to the eye.

As a final finish to your garden, you will probably want to have some large object at the far end of the walk to pull your eye down the line, as a focus. This could be a bench—and in the old days the bench would have been made of turf with the top planted to some low-growing fragrant herb, such as creeping thyme, so that every time you sat on it you would smell the fragrance. This is still a good idea if you're ambitious, but an iron bench would be very handsome and a pleasant place to sit and contemplate your work. It could be a sundial or even a bird-bath. It could be a garden figure, but the figure should be at least 18 inches high; otherwise it would look like a toy and accomplish nothing. It could be a collection of flowers in large pots, such as large geraniums. It could even be a large tub of bay. Admittedly this is a grace note, just fun for the eye.

Up to now we have arbitrarily assumed you would make a larger planting of the eight herbs in Bed A and match this with eight herbs out of the new fourteen. But there is no reason for this arbitrary sixteen total. Maybe you will want to plant all twenty-two. In that case the planting plan I have suggested would still apply—you would plant eleven herbs in one bed and eleven herbs in the other. If you *don't* want to plant all of the new fourteen, then these suggestions may help you in eliminating some of them. First of all, we must remember that bay is a *very* delicate plant except in the deep South. Unless you have a greenhouse or a semiheated sun porch, you would be well advised to forget bay. There is some question as to whether you need to plant both chervil and anise, since both have an anise taste. Chervil is harder to grow, so you could skip it. Some people would argue that it is footless to grow caraway when you can get perfectly good caraway seeds in the store (remember seeds keep their flavor far longer than leaves). And it could be argued that there is no point in growing winter savory when you already have summer savory, and no point in growing sweet marjoram when you already have oregano, since the flavors, while not identical, are similar. I said earlier that in this chapter I would not dictate which herbs to grow but would let you do your own selecting. So now you're on your own.

If you should elect to grow a total of sixteen, then your herb garden would be laid out as shown in Fig. 4. If you want eighteen, then add one to each side at the bottom, and so on.

HOW TO PRESERVE HERBS BY DRYING, SALTING, OR FREEZING

If all goes well with your herb garden—and it almost certainly will; most herbs are easy to grow, remember—there will come the happy day when you can harvest your crop for preserving. Needless to say, this will vary from herb to herb. In general, perennials can be harvested in early summer and annuals in mid-

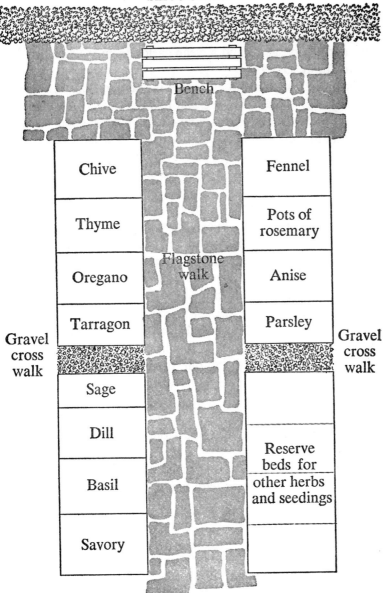

Figure 4

73

summer. But it's very easy to tell. The golden moment is *just* before the flowers start to bloom. Provide yourself with a pair of large and heavy shears and a clean carton from the supermarket, and you're in business.

The traditional time to cut herbs is "midmorning of a sunny, dry day, after the dew is gone and before the sun has baked out the volatile oils." Now, the "sunny day" is right enough—and the less humidity the better, because the leaves must be *absolutely dry* when they're cut, otherwise they may mold. Indeed if you're feeling reasonably at peace with the world, cutting herbs on a sunny day is one of the great minor pleasures of life—you have the satisfaction of harvesting your own crop, and the crop smells so good! But from my experience there's nothing wrong with noon or midafternoon. If the sun really did bake out the volatile oils, then they wouldn't be there the *next* midmorning. So forget about "the volatile oils"—they stay in the herbs all right.

You can cut off more from annuals than from perennials. With basil, for example, you can cut almost all the way to the base, simply leaving enough leaves at the base—ten or twelve maybe—to allow the plant to start up again. With, say, sage or thyme, it is advisable to leave the bottom third of the plant uncut. There is no trick about cutting. Simply gather the plant together with your left hand and cut through below your hand. In a normal year—that is, a nondrought year—you can expect to get two cuttings from annuals and three from perennials (I've had as many as four).

So now you have a carton partly filled with herb leaves and stems, and what do you do with them?

DRYING

By long odds, the best and simplest way to preserve most herbs is by drying. It's easy, and they keep nearly all their flavor. Indeed the only justification for the large amount of trouble in freezing is that a few herbs don't dry well—that is, they don't keep their flavor.

Of course, by drying I don't mean hanging bunches of green herbs from the kitchen ceiling! This is a good way to perfume a room, but it is not a good way to preserve a crop. I am talking about drying herbs on screens—30-by-30-inch window screens—which I call trays. Successful drying needs these conditions:

1. absence of sunlight;
2. circulating air;
3. dryness;
4. heat (preferably);
5. a place where they can be undisturbed for ten days to two weeks.

Thus, to dry a tray of herbs on the lawn would not work—the sun would provide heat but would bleach out the green color, even a light wind would blow the herbs off the tray, and the first rain would ruin the crop. An ideal drying shed is one I was lucky enough to find on my farm when I bought it. It has six windows and a garage-sized door; it has roof and sides of galvanized iron so the sun makes it uncomfortably hot in summer. For people who haven't got such a building—and that means practically everybody—the garage is usually the best answer if this has good circulation of air. This is a vital consideration—on damp days the green herbs can mold unless there is air moving across them.

So, for drying, the simple equipment consists of several trays (I think I started with four) and a place to put them. If you want to start very modestly—just dipping your toe in the water—you can buy a couple of adjustable screens for very little money and try balancing them in any free space in the garage. However, this is not very satisfactory, as you will agree after one is accidentally knocked over and all the crop is lost on the floor.

Building the equipment. If you don't mind paying a carpenter, you can simply say to him, "Please make me X number of screens and a rack to hold them."

However, if you want to make them yourself, or get some handyman friend to do it, here is the easiest way to go at it, from my experience:

Start with buying some aluminum screen wire. Years ago I settled on wire 30 inches wide, because this was big enough to hold a lot of herbs but small enough to handle easily. Multiply the number of screens you want by 30 inches, and this is the amount you will want to order. Cut the screening into 30-inch squares, using tinsmith's shears.

Parenthetically, some herb books suggest drying on cheesecloth stretched on a frame. This is most unsatisfactory, from my experience. The life of the cheesecloth is very short, and it must soon be renewed. When it gets dirty, there is no good way to clean it, whereas aluminum can be brushed with a whisk broom or simply rubbed across the grass. Cheesecloth will quickly sag in the middle, and sometimes it mildews. You're far better off with aluminum screening. And it has absolutely no effect on the herbs, as my palate assures me.

Next, buy some 1-by-2-inch lumber, of some inexpensive, soft wood in 12-foot lengths. Each length will make one screen. The most efficient way to join the pieces to make a square frame is to cut the ends diagonally, the way a picture frame is made. If you are going to make more than a couple of screens, it will save time to borrow a miter box—or buy an inexpensive one, or make one yourself—to get your diagonal cuts true and accurate. You should make the *outside* edge—the longer edge—of your 1-by-2 stock 31 inches long. This, obviously, will give you a frame 31 inches square, outside measurements. The corners can be joined tightly and firmly by only one 2½-inch finishing nail from each side, two to a corner. You will, however, need a vise to do this. Now fasten the screen wire to the frame, using rustproof staples (much better than tacks). To get a trim, neat job, the screening should be stretched as tightly as possible. The best way to do this is to fasten the screening on one side, making sure the edge of the screening parallels the edge of the frame; then fasten the opposite side, using your left hand to pull the wire as hard as you can *toward* you and *away* from the last staple, while you pound in the staple with your right hand. Use the same procedure on the other two sides. Now you have a very sturdy screen (the screen wire acts as a brace) except for one thing. If you are going to rub your dried herbs through a screen—and more about this later—it is good insurance to buy some ¾-inch half-round molding and cut four pieces of it so they will cover the screening on the *inside edges* of the frame. Then nail it firmly at 4-inch intervals with small wire nails. This is to make sure none of the staples works loose from the pressure on the other side as you rub down the herbs. I had to find this out the hard way. Years ago, when I was starting out and very proud of my nine-herb blend, my sister was working for the McCormick Spice Company and thought they would be interested in my handiwork. Beaming with sisterly pride, she handed her boss a jar of my Mixed Herbs. When he unscrewed the top, there on the herbs was a copper tack! It isn't necessary to fortify every screen this way, but it is a good idea to have a couple of them—so labeled on the edges.

So now you have a certain number of screens—let's say six. Where are you going to put them where they can sit undisturbed while the herbs are drying on them for two weeks, more or less? By trial and error, I worked out a screen rack which is simple to make and as economical of lumber as possible. It is shown in Fig. 5.

The four uprights are 2 by 2 inches, cut from 14-foot stock. All the other lumber is 1 by 2 inches. You cut the 2-by-2 pieces to get four uprights each 7 feet long. Then cut two pieces of 1 by 2 each 24 inches long. Nail these to the 2 by 2's to make a frame. This would collapse by itself, so you add a diagonal as shown. Now turn the reinforced frame over and nail the "sliders" —the pieces to support the screens—at whatever interval you choose on to the 2 by 2's. One 3-inch finishing nail per end will do it, since they will carry very little weight.

Now you have two finished sides. Join these to make a box by using four pieces, 36 inches long, as shown. As it is now, the frame will wiggle from side to side, so add a diagonal to the back, nailed to the 2 by 2's. And there is your herb-drying rack.

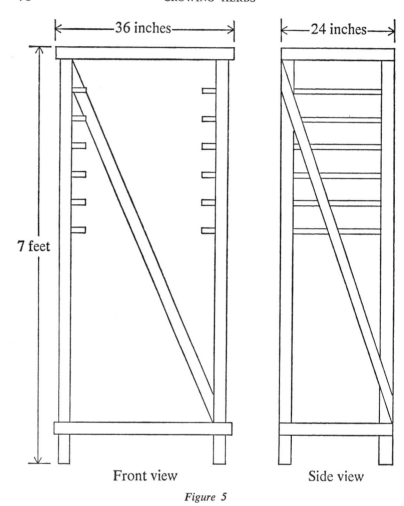

Front view   Side view

Figure 5

I rush to say I have given you the dimensions of one of my own racks, which holds eighteen screens, three inches apart. They are this close together, because I need hundreds of screens and my drying sheds have limits. I'm sure you won't want to start with as many as eighteen screens, and it's a good idea to have them farther apart than three inches. You can, of course, cut the height of the rack down from 7 feet to 6 feet or whatever height you wish.

There is one final finishing touch. I have a top for each of my racks, made of ¼-inch plywood, cut to give an overhang of 4 inches on all sides. You may want to have this too. It does, in whatever degree, help keep the dust off.

Processing. Let's assume you have cut your basil crop. Now place one of the screens on any convenient table or box or whatever will support it at table height. Lay the basil branches on the screen a few at a time, starting at the top and working down—somewhat as though you were thatching a roof, but thatching it to let a lot of water through it, because you want to let a lot of air through it. In other words, don't lay the basil on thickly. This is very important, because the leaves which are not exposed to the air will rot. If you have basil left over after laying it out this way on one screen, don't pile on any more but use another screen.

How long will it take to dry? One to two weeks, depending on the weather—a week if there's a stretch of hot, dry days; two weeks, or even more, if there's a stretch of damp, humid weather. You can tell when the basil is dry very simply—pick up a leaf and roll it in your fingers. If it crumbles into tiny pieces or into a powder, it's dry.

Now place some sheets of full-sized newspaper (not tabloid size) on any convenient worktable, put your tray of dried herbs on top, and peel the leaves off the stems. You will need leather gloves for this; some herbs with tough and wiry stems, such as thyme, can puncture the skin. You can either throw away the deleaved stems, or you can save them for making vinegar; your option. (*Note:* Some people save dried herb stems to burn in the fireplace. It's a good idea—they are very fragrant.)

One school of thought says to put the leaves in airtight glass jars just at this point. A better procedure, to my mind, is to keep going and reduce them to flakes so that they will be easier to use. This is easy. Just rub the leaves between your gloved hands and also rub them against the screen, until finally all have gone through the screen except a small residue. The ideal thing for this is to wear leather mittens, such as farmers used to wear for winter driving (driving horses, that is). These are hard to come by except in country hardware stores, but leather gloves are the next best thing.

Now you're really ready for airtight glass jars. Be sure to label them. And be sure you store them in a dark place—sunlight bleaches out the green color.

SALTING

Salting was the prefreezing method of preserving certain herbs which don't dry satisfactorily, such as parsley and dill leaves. The procedure was to fill a wide-mouthed crock with alternating layers of the herb and salt, and the crock was kept in the cellar. This last point is important because very few houses nowadays have the old-fashioned cellar where the preserves used to be stored. It had great virtues for the refrigeratorless days—it was cool, even cold, but it never froze. This means that salting can be characterized as old-fashioned and European, since it is still used there.

It has the advantage of preserving both the color and the flavor of the fresh herb. Therefore, if you want to live dangerously and try it on a small scale, here is what you do:

1. Buy several pounds of coarse butcher's salt.

2. Get a glass jar with as wide a mouth as possible (a quart Mason jar is fine for width but is too deep).

3. Put a thin layer of salt in the bottom of the jar.

4. Add a layer of the herb—say, sprigs of parsley—about 1 inch deep.

5. Alternate Number 3 and Number 4 until the jar is full, and make the top layer salt.

6. Seal tightly and store in the refrigerator.

If you try it and like the results—and would like to do it on a full-scale basis—you must first consider where you are going to store your wide-mouthed crocks. You won't have success if you keep them in a house with a seventy-degree temperature. What they need are the same conditions as for wintering a bay tree—a temperature between 36 and 50 degrees. So unless you have a cool greenhouse or a *partially* heated sun porch or garage or a cool basement, you would be well advised to forget salting, and dry or freeze—or both.

FREEZING

As I said before, drying is the simplest, easiest method for preserving herbs. However, there are some herbs which simply can't be dried with any success. Chives is one; dried chives are absolutely tasteless—it's like eating hay. Dried tarragon has a pleasant, rather sweet taste, but it bears absolutely no resemblance to the true taste of tarragon. And I have yet to taste any dried parsley which had enough flavor to be worthwhile using. These three herbs simply cry to be frozen, and while you're about it, you might experiment with a few dill, basil, and sweet marjoram leaves to see whether you like the result enough to warrant the trouble.

There are three methods for freezing—with blanching, without blanching, and a new process which I call the Guthrie method, after its inventor.

With blanching. The orthodox procedure for years has been as follows:

1. Cut your herbs with long enough stems to be able to tie them in little bunches.
2. Tie a loop of light string around the stems of each bunch so you can immerse it in hot water without burning your fingers.
3. With the water at the boiling point, immerse the bunches, two at a time, for one minute.

4. Plunge the two bunches into ice water for two minutes, until thoroughly chilled.

5. Drain the leaves of excess water.

6. Place in small plastic freezer bags.

7. Fill a small freezer box with the bags, and label the box.

8. Place the box in the freezer.

Note: Optional—instead of tying herbs into small bunches, put six or eight sprigs into a strainer, and then proceed as above.

This is the blanching-chilling method, and it has been used since freezers came on the market.

Without blanching. A simpler and newer method is to freeze herbs fresh from the garden. The only points to observe here are to wash the herbs, chop them up into the form you will want to use them, and place in each freezer bag only the quantity you will need for one meal. Then, just follow directions Number 7 and Number 8 above. As far as Anderson Farm is concerned, the results are quite as satisfactory as the blanching-chilling method—and it's vastly easier.

The Guthrie method. Dennis and Ruth Guthrie have been my neighbors in Bucks County, and New York City, for many years. They are authentic gourmets and get a deep pleasure out of the herbs they grow, so it is not surprising that they should devise a better way to freeze herbs than any so far. Their method is essentially for herbs they use in cooking. Here is how it works, with tarragon as an example:

1. Wash the tarragon and chop it into the form you will want to use.

2. Place the amount needed for a recipe, or meal, in one compartment of an ice tray. If you use a lot of tarragon you might fill all compartments.

3. Fill the ice tray with water, and pop it into the freezer.

4. When the "tarragon cubes" are frozen solid, dump them out of the tray and into a plastic freezer bag, and return to the freezer.

Most recipes take some liquid (cooking Chicken Tarragon, for example). Therefore, when you are ready to use the frozen tarragon, drop the frozen tarragon cube into the pot (using that much less liquid in making the recipe itself).

What I know of my own knowledge is that this method really works. The herb loses less flavor than with the two foregoing methods. While I'm not sure exactly *why* it works, I suspect it is because it is more effective in keeping air from the herb. When a herb leaf is frozen in an ice cube, there is no possible chance for oxidation. In any case, whatever the chemistry may be, I commend this to you as the "postgraduate" system of freezing.

You can also use the Guthrie method for herbs used in salads or for chives to be served with baked potatoes. The easiest way to defrost the ice cube is to:

1. Put one or more cubes in a plastic bag and seal tightly with a tie band.

2. Hold the bag under hot water until the cube melts, or drop the bag into a small pan of hot water and leave it for a few minutes, until it is completely melted.

3. Carefully open the bag and strain off the water in a tea strainer.

4. Place the strained herbs in a dish in the refrigerator until ready to serve.

HOW TO PROPAGATE

Seed. Most plants can be and are propagated by seed—not only the annuals, which *must* be, but some perennials, too, such as sage and thyme. Starting plants from seed was discussed in Chapter 3 and needs no more comment here, except perhaps to make this suggestion: If you are thrifty you may want to plant your own seed. If you make the kind of plantation we have been talking about in this chapter, you will have enough plants to designate several for seed purposes. After the plant has flowered, keep an eye on it until the seed head starts to turn brown, but make sure you don't wait so long that the seeds begin to drop of themselves. Cut the entire seed heads. Lay a cloth on one of your drying screens and place the seed heads on it. After a week or ten days, they will be completely dry, and you can separate the seeds from the chaff by rubbing between your hands. Put the seeds in an envelope—and be sure to label the envelope—and you're ready for next spring.

Runners. Some perennials can readily be increased by runners, especially the mints and lemon balm. As you dig around a mint plant, you will see that the main plant is connected to the smaller shoots around it by horizontal roots, or runners. Select the shoots you want to transplant and cut through the runner before you dig up the plant. After you set it out, be sure to water well and regularly until it has established itself.

Root division. Tarragon is one herb which you can increase best by root division—in fact, if you don't divide the roots about every three years, the plant will die out. First, cut the foliage back to about 4 inches from the ground. Then, using a shovel, lift the plant out of the ground—and this means stamping the blade into the ground as far as it will go, so that you can lift the whole plant out cleanly, not chop into the roots. If the roots don't come apart easily, cut the whole plant into halves or quarters with a sharp knife. When you replant the sections, be sure to water well until they establish themselves.

Layering. Oregano, sage, and thyme are three herbs which can easily be increased by layering. You simply fasten a stem to the ground, cover the section where it touches the ground with plenty of soil and make sure it can't spring up again. You can hold it down with a stone, or with an oversize staple you can bend out of a piece of wire. After the stem has been putting out a good growth for a couple of weeks (spring is the best time for this), cut it away from the main plant, dig it up and set it out where you want it. Repeat: Water it faithfully.

Stem cuttings. Stem cuttings work especially well for woody plants, such as mint, rosemary, sage, thyme, lavender, winter savory, and such. Before you cut your stems for propagating, have everything ready so that the shoot will have only a minimum time to wilt. "Everything" simply means a little flower pot filled with moist sand—or vermiculite, which is slightly better. Instead of pots you can use plastic or waxed boxes, but be sure these have several small holes in the bottom for drainage. Now with clippers cut a stem five or six inches long, cutting just below where a leaf is attached. Make a hole in the wet sand with a pencil. Trim off the leaves on the lower end and dip the base of the stem into a hormone powder such as Rootone. Bury the stem for two thirds of its length in the hole, press the sand firmly around it, and soak the sand.

Now it will require a little nursing. The sand must never be allowed to dry out but should not be kept soggy. It will need ventilation, but it must be protected from direct sunlight by a covering of plastic or paper, which should not press down on the plant. After five or six weeks, the new herb plant will be ready to set out in the garden.

If this seems like a great deal of trouble, you can reflect that you won't have to do very much of it unless you want to have a far bigger herb garden than this chapter describes.

5

A Small Salad Garden

YOUR OWN SPECIAL GREENS AND YOUR OWN SPECIAL DRESSING

If you don't really like salads, you would do well to skip this chapter entirely.

But if you are interested in them—or think you might be—then you may well find it rewarding, because I will suggest how you can get a reputation as a true gourmet by serving your own special individual salads, absolutely unduplicated by any neighbor. As they might have phrased it in advertising a while back: "You can be the salad queen of your block!"

There have been some very dreary concoctions served as "salads" in America. For example, the salad of World War I days was, prevailingly, one quarter of a head of iceberg lettuce (which is tasteless) and two slices of tomato topped by a blob of mayonnaise. And the "tea shoppe" salad of the 1920's was usually a leaf of lettuce (still iceberg) topped by a ring of pineapple, topped by a ball of cottage cheese, topped by a sprinkling of ground English walnuts—and sometimes, I swear it, even topped by a maraschino cherry. I always wondered why it was called a salad.

The old boys of past centuries went at it much better. The word had been passed on to them that people should eat salads because it was healthy to do so. Therefore it seemed good sense to make their salads as varied and appealing as possible. It seems to me that we could profitably take some hints from them to make our salads more varied, more interesting, and better tasting.

The most definitive work on the salads of the olden times is a book called *Acetaria: A Discourse of Sallets,* by John Evelyn, published in London in 1699. Evelyn was a friend of Samuel Pepys and both held offices in the Government. He was a country gentleman, who knew gardening, and was quite capable of instructing his cook in preparing new dishes. *Acetaria* lists an astonishingly large number of plants which he considered suitable for "sallets." Here are the ones now available to us:

artichokes

asparagus

basil ("the tender tops to be very sparingly used")

beets

borage

cabbage

carrots

celery

chervil

chives

corn salad

cucumber

dandelion ("macerated in several waters to extract the bitterness")

endive

fennel

flowers: of clove pink, elderberry, cowslip, rosemary, sage, nasturtium

garden cress

garlic

hops ("the buds and young tendrils may be eaten raw; but more conveniently being boiled, and cold like asparagus")

leeks

lemon balm

lettuce

melon

mushroom

mustard (wild mustard: "so necessary an ingredient to all cold and raw salleting, that it is very rarely, if at all, to be left out")

nasturtium

onion

orange

parsley

parsnip

peas

pepper

purslane (portulaca, or the common weed called pussley in the South)

radish	spinach
rampion	stonecrop
rosemary (especially the flowers)	succory (chicory)
sage	tansy ("sparingly mixt with our
salad burnet	cold sallet")
skirrets	tarragon
sorrel	turnip
spearmint	watercress

He adds several more, formerly thought to be delicious, "since grown obsolete or quite neglected with us": tulip bulbs, narcissus bulbs, the tops of wormwood ("eaten by the Spaniards . . . with oil alone, and without so much as bread. Also coriander and rue, which Galen was accustomed to eat raw, and by itself, with oil and salt, as exceedingly grateful, as well as wholesome, and of great virtue against infection").

I rush to say that I am not suggesting a salad garden of the forty-eight plants above! Nor even half that many (although you may be planting quite a few anyway, as vegetables or seasoning herbs). My suggestions are modest, and are these:

burnet	nasturtium
garden cress	sorrel
lovage	violet

Burnet has a strong cucumber taste, lovage a strong celery taste. Garden cress and nasturium are spicy and peppery. Sorrel leaves are sour. Violets have a pleasant, mouth-filling succulence, both leaves and flowers. And don't be shocked at the idea of eating flowers—we are told that Disraeli, the prime minister of England about a century ago, ate primroses as his favorite salad.

As two possible additions or alternates you can use rue and coriander, the two that Evelyn said were used by Galen, the Greek physician and writer who was attending physician to Marcus Aurelius. Rue contributes a bitter taste which can at times be pleasant, as the bitter taste of green olives is pleasant—just as a change. However, you don't have to have rue for bitterness; dandelion or chicory will give it to you. As to coriander, I said, when describing it in the last chapter, that I'd only known one American who relished green coriander leaves, a New York food editor. Since writing that, I have read in a column by the same food editor that the "delectable odd-tasting leaves of fresh coriander [are] popular in many Chinese dishes and almost always available in Chinatown." They are indeed; they're called "Chinese parsley." So I suggest using coriander to add an odd taste, but do experiment cautiously.

Let's find out something about these herbs.

BURNET, OR SALAD BURNET (*Sanguisorba minor*)

Burnet is a perennial, almost an evergreen, growing 1 to 2 feet. The leaves are about 1 inch long, nearly round, with serrated edges. The flowers are reddish, in umbels. You can grow it easily from seed sown in early spring, and germination takes about twelve days. It prefers full sun and has no special soil requirements. Plant it where you want it to grow because it does not transplant satisfactorily. Pinch off the weaker seedlings so that the plants will stand 8 to 10 inches apart. Burnet makes a handsome little bush and has the special virtue of staying green through much of the winter. It will self-sow if allowed to go to seed. If you prefer to grow it as an annual, as some do, plant seeds in the fall, and pinch the flower buds off before they open the following spring.

Uses. Its greatest use, of course, is as a salad green, because of its cucumber flavor. Thus it is really useful to people who like cucumbers but find them hard to digest. Also excellent in soups —celery, pea, bean, asparagus, cooked with the soup. Add it, chopped, to cream cheese. In iced drinks. It is very attractive as a garnish. It makes an excellent cucumber-flavored vinegar. It cannot be dried successfully, but it freezes well—that is, not much flavor is lost.

Background. Burnet originated on the shores of the Mediterranean, as did so many herbs, and has been used time out of mind, for thousands of years, both as a food and as a medicine. The medicinal use came first, and the ancient Chinese applied the green leaves to wounds to stop bleeding. In the Middle Ages, it was also used as a vulnerary, either as a salve prepared from the juice of the leaves, or the application of the green leaves directly on the wound. The leaves have an appreciable tannin content which may explain their styptic quality. It is not known exactly when people started eating the leaves as a salad, but they certainly were by the sixteenth century. Evelyn says of it in his *Acetaria:* "Pimpinella, eaten by the French and Italians, is our common Burnet; of so cheering and exhilerating a quality, and so generally commended, as (giving it admittance into all Sallets) 'tis passed into a Proverb." He then gives a couplet in Italian which can be freely translated as:

> A salad is not good or attractive
> If it does not contain pimpinella.

In his essay on gardens, Francis Bacon mentions three herbs "which perfume the Aire most delightfully. . . ." Burnet is one (the other two are "Wilde-Time and Water-Mint"). Culpeper wrote of it, ". . . a most precious herb; the continual use of it preserves the body in health, and the spirit in vigor. . . . Two or three of the stalks with leaves put into a cup of wine, especially claret, are known to quicken the spirits, refresh and clear the heart, and drive away melancholy." It is interesting to reflect that, three hundred years later, burnet is still much used in England in claret cup.

LOVAGE (*Levisticum officinale*)

Also called smallage, this is a tall vigorous, hardy perennial, reaching 3 feet up to 6 feet, depending upon where it is planted. Leaves are large and dark green, looking much like celery leaves, and tasting and smelling like celery. The flowers are small and greenish-yellow, growing in umbels. Lovage is basically a swamp plant and does best in rich moist soil in full sun. It is a vigorous plant and will grow almost anywhere but the only 6-foot plants I have seen were growing in a damp spot. Because of its height, it should not be planted with other herbs unless it is at the north end of a herb garden running north and south; it would give too much shade. Also because of its height, a good place to plant it is next to a fence. Sow the seeds in the autumn, cover them with ¼ inch of soil, and they should germinate the following spring. You can also propagate by root division in the spring. Four to six plants should be enough for most families.

Uses. Although the leaves are excellent in green salads, it is unfair to the plant to limit it to that. Use the leaves as you would celery leaves in any soup or stew. Excellent in sauces, especially fish sauce. Good in chicken potpie. Good with cabbage and potato dishes. Try it in potato salad. Very good with seafoods. The leaves can be cooked as you would spinach. The stems can be blanched and eaten as celery. The seeds can be sprinkled in meat stews and on biscuits. In England, they brew a tea from the leaves.

Background. Lovage is a native of southern Europe, the south of France, Italy, Greece. It is one of the oldest of salad herbs. The Greeks and the Romans knew lovage and ate the whole plant—roots, stems, leaves, seeds. Aside from using them for flavoring, they chewed the seeds because they thought this helped digestion. This was one of the herbs grown in the monastery of St. Gall in the Middle Ages. For centuries, beginning with medieval times, an infusion of lovage leaves has been used as an aromatic and soothing bath, which was thought to help one's circulation and act as a kind of primitive deodorant. A tea made of the leaves was thought to benefit rheumatism. Culpeper gives it numerous uses: "It is a known and much praised remedy to drink the decoction of the herb for any sort of ague. The distilled water of the herb helps the quinsy in the throat, if the mouth and throat be gargled and washed therewith, and helps the pleurisy, being drank three or four times. Being dropped into the eyes, it takes away the redness or dimness of them; it likewise takes away spots or freckles in the face."

GARDEN CRESS (*Barbarea vulgaris*)

Garden cress is also called spring mustard to distinguish it from watercress (*Nasturtium officinalis*). If you have a brook or a pool or pond in which you can grow watercress, by all means do so. But if you're not so fortunate, then garden cress will have to substitute. It is one of hundreds of species of the mustard family. It is an annual and grows 6 to 12 inches. Leaves are dark green and glossy. Flowers are small and yellow, in racemes. It will grow almost anywhere, in sun or partial shade. You can grow it from seed planted in the spring.

Uses. Its principal use is as a sharp-flavored salad green. Sometimes it is used as a vegetable and cooked in the same way as spinach. Indeed, spinach is improved by the addition of garden cress.

Background. Both garden cress and watercress have been in use for many centuries, were both used by the early Egyptians, the Greeks, and the Romans. However, the lore of cresses refers for the most part to the spicier cousin, watercress. When Culpeper said, "Those who will live in health may use it if they please. If they will not, I cannot help it," he was referring to watercress, not garden cress. However it is very much worth growing as a salad herb.

NASTURTIUM (*Tropaeolum majus*)

This is an annual climber. There is a dwarf variety (*T. minus*) which is also useful for salad greens—and, incidentally, is an attractive border plant. The leaves are kidney-shaped. Nasturtium is very popular in the flower garden because of the brilliance of the bell-shaped flowers, in various shades of yellow, orange, and red. The soil should be rather sandy, and if you are growing for flowers, it can be poor and thin. But if you're growing for leaves, as you are, you will get best results by a lavish use of compost. Sow the seeds where the plants are to grow, after the danger of frost is past, then thin the seedlings to stand 8 inches apart.

Uses. Both the leaves and the flowers are excellent in salads and add a delicious spicy, peppery taste. The chopped leaves add this flavor to bland cheeses—cream cheese and cottage cheese, for example. (*Caution*: Mix shortly before serving; otherwise a bitter taste will result.) The leaves are sometimes used as a garnish. If the seeds are pickled when green, they make a useful substitute for capers. Interestingly enough, nasturtium has a very high Vitamin C content. For this very reason it is regarded as a sort of herbal antibiotic in Germany and Austria, and valued accordingly. The flowers cannot be dried but the leaves dry very satisfactorily.

Background. The word "nasturtium" comes from Latin words meaning "to twist the nose," stemming from its pungency. The leaves have been used in salads for centuries. It was originally called Indian cress, doubtless because it originated in South America, but in 1574 the Spanish physician, Niccolo Monardes, gave it its present name. It was taken to Europe from South America and was planted in the kitchen garden of Louis XIV. And the French still use it as a sophisticated salad green.

SORREL, OR FRENCH SORREL (*Rumex scutatus*)

Sorrel is a hardy perennial reaching to 2 feet. It grows as a weed in Europe and the United States, which suggests that it will grow in any kind of soil. The leaves are long and shield-shaped and light green. Flowers are spikes of reddish-green. It is easily grown from seed sown in the spring, in moist soil, preferably, and full sun. Thin the plants to stand a foot apart. Sorrel must be watched to keep it from becoming a pest, because its spreading roots make it increase quickly. For an average family 6 or 8 plants should be enough.

Uses. Its best-known use is as the main ingredient of the French sorrel soup, *soupe aux herbes.* However, it has been used as a salad green time out of mind. For example, the Romans used to eat a salad of lettuce and sorrel as an appetizer before a heavy banquet—and, using sorrel sparingly, this is an excellent salad for today. Good in omelets. In England a sorrel sauce is served with beef and mutton. You can cook sorrel with other greens—cabbage, lettuce, beet tops, spinach for additional flavor. Indeed it improves spinach remarkably.

Background. The history of sorrel goes back at least to 2000 B.C., since the Egyptians used it in combination with other greens because it improved their flavor. It originated, probably, in western Asia and eastern Europe. It has diuretic properties (though only mildly so), and for this reason Roman doctors employed it as a medicine. The sour flavor comes from its acid content, since it contains citric, tartaric, and oxalic acids, among others. Culpeper said that it would "cool any inflammation and heat of blood in agues—and is a cordial to the heart." Evelyn went all out: "Sorrel sharpens the appetite, assuages heat, cools the liver and strengthens the heart; it is an anti scorbutic, resisting putrefaction; and in making of sallets imparts a grateful quickness to the rest as supplying the want of oranges and lemons. Together with salt, it gives both the name and the relish to sallets from vapidity which renders not plants and herbs only, but men themselves and their conversations, pleasant and agreeable."

VIOLET (*Viola odorata*)

Culpeper says so correctly of violets, "Both the tame and the wild are so well-known, that they need no description"—and I repeat his thought. This is a hardy perennial, with heart-shaped leaves and deep violet flowers. It will grow in almost any soil, especially poor soil, and prefers partial shade. There are some six hundred species, including those with flowers of white, rose, lilac, and yellow.

Uses. The violet is a good example of a plant we know as a flower—and grow as a flower—which was used in the olden times both as a food and a medicine. In the fifteenth century, for example, violets were listed as "herbes for potage" and "vyolette flourez for a salade." There were even violet fritters and violets put in omelets. As late as the nineteenth century violets were cooked with thyme, savory, and fennel to make a broth. And were served with lettuce as a salad—which is exactly the use I'm suggesting. Candied violets have decorated cakes for centuries.

Background. From Hippocrates on, the violet has been used medicinally. It still appears in many pharmacopoeias. In the last century a syrup of violets was sold in pharmacies as a mild laxative. An infusion made from leaves and flowers is thought to help a spasmodic cough, as Culpeper noted in 1684: "The herb or flowers, while they are fresh, are effectual in the pleurisy and all diseases of the lungs." He also said that the flowers, "only picked and dried and drank in water, is said to help the quinsy, and the falling-sickness in children. The green leaves are used with other herbs to make plasters and poultices to inflammations and swellings, and to ease all pains whatsoever, arising of heat." The violet has been used symbolically countless times. One such relates to Napoleon. When he was confined on the island of Elba he said he "would return with the violets in the spring"—meaning he would escape and return to France. Therefore the French Resistance of that day adopted the violet as the symbol of their membership and their allegiance to him.

RUE (*Ruta graveolens*)

Rue is a beautiful plant to have around. It is a hardy perennial, reaching 2 to 3 feet. The leaves are blue-green, about an inch long and ¼ inch wide, divided and notched. The flowers appear

the second year and look like tiny yellow stars. It is a sub-shrub
and almost an evergreen; it stays green well into the winter and
is one of the first plants to put out green shoots in the spring.
You can grow it easily from seed planted in the spring, and you
can also propagate it by cuttings and root divisions. It will thrive
in poor soil and is very tolerant as to sun and moisture. Because
of their large size and bushiness, the plants should stand a good
18 inches apart.

Uses. The taste of rue has been described as "musky" and
"strangely bitter," both accurate according to my palate. Thus
the leaves can help produce what might be called chords of taste
in a green salad. If you want to experiment, you might try the
chopped leaves—used sparingly—in a mushroom omelet. Try
them also with certain vegetables, such as eggplant and asparagus
and peas. In fact, try rue in any dish where you think a faint
touch of bitterness might round out the total taste.

Background. Rue has an ancient history. Probably no other
herb, except possibly rosemary, has appeared as often in literature. This started with the Bible (Luke 11:42): "But woe unto
you, Pharisees! for ye tithe mint and rue and all manner of
herbs. . . ." To the ancient Greeks rue represented protection from
disease, and they—and the Romans—strewed it on the floors of
public buildings and carried sprays of it in their hands, to ward
off infection. This idea persisted in an unbroken line for nearly
twenty-five hundred years, because up to the nineteenth century
English judges kept a bunch of rue on their benches to protect
them from the "gaol fever" of the prisoners. Rue has also been
called herb of grace, probably because in early times sprigs of it
were used to sprinkle holy water. The word came into our speech
centuries ago to mean regret and sorrow, as "he will rue the day."
In medieval times it was used in salads, in fish sauces, in omelets,
and to flavor beer (perhaps as a forerunner of hops); and was
used too as having magical powers to keep away witches, evil
spirits, and the plague. It was thought to be especially valuable
in curing ailments of the eyes—and this, by extension, led to the

belief it would give "second sight." It was also thought valuable in treating the stiffening joints of old age—and by some believed to "cure old age"!

CORIANDER, the eighth salad herb, is described in Chapter 4.

I said earlier that I thought we could profitably take some lessons in salad making from the old boys of past centuries. It might be interesting at this point to look at an actual salad recipe from 1390. Years ago I bought an old cookbook, privately printed in London in 1849, because I was drawn by its title, *English Cookery Five Hundred Years Ago*. The title page says: "From a Manuscript, compiled about 1390 by the Master Cooks of King Richard the Second entitled 'The Forme of Cury' etc." It made fascinating reading—for example a recipe which was for medieval scrapple and called "For to make grewel forced." But the one I tried first was headed simply:

SALAT

Take parsel, sawge, garlec, cibollas [young onions], leek, borage, myntes, porrectes [a form of leek], fenel, and ton cressis [cresses], rew, rosemarye, purslarye [purslane]; lave and waisshe them clene; pike them, pluk them small with thine hande, and myng [mix] them well with rawe oile. Lay on vynegar and salt and serve it forth.

I could hardly wait to grow the herbs to make it! Finally the big day arrived, and I tasted it, and—anticlimax—it was much too strong and bitter. But I had, you see, made a lot of mistakes. First, I had ignored the fact that my palate was used to a bland salad of lettuce, whereas the old boys had much more robust taste buds. Also I had been so foolish as to use sage and rosemary and mint as salad *greens* whereas they are very strong *seasonings,* especially sage. And I had used much too much rue, which, we have just seen, is bitter in its own right. What I should have done was to start with a base of Bibb lettuce and add just a few leaves of parsley, borage, fennel, and cress (watercress or garden cress), a few slices of young onions and leeks, almost no garlic, plenty of purslane (which is portulaca or the weed pussley) because it's very bland; chopped up a leaf of spearmint and half a leaf of sage; and added a pinch of rosemary. If you follow these suggestions, you can serve with pride a 1390 salad for twentieth-century palates—and it's rather a good one.

I put this recipe in at this stage not only because it's an interesting antique but because I thought it might encourage you to experiment with your own salad greens. The first thing to remember is that only your own palate can be the judge. In other words, it would be footless for anyone else, including me, to give you precise formulas for salad greens. But here are some suggested combinations just to get you started. Begin with a base of Bibb lettuce and add a few (say four to six) leaves of each herb in the groups below—remembering to use rue and coriander with caution:

> nasturtium, cress, burnet
> cress, lovage, violets (leaves and flowers)
> burnet, sorrel, cress
> burnet, lovage, cress
> nasturtium, burnet, rue
> lovage, nasturtium, coriander
> basil, burnet, sorrel
> and so on

You don't have to confine yourself to a group of three—for instance, you can add a little rue to the last one, making sure you have plenty of basil and burnet, since they are more "couth" to the palate. As you see, you can get countless variations in taste —thousands, really. And someday, if you're a true experimenter, you'll shoot the works and use them all! (*Note:* If you're going to pick the salad greens four or five hours before using them, here's what to do. Wash the leaves, shake out the water in a French wire basket, wrap loosely in a paper towel, and place in the vegetable bin of the refrigerator. They come out crisp and fresh. We have kept chives this way as long as two weeks.)

It is time now to consider a dressing for your salad. Nowadays there are dozens of prepared dressings on the shelves of a super-market, some of them quite good. But if you are—or become—a true salad fancier, you'll certainly want to make your own dress-ing. The basic salad dressing is just the same as it was in 1390: "oile, vynegar and salt," known to us as French dressing. In Paris in 1938 I had the good fortune to be given a special recipe for French dressing, which I've been using ever since because it's the best I have ever tasted—and I am glad to share it with you:

½ cup Italian olive oil
¼ cup vinegar (wine vinegar is
  best; malt is also good)
¼ teaspoon salt
¼ teaspoon sugar

¼ teaspoon mild prepared
  mustard
1½ teaspoons fresh minced herbs
  (or ¾ teaspoon dried herbs)

Blend thoroughly by shaking in a bottle—or, better still, by mixing in a blender. Rub the salad bowl with a clove of garlic. The elements that make this unusual—and great—are the sugar, mustard, and herbs. But what kind of herbs? Here, again, your own palate will tell you what to use, after you have become familiar with your herbs and started to experiment. In the mean-time, here are some suggestions to help you get started:

There are certain herbs which can be used interchangeably in a green salad with very happy results. The principal ones are these:

> basil
> savory
> sweet marjoram or oregano
> tarragon (fresh only; it cannot be dried successfully)
> thyme

A special word about basil: It is the supreme seasoning for salads—in fact, as I suggested earlier, you can use a few leaves of basil as salad greens. You will very likely want tomatoes in your green salad, and the Italians, very perceptive cooks, feel that tomatoes need basil. So, in a word, you can't go wrong with basil in a salad. But the other herbs are excellent also; it all depends on what you fancy on a given day.

It is also possible to get a perfectly delicious flavor by combining certain herbs, and here are some excellent combinations:

FOR FRESH HERBS ONLY

> parsley, thyme, chives
> lovage, chervil, marjoram, chives
> thyme, basil, savory, chives
> parsley, basil, thyme, marjoram

Let me carry this a step further and suggest several definite formulas:

FOR FRESH OR DRIED HERBS

Mixture A: equal parts of basil, thyme, oregano

Mixture B: equal parts of thyme, savory, basil, dill, fennel (if the mixture is for dried herbs, use dill seed and fennel seed, ground)

Mixture C: 3 parts of basil
1 part thyme
½ part sage
½ part savory
½ part lovage
½ part oregano

Any one of these mixtures will give your salad a superb flavor.

So now you're equipped to make your own varied and individual salads, and your own varied and individual dressings. *Bon appétit!*

6

Fresh Herbs for the Winter

AN INDOOR HERB GARDEN AND A COLD FRAME FOR AN EARLY START NEXT SPRING

As we saw in Chapter 4, you can freeze herbs with relatively little trouble and with retention of most of the flavor; thus your winter need of "fresh" herbs can be provided for. An alternative method—or an additional method—is to grow herbs indoors.

This is not hard to do if certain basic conditions are provided for them. These are:

1. sunlight;
2. moderate coolness;
3. moist air;
4. moisture for the roots;
5. fresh air.

The place. The traditional place for a few pots of chives and parsley is in a kitchen window—if it faces South. However this is by no means the best place to grow them, because it is usually too hot, and often too dry, and the cooking fumes can damage the leaves. The proper temperature range is 50 to 65 degrees. Where in your house can you find a room which can be kept in this range—a small greenhouse, a sun room, a spare bedroom, a cool basement, a semiheated garage? Coolness and sunlight are the two most basic needs, and if you have a sun room which gets at least five hours of direct sun a day and can be kept at the proper temperature, you're in fine shape. But if you get the right temperature and you lose sufficient sun, you're still not defeated. You can install artificial sunshine—fluorescent lighting. You can buy a fixture called a Gro-Lite, for instance (there are various names for it), which consists of two fluorescent tubes, each of 40 watts, backed by a reflector. The fixture is meant to be suspended about 16 inches above the herb pots. The light should be turned on about fourteen hours a day. (*Note:* Not twenty-four hours, which would break down the plants.) A 40-watt tube means a length of 4 feet, so your growing table can be slightly over 4 feet long. It can also be slightly over 3 feet wide, depending on the precise distance of the fixture above the plants. Admittedly this is getting "sunshine" the hard way. But if you have a room which fits all the conditions except that it is dark—and you really are determined to grow herbs indoors—why not?

Let's assume you have a cool, sunny sun room and go on from there. The plants will need fresh air, and presumably enough will come in around the windows, but they must be protected from sudden draughts or sudden temperature changes. The air can be kept moist by an inexpensive humidifier or by numerous pans of water kept on radiators and other suitable spots.

Containers. The basic container for an indoor garden is a pot —and make sure the pot is large enough. Chives, for example, are often sold in 2- or 3-inch pots—and thus soon dry up and die. Be sure to use pots of no less than 5 inches in diameter. Some people prefer to use a window box as being more decorative. In that case, one can buy or have made a redwood box about 12 inches wide, 12 inches deep, and of a length to fit the window sill, say, 30 inches. Fill this with gravel to a depth of 2 inches for drainage. Then you can plant your herbs already in pots in the window box and surround them with sphagnum moss, kept moist to increase the humidity. Or you can plant your herbs directly in soil in the box.

The soil. Plants grown indoors exhaust the soil faster than those grown outside, so it is advisable to provide them with a richer soil to start with. A good mixture is:

> 1 part garden soil;
> 1 part peat moss;
> 1 part sand;
> 1 part compost;
> ½ part dehydrated cow manure.

Additional feedings during the winter can be of small quantities of the cow manure—say, ½ teaspoon per plant—well scratched and watered in. Note that this mixture must be changed at least once a year. It is possible to buy prepared potting soil from a commercial greenhouse. If you do, it is well to mix ¼ as much sand with it because otherwise it will probably be too rich for most herbs. The point is to get a potting soil richer than you would use outdoors but not *too* rich.

The plants in your garden you are going to grow indoors should be prepared in advance. In late August they should be cut back about one third of their growth, put in pots (or in a window box), and left outdoors to get adjusted to their new surroundings. Then the latter part of September, before the first frost, they can be moved inside and should be off to a good start. This assumes you are going to use mature plants. Another way is to plant seeds of the plants you want, in early August, so that what you bring indoors is young seedlings. This method is particularly good for annuals—although it is perfectly possible to grow a mature plant of, say, basil indoors if you keep it cut back. Remember that once annuals mature their seed, they die.

Watering. The main thing to keep in mind in watering your herbs is a happy medium—they've got to have water or they'll die, but you can easily kill them by giving them too much. In other words, the aim is to keep the soil moist but not wet. A simple gauge for when to water is when the soil on top of the container feels dry. Then water thoroughly, not lightly; water until it seeps out the bottom of the pot. But if the seepage partly fills the saucer, then be sure to empty the saucer because a plant cannot stand very long in water without fatal results. It is true that the usual way to water plants in a commercial greenhouse is from the bottom. The pots are put in a big tray of water every few days and allowed to stay there about an hour—and they thrive. But if they stayed there for very *many* hours they would die. The best way to make sure a plant is not standing in too much water is to have large trays, filled with gravel or pebbles about 1½ inches deep, in which the pots can rest—as opposed to the usual pottery saucer. The tray should have water in it at all times but never up to the level of the pot. The tray thus serves a double purpose: It provides drainage for the pots in it and also, by the evaporation of water from the surfaces of the pebbles, gives the plants at least part of the humidity they must have to be healthy.

WHAT PLANTS TO GROW INDOORS?

The very first ones to grow, it seems to me, are those which cannot be dried successfully: chives, parsley, dill, tarragon.

Chives. If you are growing chives outdoors, as you probably are, simply dig up a small clump and plant it in a 5-inch pot in the pointing mixture already described. (*Note:* The hole in the bottom of the pot should be covered with a piece of pottery with convex side up; add a layer of gravel 1-inch thick and fill with potting mixture up to ½ inch from the top.) For some reason it helps chives to go through one killing frost outside before they are brought indoors. Then simply trim down your clump to compensate for moving it, and you're off. Chives are sturdy and will do very well for you if the conditions I described before are met.

Parsley. One thing to note about parsley is that it has a long tap root. Therefore the plant you pick to bring indoors should be a small one so that the tap root won't be damaged. You can make sure of this by sowing a few seeds especially for this purpose in late July or early August. Parsley especially likes a cool temperature.

Dill. For dill, I would suggest a special treatment. In mid-August sow a few dill seeds, outdoors, in a 10-inch pot filled with potting mixture. When the seedlings come up, leave about four or five when you thin out, and you'll have a handsome pot to bring indoors. If you are growing it for the leaves—and you must be—be sure to pinch off all flower buds before they start to bloom.

Tarragon. This herb, also, needs special treatment for indoor growing. The first point is the size of the pot; it simply won't thrive in a small pot, and one 10 inches in diameter is as small as one should use. This is because the roots grow very shallowly and to compensate must spread out to the sides. The second point is that tarragon, although a perennial, is herbaceous. This means it dies to the ground after a killing frost—it is going into "hibernation" for the winter. Well, let it freeze and hibernate for a few days; then pot it, cut off the old stems and bring it indoors. It will quickly pop out new shoots, believing another growing season has started.

There are a number of other herbs which can be dried and keep their flavor but which are a pleasure to grow indoors if you can make room for them:

Rosemary. Perhaps this herb should have been mentioned first of all, because you've *got* to bring it indoors for the winter or it will die. Rosemary is, by nature, a large plant. When it grows in a warm climate—Arizona or Sicily or southern Spain—it grows 3 to 5 feet high. Therefore, even if your plants are new and small, *don't* try to cramp them in a 5-inch pot; use a pot at least 10 inches in diameter. If you want to, you can pot your rosemary in the fall and then plant it in the garden again in the spring. However, I find it much more convenient to leave them in 10-inch pots at all times. They spend the winter in the greenhouse and are taken out to the herb garden in the spring after the frosts are completely over. You can sink the pots to their full depth in a bed of sand or simply let them sit on top of the ground.

Basil. As I have said, basil dries beautifully, but it's a special treat to be able to use the green leaves. You can pot a sturdy plant already growing in your garden—and be sure to cut it back from ⅓ to ½ of its height. Or you can sow a few seeds in early August and start the fall with one or more young seedlings. If you enjoy using a few leaves of basil in a green salad—and they are delicious—you would do well to bring in three plants.

Marjoram. Although marjoram dries well, the green leaves have considerably more flavor than the dried ones, so this is a rewarding plant to grow indoors. Simply select a strong plant and pot it.

Savory. The unique flavor of savory is somewhat stronger fresh than dried. Since it doesn't transplant very well as a mature plant, it is well to plant a few seeds in early August and bring in young plants. You can, if you like, plant three or four seeds directly in the pot and then pinch off all but one seedling.

Thyme. You don't really need to grow thyme indoors, because it dries so well. But it is a nice little plant to have around, because it is handsome and very fragrant—and a lot of people grow it indoors for this reason.

Now, if you still have available space—and would rather use it to grow additional herbs than to double or triple those above— here are four more desirable ones:

Burnet. This herb is pleasant to have around for winter salad greens. As you will remember, burnet tastes like cucumber. All you need do is to pot a sturdy plant from your garden.

Borage. This also is for winter salads and also tastes like cucumber. If you must choose between the two, my choice would be burnet. Borage cannot be transplanted from the garden in late summer, because the plants have become too big and bushy. Therefore, you will need to sow seeds in early August and pot a plant in early September; or you can sow several seeds directly in the pot and pinch off the seedlings you don't want.

Mint. Spearmint, especially, can be a good and fragrant house plant—and delicious in many foods. Just dig up a small plant from your garden.

Anise. This will not transplant well as a mature plant, so you will need to sow a few seeds in early August, in the ground or directly in the pot.

Note that all these plants must never be allowed to flower and set seed—or good-bye house plant.

To repeat: If you have trouble growing herbs indoors, it will be because of one or more of these conditions:

1. too much heat;
2. not enough light;
3. not enough humidity;
4. too small a pot;
5. not enough fresh air.

A COLD FRAME FOR AN EARLY START

The purpose of a cold frame is to get an earlier start with the plants you grow from seed than you can if you sow the seed directly in the ground. This means, of course, a longer growing season, a longer time to enjoy the fresh leaves, and possibly even an extra cutting if you are growing them to dry. If you have a greenhouse, you certainly don't need a cold frame, because permitting one to plant seeds early is one of the purposes of a greenhouse. So you could really define a cold frame as "a small partial approximation of a greenhouse which costs almost nothing."

A cold frame is intended to protect the seedlings from cold winds and the bitterest cold. Therefore its location is of paramount importance. It needs to be against the wall of a building on the leeward side to protect it from the wind, and it needs a southern sun for warmth. Thus, if the only space you can find for a cold frame is the north side of a building, do spare yourself the trouble of making one. But if you can place it against the southern wall of a house or garage, on level ground so that it won't be flooded in a heavy rain—and want to take the trouble— then here is what to do:

The best top for a cold frame is window sash. Thus its dimensions will reflect the dimensions of the window sash you use. For instance, a usual sash in this part of the country is 24 by 28 inches. Therefore, if you wanted to use two of these sashes, your frame would be 24 by 56 inches; if you wanted a bigger one, you would use three sashes and your frame would be 24 by 84 inches, and so on. Let's assume you elect to use two sashes, 24 by 56 inches—which by the way, will give you a lot of seedlings. You will need 1-by-12-inch lumber to give you two pieces, each 56 inches long, for the front and back, and two pieces, each 24 inches long, for the sides. Now the back should be higher than the front, so that the top will be tilted. Therefore you will need 1-by-6-inch lumber to give you one piece 56 inches long (for the back) and one piece 24 inches long (for the sides).

Use metal straps to fasten one long 12-inch and the long 6-inch pieces together, so that you will arrive at a piece 18 by 56 inches. (Use two straps on one side and one on the other, for rigidity.) Now cut the piece 6 by 24 inches in half diagonally, using a rip saw (so that you get two long, skinny, right-angle triangles). Fasten each half to a piece 12 by 24 inches, so that you get two sloping sides for the box.

Now you have four sides, so simply nail them together, and your frames will be ready to take the two sashes, which you will fasten to the top with hinges. And there you are, in business. The cold frame can simply rest on the ground. If you're afraid the wind will blow it away, then your location is too windy. But you can, if you like, as a precaution, drive a stake into the ground at one corner and nail it to the frame.

The soil in the cold frame should be a mixture, about 4 inches deep, of ⅓ garden soil, ⅓ peat moss, ⅓ sand, over which is spread a layer about an inch thick of vermiculite. The vermiculite is important; germination is much more certain.

The cold frame should not be airtight, because plants must breathe. But it won't be unless you've used exquisite cabinetwork in making it; there will probably be enough little gaps in it to let in all the air needed when the weather is very cold. When the sun shines on the frame and warms the air, the sashes should be propped open slightly and as the weather gets warmer, they should be opened wider. Then, a week or two before you intend to transplant the seedlings to the garden, the sashes should be propped wide open so that the plants can get used to the great outdoors. The thing to keep in mind is that the seedlings shouldn't be allowed to freeze, but neither should they be baked to death by a hot sun shining on a closed box, and you can regulate this by the aperture of the sash.

If you like, you can carry a cold frame a step further—and make it a hotbed! You can find in mail-order catalogs and garden magazines ads for a device called a hotbed heater. It consists of a length of electrical cable which you bury in the cold frame, so that you can plant your seeds over it, and attach to your house current. I am looking at one such ad which says that for $6.45 you can get forty-nine feet of cable which will keep a bed 3 by 6 feet at a 70-degree temperature (thermostat attached). The advantage of such an arrangement is that you can plant seeds earlier —in late February if you like—and be sure they won't be ruined by frost. It's your option!

7

A Herb Garden for Fragrance, Beauty—and Curiosity

As far as the title of this book is concerned, *How To Grow Herbs for Gourmet Cooking,* we have had it. We have discussed thirty different herbs for seasoning or eating or both, and gourmet cooking just plain doesn't require any more.

However, for centuries, herbs have had other uses than as food. I'm not referring to their medicinal uses, which were primary. Ten incidental uses are given in Chapter 8, and quite aside from these, certain herbs are and have been grown for their fragrance and the pleasure they give to the eye.

By "curiosity" in the chapter heading, I mean the curiosity of the grower. Are there certain plants you have heard about which you'd like to see growing? For example, having read as a boy that the original Britons painted their skins blue with woad, when I started to grow herbs, I was eager to set out a few woad plants to see whether the leaves really do stain the skin blue. (*Answer:* They do.) For example, I was curious to see what linen looked like in its raw state and so grew several flax plants. Also, for example, I was somewhat intrigued by the legend that when Helen of Troy was "kidnapped," she was gathering elecampane —so what does elecampane look like? (The legend is at least

110

partly borne out by the Latin name of the plant, *Inula helenium.*)
But, of course this sort of curiosity is strictly nontransferable;
what is one man's interest is another man's total boredom.

Actually, this chapter is for people who have become thoroughly interested in herbs, who have plenty of space for planting, and who have plenty of time and energy—or have a gardener.
If you have planted all, or even half, of the thirty herbs I've
talked about, in enough quantity to supply your family's needs,
you have a very presentable herb garden, indeed, and you need
have no qualm of conscience at stopping right there. But if you
care to go on, then here are some suggestions as to what—and
how—you might plant.

As a start, we can't do better than go back to the Elizabethans
for ideas, because they invented the pleasure garden, and that's
what we're talking about here. Up until their time, the herb garden was strictly for utility. You grew herbs for food (potherbs)
and to season food, for cosmetics, and most importantly for medicines, since all medicines were based on herbs. I'm not, of course,
talking about the fabulously rich kings and princes; they had had
pleasure gardens for thousands of years. The Babylonian and the
Persian and the Roman rulers had fantastic ones; King Solomon
had a real showpiece. But the common people, no.

The Elizabethan period, as everyone knows, brought a flowering of the spirit to England. This was a compound of many
causes. Perhaps a ruler who inspired great confidence and devo-
tion was one. Perhaps a greater feeling of national security, stemming from the Spanish Armada incident, was another. In any
case, it was a time of great bounce and exuberance. One mani-
festation of this was an awakened interest in gardening, a peace-
time pursuit, on the part of the country gentlemen—or, as Parkinson phrased it, "Gentry of the Land." They "discovered" flowers
and began to plant them in separate plots in the herb garden.
That is, they discovered that flowers were rewarding in their own
right, for beauty and fragrance, and were not simply the raw
materials for medicines. They began eagerly to import flowers

from other countries to add to their herb gardens—daffodils, hyacinths, tulips, and such. And they began to write about this new element in gardening, calling it "The Garden of Pleasure" (Parkinson); the "Garden for Flowers and Sweet Smells" (Markham); and "The Garden of Pleasure and Delight" (Hyll). The old-time practical herbs were by no means dropped; the aesthetic herbs were simply added. And one prevailing rule was that the most fragrant were to be planted closest to the house.

Various writers had their own special favorites for a garden of pleasure and delight. It will be instructive to combine some of these favorites for our own guidance. If we put together those preferred by Thomas Hyll, William Coles, William Lawson, and Richard Surflet, all writing around 1600, we arrive at the following list of herbs, not already described in this book:

angelica	horehound
camomile (or chamomile)	hyssop
carnation	jasmine
catnip (nepeta)	lavender
clary sage	mugwort
costmary	pellitory
cowslip	pennyroyal
daisy	rose
elecampane	southernwood
fumitory	tansy
Good King Henry	wormwood

These men, and others who thought and wrote like them, were many-faceted people, not unlike our Thomas Jefferson; so their preferences are a good takeoff point for our garden of fragrance and beauty. We will not follow this list slavishly but simply borrow from it for ideas.

A GARDEN OF FRAGRANCE

Let's start with fragrance, as being the most important quality. Perhaps the best introduction to this section and the next was written by William Coles in 1657:

As for recreation, if a man be wearied with over-much study (for study is a wearinesse to the Flesh as Solomon by experience can tell you) there is no better place in the world to recreate himselfe than in a Garden, there being no sence but may be delighted therein. Neither doe the Herbes onely feed the Eyes, but comfort the wearied Braine with fragrant smells, which yield a certaine kind of nourishment.

Perceptively said! And this leads us directly to:

LAVENDER (*Lavandula vera* or *L. officinalis*)

This, without doubt, is the king of fragrant herbs, and you really should have a few plants growing in your garden even if your interest in herbs is strictly culinary. The fragrance is so delightfully fresh and clean—but moths hate it! It is not hard to grow lavender; the main secret is to use a great deal of pulverized limestone. If you have a clay soil, as I have, add as much limestone as soil and mix in until your planting soil is nearly white. The other essential is good drainage. Ideally it should have the protection of growing on the lee side of a stone wall, but this is not necessary. Lavender is a hardy perennial, growing 2 to 3 feet, a semi-shrub. The leaves are gray-green, 1 to 2 inches long, the flowers are tiny and lavender on long thin spikes. It is best to start with one or more plants, and thereafter you can propagate by cuttings. However, you can grow from seed, but be sure to plant in the fall, preferably October, and be careful not to disturb your plantation in the spring, because germination is slow.

Lavender was used by the ancient Egyptians, the Greeks, and Romans—and for much the same purposes it is used today: to scent linens and bath water and for perfumes. In Elizabethan times and before, there were such exotic things as lavender tea, lavender jelly, lavender sugar, lavender wine, and lavender vinegar. It was also quilted into a cap and worn to cure a headache! It was used as a strewing herb and was a popular bee plant. But its prevailing use has always been to scent clothing, and thus its fragrance came to be associated with a well-kept house. As one writer of the last century said, "The odor of domestic virtues."

LEMON VERBENA (*Lippia citriodora*)

This plant may well be the next choice for fragrance. It could not have appeared in an Elizabethan garden because it did not reach England until about 1785. It originated in Chile and very probably was brought to Europe by the Spanish conquerors of South America. It is a tender perennial and thus must winter indoors. Grown in a tub, it may reach 5 feet in height. The leaves are 3 to 4 inches long, of a yellowish green; the flowers are tiny and white or lavender. The leaves have a delightful smell, and taste of lemon. Thus they are useful as a tea and as a flavoring for jam and jelly. You might try a few leaves in a green salad and add to lemon in a fish sauce. The leaves, dried, are excellent in a potpourri. They are also used as a tea. And all this in addition to being a fragrant plant for the garden.

ROSE GERANIUM (*Pelargonium graveolens*)

This plant, also, could not have been in an Elizabethan garden, because it originated in South Africa and was not introduced into England until the 1630's. Once there, it became very popular and was brought to America during the next century. During the 1880's and '90's it had a tremendous vogue, and every collection of potted plants had one or more varieties, of which there were more than two hundred. The reason for the great popularity of rose geranium is simply that the leaves are so very fragrant when touched—they smell of roses with a hint of spice. This is a tender perennial and must winter indoors. Where it can grow outside all year round, as in the deep South, it reaches 4 feet; but grown in a pot, about half that. The leaves are lobed and notched and rough to the touch; the flowers are small and lavender. It needs sun and will grow in any good garden soil.

The leaves are used to give a slight rose flavor to such things as jams and jellies and custards. You can make a delicious apple jelly by putting a leaf in the bottom of a jelly glass, pouring hot apple juice over it, and putting another leaf on top. The leaves are also used in tea blends and to make vinegar. A leaf under canned peaches or pears adds an exotic flavor. This is a valuable addition to potpourris.

There are many other varieties of scented geraniums, each with a wonderful fragrance of its own. *P. tomentosum* smells strongly of peppermint and thus is used to flavor desserts and jellies. *P. torento* smells like ginger; *P. odoratissimum* smells like apples. *P. crispum* has a delicious lemon scent. *P. fragrans* smells like nutmeg. *P. nervosum* smells like limes. In short, these are superb additions to a garden of fragrance.

COSTMARY (*Chrysanthemum balsamita*)

This plant used to be known also as Bible leaf and mint geranium, the former because a leaf of it, being large and sturdy and fragrant, was often used as a marker in Bible or prayerbook. It was also known in the Middle Ages as alecost, because it was important in flavoring ale and beer. It was a strewing herb and, together with lavender, was "to lye upon the toppes of beds, presses, etc. for the sweete sent and savour it casteth," as Gerard said. It originated in western Asia, is a very ancient herb, and was used by the Egyptians, Greeks, and Romans, and was grown by Charlemagne. It is a hardy perennial, 2 to 3½ feet, and wants full sun and well-drained soil. Leaves are about 6 inches long and toothed, flowers yellow and buttonlike and rather attractive. Plants can be started from root divisions. If you set them out 2 feet apart, they will fill in the gap in two years. About every three years the plants should be dug up and divided.

Some people brew tea from the leaves, either fresh or dry; they also use them to flavor meats. However, I can't honestly recommend either; I find the taste too bitter. The best use for costmary is to add a pleasant smell to bureau drawers and closets, and to add to potpourris.

SOUTHERNWOOD (*Artemisia abrotanum*)

This branch of the artemisia family is both attractive and fragrant; in fact the fragrance comes in three flavors—lemon, camphor, and tangerine. The lemon variety (*A.a. limoneum*) is the best known, and indeed southernwood is called *citronnelle* in France. This is a plant of southern European origin. Culpeper says of it, "The ashes [of the leaves] mingled with old salad oil helps those that have their hair fallen or are bald, causing the hair to grow again either on the head or as a beard." From this belief developed the folk name for it, lad's love—or, as we might have phrased it, "Help for the adolescent boy." Its believed efficacy for baldness may have inspired another common name for it, old man. Several centuries ago southernwood was used with rue to protect judges from the "gaol fever." But its prevailing use, time out of mind, has been to drive away moths and ants, and thus branches of it were put in closets and chests. This is a hardy perennial, growing 2 to 3 feet. Its lacy branches are an addition to the garden, quite aside from its fragrance.

WOODRUFF (*Asperula odorata*)

Also called hay plant, woodruff's claim to fame is that it is one of the sweetest smelling of all herbs. It contains coumarin, which gives off the delicious smell of new-mown hay. For this reason it has been used for centuries as a strewing herb and to put in linen chests, both for perfume and to keep away moths. It grows wild in the forests of Europe, particularly along the Rhine and in the Black Forest, where it is known as *Waldmeister*, "Master of the Woods." It is a hardy, creeping perennial, growing to about 10 inches. To cultivate it, its forest background should be remembered, and it should be planted under a tree.

Growing from seed is not satisfactory, and one should start with several plants, to be set out about a foot apart. When the plants mature, cuttings can be taken and set in wet sand.

The principal use of woodruff is in may wine, or *Mai Bowle* a dry white wine in which woodruff has been steeped. It is excellent in fruit drinks. It is also used as a tea, either by itself or added to packaged tea. C. Loewenfeld currently says of it: "In the Highlands of Scotland . . . and in France, woodruff tea has been appreciated for increasing perspiration to ward off colds. . . . The length and depth of sleep will also be improved. . . . Taken as a tea it relieves headache and migraine and is supposed to dispel accompanying melancholy."

CREEPING THYME (*Thymus serpyllum*)

This is the well-known wild thyme or mother-of-thyme, which is so tough and rugged it almost begs to be walked on. And when you do walk on it, as you know, the wonderfully pungent thyme smell comes up to you. You can plant it between the flagstones or bricks of a walk, and it grows well in rock gardens. Two useful varieties are white thyme (*T.s.albus*) with tiny white flowers and crimson thyme (*T.s.coccineus*). Creeping thyme is indeed hardy and will grow well almost anywhere except in the shade and in damp places. Once established, the plants will spread themselves by creeping roots and self-sowing. A most rewarding little plant.

CATNIP (*Nepeta cataria*)

This was one of the Elizabethan favorites, but whether or not it is fragrant is a matter of personal taste. When I rub a leaf between my fingers, I find the smell fresh, pleasant, and pungent. On the other hand I have more than once stepped on a small plant accidentally—and then looked around for a skunk. Which, I suppose, at least says the plant is pungent. This is a hardy perennial of 2 to 3 feet. It grows wild in most of the United States and is very difficult to make grow where you want it to. It likes sun, prefers a sandy soil, and grows best in an abandoned chicken run, which seems to say it likes a rich soil. It is a good tonic for cats, which love it. And it is still used in the United States to a small extent as a tea, which is believed to be relaxing and a help in warding off a cold. It is also used, sparingly, in soups and stews.

ORANGE MINT (*Mentha citrata*)

This is a very pleasant species of mint to grow because of its spicy fragrance. Like other mints, it prefers a moist soil with plenty of humus. It is excellent in vinegars, jellies, and teas. In giving the Elizabethan list above I said that other herbs had been mentioned but had not been included because they had been discussed earlier in the book. These were: lovage, fennel, anise, thyme, savory, mints, sage, rue, marjoram, rosemary.

These are all fragrant herbs, as you know, and there is no reason why you can't plant some of them specifically in a garden for fragrance. But whether you do or not, if you grow the nine herbs described briefly above, you will have a fragrant garden!

A GARDEN FOR BEAUTY

Beauty in a herb garden is an elusive quality, because it does not refer to the colorful and self-evident attractiveness of a rose or an iris or a peony. Rather, it refers chiefly to subtle differences in the color and design of *foliage,* since most herb flowers are inconspicuous. Also, it is a highly subjective quality. I may find beauty in the lacy, dark-green foliage of tansy or the silvery "velour" of lamb's ear, whereas they may inspire you to no more than a yawn.

The plants I shall describe very briefly are generally considered to be among the most attractive herb plants—but only your own eyes can decide for you. Of course there is no reason why you shouldn't plant roses and iris and peonies and daisies and the rest in your herb garden, since they were all regarded as herbs for many centuries.

LAVENDER COTTON (*Santolina chamaecyparissus*)

This is a hardy perennial of 1½ to 2 feet which originated in southern Europe. It has a pungent smell and is very decorative. The leaves are grayish to nearly white, lacy, and in their convolutions resemble finely cut coral. Flowers are globular and lemon yellow. It will grow in average soil and full sun. Propagation is by cuttings, rooted in damp sand. In a season or two a plant will grow into a large clump. You can also propagate by layering.

WOAD (*Isatis tinctoria*)

Woad is a handsome plant growing 3 to 4 feet. The leaves are blue-green, shaped rather like an arrowhead. Flowers are small and yellow, in panicles. It is a hardy biennial and will self-sow, and should have a fertile soil for best growth. It should be sown in September for bloom the following season. It used to be called dyer's woad because for many centuries a blue dye was made from the leaves. When the Romans invaded Britain, they found that the natives painted themselves blue with woad and therefore called them Picts, from the Latin meaning "painted." Their purpose in painting themselves may have been to frighten enemies, or it may have been part of a religious rite.

ANGELICA (*Angelica archangelica*)

This is a native of northern Europe—it grows in Iceland—and gets its name from the old folk belief that an angel called attention to it as a cure for the plague. It is an excellent plant for the back of a border, because it grows 5 to 7 feet and looks lush and tropical. The leaves are large and deeply cut, somewhat like celery leaves. Flowers are whitish green in large umbels. It is a biennial, but if allowed to self-sow, can be grown as a perennial, the new seedlings replacing the old plant. It prefers a moist rich soil and at least partial shade but can grow in sandy soil. It is safest to start with plants, because the seeds lose viability quickly, but if you plant seeds, be sure it is in the fall, preferably September.

The leaves, stalks, and seeds of angelica have the pungent, spicy smell of juniper berries, and it is one of the many herbs used in making chartreuse and vermouth. The stems are sometimes cooked with tart vegetables such as rhubarb. The leaves are used for tea and potpourri.

TANSY (*Tanacetum vulgare*)

A hardy perennial, tansy grows to about 3 feet. The leaves are dark green and fernlike. Flowers are bright yellow and like buttons, growing in clusters—doubtless the origin of the folk name bitter buttons. It will grow in any well-drained soil and prefers sun. It spreads avidly, so don't let it get away from you. The name is derived from the Greek word for immortality, and it was used as a symbol of immortality at Greek and Roman funerals. It was one of the herbs in Charlemagne's garden and for centuries was thought to have medicinal and tonic properties. Culpeper says, "The herb fried with eggs (as it is the custom in the Springtime) which is called a Tansy, helps to digest and carry downward those bad humors that trouble the stomach." It was also used as a spring tonic in cakes and as a bitter tea. Aside from this, it is, to my eyes, a very handsome plant.

LAMB'S-EAR (*Stachys olympica*)

This is a pleasant little plant—indeed you could call it a cute little plant. It is a hardy perennial, growing 8 to 12 inches. The leaves are, in fact, shaped like a lamb's ear and look like pale gray velour. Flowers grow in spikes and are purple. It will grow in any well-drained soil and prefers sun. As far as I know, lamb's-ear has absolutely no use except to be looked at.

MARIGOLD (*Calendula officinalis*)

As Culpeper said so often, "This plant is so well-known, that it needs no description." Anyone who has ever grown flowers has certainly grown marigolds, because they are very handsome and virtually mistake-proof. (Plant them in full sun, in any soil—the richer the better—and thin to at least 1 foot apart.) But many people don't know that marigold flowers have been used for two thousand years as a substitute for saffron. The plant originated in India, and the Romans early caught on to its value as a coloring and flavoring agent. Saffron was so expensive that only the very rich could afford it; so, often people used marigold petals. (Parenthetically, saffron is still very expensive and for a very good reason—it consists of the dried stigmas of the *Crocus sativus,* and it requires some seventy thousand blossoms to make a pound of stigmas.) Legend says that the Romans took the marigold to Britain, because they found it too difficult to carry saffron there.

Marigold petals are used today as a saffron substitute in soups, stews, chowders, and roast meats. Also in bread and rolls; I was served a bright yellow "saffron bread" (made with marigolds) by Swedes in Minnesota years ago. Some adventurous people use both the flowers and the leaves in salads.

Marigold flowers were also valued highly in medicine. Thomas Hyll in 1577 said that the juice of the petals with vinegar was to be rubbed on the gums and teeth and thought it "a soveraigne remedy for the aussuaging of the grevious pain of the teethe." A marigold ointment was thought excellent for wounds. William Coles in 1657 wrote, "The Flowers of Marigold comfort and strengthen the Heart exceedingly . . . are good in pestilent and contagious Feavers as also in Jaundice."

The marigold serves as an interesting example of how plants

we call flowers and grow for decoration were valued in past times as medicine and food.

HYSSOP (*Hyssopus officinalis*)

This is a hardy perennial, virtually evergreen, growing to about 2 feet. Leaves are narrow and dark green and have a spicy smell and taste. The flowers are usually blue, but *H. rubra* has pink flowers and *H. alba* white. Hyssop will grow readily from seed and wants full sun but is not particular about soil. It can also be propagated by cuttings. The name comes from the Greek, meaning "aromatic herb"; and in ancient times it was valued for its cleansing and medicinal properties. It is mentioned frequently in the Bible.

Hyssop is useful, chopped, in salads where it contributes a minty and faintly bitter taste. It is also good in soups, stews, and roasts, and goes particularly well with pork and fat fish, because, like sage, it seems to have grease-cutting qualities. It is an ingredient of the much-herbed chartreuse. Good in fruit cocktails and fruit pies. However, its principal use for years has been as an attractive sub-shrub, often clipped and grown as a border. It was used this way in Elizabethan knot gardens and in the formal gardens of eighteenth-century Virginia, such as Williamsburg. It does, indeed, belong in "a garden for beauty."

WORMWOOD (*Artemisia absinthium*)

It is the principal ingredient of the French liqueur, absinthe. A hardy perennial sub-shrub, growing about 3 feet tall. Its attractiveness lies in its lacy, feathery leaves and its grayish color, an interesting contrast to the prevailing greens of a garden. It will grow almost anywhere, in sun or partial shade. It originated in southern Europe, and from the first century on was highly regarded for its supposed tonic and medicinal properties. It was

BROOKLYN BOTANIC GARDEN

Elizabethan knot garden

Formal colonial garden

PHOTO BY FRED A. ANDERSON

Contemporary informal garden

THE METROPOLITAN MUSEUM OF ART, THE CLOISTERS

Medieval cloister garden

believed helpful for indigestion, rheumatism, gout—and falling hair! Dioscorides thought it was a good hangover remedy. It was thought to repel moths and other insects, as Thomas Tusser forthrightly put it in 1573:

> When chamber is sweeped, and wormwood is strown,
> No flea, for his life, dare abide to be known.

Culpeper added, "This herb Wormwood being laid among cloaths, will make a moth scorn to meddle with the cloaths." Indeed, Culpeper was very high on wormwood and recommended it for countless ailments, from melancholy to jaundice: "The sun never shone upon a better herb for the yellow jaundice than this." The fact is that wormwood is a narcotic poison. Taken in small quantities, it is harmless enough, but taken in quantity and consistently, it has a deteriorating effect on the nervous system. In short, wormwood is a herb best looked at.

SWEET CICELY (*Myrrhis odorata*)

This is a tall, handsome, eye-filling perennial, growing to 3 feet and even more with age. It has also been called anise fern and sweet chervil, the former being particularly descriptive since the leaves do resemble a fern, and smell and taste like anise. Flowers are white and grow in umbels. It grows best in partial shade in fairly rich soil, but if you're obliged to plant it in the sun, then the soil should be moist. You can grow it from seed, best planted in the fall. When you transplant, you should set the seedlings 1½ feet apart since this is a rampant plant.

Sweet cicely is delicious in tart stewed fruit, either added as chopped leaves or put in the boiling water. The leaves are excellent in salads. Good in soups, stews, and omelets. Very good with root vegetables. This is another herb used to make chartreuse. Both the leaves and seeds are a fragrant addition to potpourri. An infusion of the root is thought good for coughs.

A GARDEN OF CURIOSITY

As I said earlier, curiosity about certain herbs is a quality which cannot be transferred; my bright-eyed interest may be your yawn and vice versa. It is impossible to read your mind, of course. Would you like to grow your own sesame seed? Your own saffron? Would you like to make your own horehound candy? Would you care to see what Helen of Troy was gathering when she was abducted? Like some camomile tea? The very best I can do for your curiosity is to describe very briefly six or eight herbs which have interested me, just to start you off.

SESAME (*Sesamum orientale*)

An annual growing 2½ to 3 feet. It is also called *benne,* meaning "grain" in Malay. You can easily grow it from seed, planted in May in a sunny spot. It needs very little care. Just thin out the seedlings and keep them weeded, and harvest the seeds in early fall. Be sure to cut the seed pods before thay become so dry they will shatter; then dry them on a screen.

Sesame is incredibly ancient. The seeds were used to flavor wine six thousand years ago in Sumer (the "Ur of the Chaldees" mentioned in the Bible as the home town of the patriarch Abraham). It originated in Asia or Africa, and has been used for several thousand years in Egypt and India as a food and for the oil pressed from the seed. The old Greeks and Romans used it, and the great Hippocrates thought highly of its medicinal properties. It is still a staple food in the Orient, and sesame oil is used in our margarine. In Spain and Sicily it is usual to sprinkle the seed on bread. If you ever make cookies, try adding a tablespoon or so of sesame seed, for a happy result. Yes, the sesame you may grow is the same seed as the "Open, Sesame" which Ali Baba's brother forgot.

ELECAMPANE (*Inula helenium*)

Elecampane is a large, coarse, hardy perennial growing to 4 or 5 feet, with yellow flowers. You can grow it from seed in a sunny spot. Webster says laconically, "The root was formerly used as a remedy in pulmonary diseases," so Helen of Troy was *digging* elecampane when she was abducted, which speaks well for her industry (assuming that there *was* a Helen of Troy). Pliny recommended it for colds, coughs, and asthma. Culpeper agreed: "very effectual to help the cough, shortness of breath and weezing in the lungs." He also thought "the root chewed, fastens loose teeth" and that "the roots beaten and put into new ale or beer, and daily drank, clear, strengthens and quickens the sight of the eyes wonderfully." But pulmonary diseases was its prevailing use. Gerard said it was very good for "shortnesse of breath and for such as cannot breathe unlesse they hold their necks upright." So apparently people suffered from colds and "shortnesse of breath" as far back as Agamemnon.

SAFFRON (*Crocus sativus*)

The word is derived from the Arabic *za'faran*—and fair enough, since it is a native of the Middle East, a small autumn crocus with slender green leaves and lavender flowers. It is not hard to grow saffron, but it is best to start with bulbs or corms, since it takes several years for the plant to blossom if you plant from seed. The corms are planted in August, about 6 inches deep. They will bloom in early October, and the flowers should be picked daily, the stigmas pulled out and placed to dry on a screen covered with cheesecloth or paper, and the flowers thrown away. Every two or three years the corms should be dug up and divided, as with other bulb plants. Saffron was known as far back as Babylon and was used by the Egyptians, the Hebrews, Greeks, and Romans. As noted earlier, even in ancient times it was very expensive and thus was symbolic of gods (burned as incense) and kings—and the very rich. In medieval times it was very popular among the well-off in England, and it is included in at least one third of the recipes in Richard II's cookbook. One writer even got emotional about it: "For hen in broth, color it with saffron for Goddes sake."

Saffron is said to have a subtle taste, and this is true enough—it is so subtle I've never been able to taste it. However, the bright yellow color gives a cheerful touch to bread, rolls, fish stews and chowders, and such. If you are making an exotic sauce, it is a good idea to add a little saffron to make it *look* exotic.

COLTSFOOT (*Tussilago farfara*)

This is included because it is a simple, which has been in use for two thousand years. It is a perennial growing to 1½ feet with bright yellow flowers. It is also called clayweed and coughwort, the latter explaining clearly its use for diseases of the respiratory tract. Dioscorides in the first century suggested inhaling the fumes of the burning dried leaves. Gerard expanded on this: "The fume of the dried leaves taken through a funnell, burned upon coles, effectually helpeth those that are troubled with the shortnesse of breath, and fetch their winde thicke and often."

This herb contributes nothing of fragrance or beauty, but you just may be curious to see what a venerable medicine looks like.

YARROW (*Achillea millefolium*)

Yarrow is another ancient simple but with an entirely different use—to heal wounds. The name is derived from Achilles who was thought to have used it to heal his wounds. It used to be called soldier's woundwort, because an ointment was made from it which aimed to cure the wounds of crusade and tournament. In the pioneer days, a tea was made from the leaves for rheumatism and fevers. Culpeper thought that "the leaves chewed in the mouth eases the tooth-ache."

Yarrow is a hardy perennial growing to about 2 feet, with finely cut leaves resembling wild carrot, and white flowers in umbels. It grows widely as a weed.

CAMOMILE (*Anthemis nobilis*)

This is another simple which has been used for thousands of years—and still is. It is also called English camomile, Roman camomile, barnyard daisy, and ground apple, the last from the Greek *chamai,* "on the ground" *melon* "apple," the two together sounding much like "camomile." The Egyptians and the Greeks valued it highly. It is a low-growing, creeping hardy perennial, with lacy, fernlike foliage, and flowers like small delicate white daisies with yellow centers. The crop is the flowers, and they should be harvested when in full bloom and dried on a screen. Camomile will grow in any well-drained sunny soil, and you can start with seeds or plants. Its uses have been in two main classes—as a soothing, calming tea for nervous headaches and "all sorts of agues," and to reduce the inflammation of wounds and sprains. It is widely used in Europe for both purposes, and it may well be effective. Nelson Coon wrote in 1963 in *Using Plants for Healing:* "An analysis of all that has been written about chamomile would indicate that here is the 'general medicine' *par excellence* which is not only efficacious but perfectly safe." I have read in a number of places that camomile tea is served "in a famous beauty salon on Fifth Avenue, New York, to soothe nervous tension." Although I have yet to track down the beauty salon, this would be a perfectly reasonable thing to do; it is probably helpful and certainly safe. It has been used in beauty shops as a rinse for blonde hair, a sort of natural dye or harmless vegetable coloring. It has also been used as a soothing bath. Culpeper wrote: "The bathing with a decoction of Camomile takes away weariness, eases pains." An incidental use for an infusion of it is as an insect repellent. It used to be called the "plant physician," because it was thought to cure the ills of other plants in the garden! To make camomile tea, add 2 teaspoons of dried flowers to 1 cup of boiling water.

HOREHOUND (*Marrubium vulgare*)

Its name is said to come from its name in Hebrew *marrob,* meaning "bitter." It has been used since the early Greeks for ailments of the lungs and throat—and so our horehound cough drops are part of a twenty-five-hundred-year-old tradition. Pliny recommended it highly, as did Strabo in the first century B.C. Culpeper praised it as an antidote "to those who have drunk poison or been bitten by venemous serpents." But he recommended it particularly as "a remedy for those that are short-winded, have a cough, or are fallen into a consumption. . . . There is a syrup made of Horehound to be had at the apothecaries, very good for old coughs, to get rid the tough phlegm and for those that are asthmatic or short-winded."

Horehound is a perennial, growing 18 to 24 inches, with ovate, gray-green leaves and small white flowers. It is supposed to be hardy but sometimes winter-kills, so it is safer to grow it as a biennial and sow a few seeds each year. It can also be propagated by cuttings or root division. Full sun and any light soil will satisfy it.

Do you want to make some horehound candy? Here is an old recipe:

HOREHOUND CANDY

    10 pounds sugar
    2 quarts water
    6 ounces (by measure) dried horehound leaves
    ½ ounce (by measure) ground anise seed
    ½ ounce cream of tartar

Simmer water and leaves until reduced to about 3 pints. Strain, and combine liquid and sugar, and boil. Add cream of tartar and anise, and boil for 5 minutes, stirring well. Pour into buttered mold.

WHAT FORM FOR THE GARDEN?

We have discussed above twenty-five different herbs. This is a lot of herbs, and even with a few plants of each, would be a large garden. It is clear that if they were set out haphazardly the result would be great confusion. We should also consider that this is a garden for pleasure, not practicality, and such a utilitarian plan as was recommended in Chapter 3 would be out of key with the purpose of the garden. Its form should add to the pleasure. Therefore it is proper to consider the form very carefully, and this means considering a wide variety of possibilities. If some of the suggestions below seem too fanciful to you, ignore them. But remember, the premise of this chapter was stated at the beginning: This is a garden to plant only if you're intensely interested in herbs, have plenty of space, have plenty of time and energy— or have a gardener.

Let's start with our old friends, the Elizabethans—because for all reasonable purposes, they invented the pleasure garden—and move forward from there. As part of their enthusiasm for gardening, they invented the fanciest planting pattern yet seen outside the gardens of princes—the knot garden. This was not the kind of knot we might tie in making a rope fast but rather the knots used in embroidery. In short, it was a translation of embroidery threads into geometric patterns of low-growing herbs, with the spaces between them filled with colored earth, flowers, or white pebbles. There was an infinite variety of patterns for these knot gardens. William Lawson in *The Countrie Houswifes Garden* (1617), the first book in English about gardening for women, said: "The number of Forms, Mazes and Knots is so great, and men are so diversely delighted, that I leave every House-wife to herself; yet lest I deprive her of all delight and direction, let her view these few, choice, new forms; and note this generally, that all plots are square, and all are bordered about with Privet, Raisins, Tea-berries, Roses, Thorn, Rosemary, Bee-

Cross-bow

Flower-
de-luce

Diamond

Tre-foy

Fret

Lozenge

Figure 6

130

flowers [borage or bergamot], Hyssop, Sage, or such like." Six of these "choice, new forms" are shown in Fig. 6.

As you can see, these are enormously complicated, and I, for one, shudder at the labor involved in planting and maintaining them. Somewhat simpler patterns are recommended in *The Gardener's Labyrinth* by Thomas Hyll, first published in 1577 and one of the earliest gardening books published in England. Four of these are shown below as Fig. 7.

Figure 7

Such knot gardens as these were usually planted in groups of four—either all four together to form one very large plot or one in each corner of the total garden (which would be occupied with kitchen herbs and simples). You can see what a knot garden actually looked like in the photograph following page 122. This is an authentic Elizabethan knot garden growing at the Brooklyn, New York, Botanic Garden. It is another design by

Thomas Hyll. The broad-leaved plants are violets, the light-colored ones are dwarf lavender, and the darker ones are thyme. In this garden the spaces between the herbs are filled with gravel or white sand. As you can see, it's a stunning garden and something of an inspiration.

Advancing in time and simplicity, we come to Leonard Meager's *The English Gardener: Or, a sure Guide to Young Planters and Gardeners* of 1699. He suggests many designs which are simple enough to be compassable for gardens today. Some of these are shown as Fig. 8. They have borrowed the geometry of the knot gardens but are not as frivolous.

So far we have looked only at English gardens, which is proper because that's where decorative gardens originated. Now let's cross the Atlantic and look at an American colonial herb garden —one that was designed by William Penn himself. On the Pennsylvania shore of the Delaware, a few miles south of Trenton, New Jersey, is Pennsbury Manor, a superb re-creation of a late seventeenth-century manor house and grounds. Penn started to build it in 1683 but was obliged to return to England and to remain there for fifteen years. But for those fifteen years he wrote many detailed letters to his agent here, giving minute instructions on construction, and laying out of grounds and gardens, and the selection of plants. On the basis of his letters, which fortunately survived, the manor was reconstructed about thirty years ago and now looks just as Penn last saw it in 1701. His herb garden is a lovely sight, and a photograph of it is shown following page 122. The planting plan is shown as Fig. 9.

Notice that the design is simply a repetition, four times, of the circle-in-a-square which we saw above in Leonard Meager's collection—most understandable, since he and Penn were contemporaries. It is also interesting that the circle in every case is occupied by rue. Rue was discussed earlier as a salad herb, but it is also a very handsome plant and contributes to the beauty of a formal garden such as this.

Although we are considering this garden primarily for form,

Figure 8

it is interesting to notice what herbs it contains. It is a well-rounded post-Elizabethan pleasure garden, which is also part kitchen garden. Most of these herbs are used to flavor food; a few are simples such as horehound, agrimony, and wormwood; and a few are for beauty or fragrance such as rose geranium,

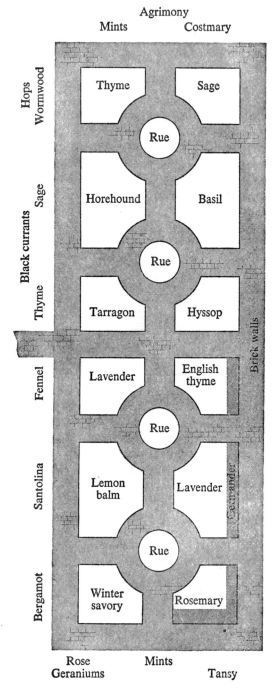

Figure 9

santolina, rue, hyssop, and lavender. (Although lavender was also a simple and was valued for headaches.)

All the plants in this garden have been discussed earlier in this book with the exception of agrimony and black currants. Agrimony will be touched on in the next chapter. Black currants scarcely belong here and are really an adjunct to the vegetable garden which is to the right of the brick walk on the right-hand side of the photograph. A row of chives six inches wide runs the entire length of the walk, and behind that are peppers, beets, spinach, onions—and all the others. The vegetable garden is about a third larger than the herb garden.

This is an authentic, old-time pleasure garden, and a visit here is a happy aesthetic experience which I commend to you. The whole manor, in fact, is a pleasure to the eye—a brilliant flower garden in front of the house with a vast lawn sweeping down to the river.

Let's now come to the present and look at an informal herb garden. A stunning example of this is the garden of the John Richardsons, friends and neighbors of mine in Bucks County, and a photograph of it is shown following page 122. Here no effort was made to use formal shapes, and the herbs are planted in clumps of however many plants the owner wanted of each herb. For example, the clump of sage in the left foreground consists of six or eight very large plants. Behind the sage are oregano, costmary, tarragon, and mint, and to the left of the herb row are flowers. Across the grass walk are thyme, oregano, artemisias, wormwood, violets, lamb's-ear, and others. So this, too, is a pleasure garden in a very real sense.

The planting plan of this garden would be similar to those shown in flower catalogs to suggest how to plant a large flower border—that is, in clumps.

We have now looked at a variety of garden forms, ranging from the vastly complicated to the simple and informal. And only your own ambition and energy can decide which form you choose.

8

Incidental Uses of Herbs

People don't have to make their own medicines anymore or their own cosmetics, so the uses of herbs nowadays are almost entirely culinary—or, to be more accurate, gastronomic.

However, there are a number of subsidiary herb uses which have nothing to do with putting herb leaves in a recipe you are preparing, and you should know about them if you don't already.

VINEGARS

By long odds the most important of these is herb-flavored vinegars. Many of them are delicious and highly useful to a perceptive cook. For instance, tarragon. I have said before that tarragon loses its flavor when it is dried. Well, tarragon vinegar was invented centuries ago by some imaginative fellow who wanted the tarragon taste but didn't have a freezer to help him keep it. It was originally a primitive way to preserve flavor, just as soy sauce was originally a primitive Chinese way to preserve soy beans.

I have read many recipes for making herb vinegar, and mostly they go like this: "Go into the garden on a sunny day and fill a pint jar ⅓ full of basil leaves. Pour in white vinegar to the top of the jar, cover, and let stand in the sun for three weeks." With all respect, there's a better way to do it. In the first place, it seems footless to go to the initial trouble and then make such a small quantity. If you really like basil vinegar—and it is superb, by the way—then by all means make enough of it to last awhile—certainly a quart and, better still, a gallon. You can buy gallon jugs of vinegar in most supermarkets, preferably malt but, failing that, white vinegar (cider vinegar has too much taste of its own). Pick a double handful of basil leaves. Now find a 2-gallon pot of porcelain or stainless steel—and don't use any other metal, or you'll get a chemical reaction with the acetic acid of the vinegar. Macerate the leaves in the bottom of the pot with an old-fashioned potato masher, and pour in a gallon of vinegar.

Now you have the choice of using the English method of steaming over a slow flame or the French method of bringing quickly to a boil. In any case, make sure the basil is cooked. Cover the pot and let stand for at least ten days—and two weeks is ideal. Then scoop out the basil leaves and strain the vinegar into the gallon jug, using a funnel and cheesecloth. (Let a few basil fragments stay in, if you like.) And there you have enough basil vinegar to keep you going for quite a while—and some to give away if you care to. You can follow just the same procedure with any herb you may fancy. In the case of seeds, such as dill, it is best to crush them first with a mortar and pestle.

There are many herbs which will make interesting and delicious vinegars. In the old days, vinegars were made of such exotics as rose petals, clove pinks, and elder flowers. Currently, people I know have made vinegars of:

anise (leaves or seeds or both)	lemon balm
	marjoram
chives	rosemary
dill (leaves or seeds or both)	savory
	spearmint
fennel	tarragon
garlic	thyme

TEAS

Herb teas or *tisanes* are used a great deal more in Europe than in the United States. To many Europeans, the perfect nightcap is a cup of camomile tea, believed to soothe the nerves—a belief which has persisted for centuries. In the early days of the United States, herb teas were much used and greatly depended upon medicinally. Boneset tea was to prevent a cold, costmary tea was for catarrh, hop and camomile teas to make one sleep at night, pennyroyal if you felt a cold coming on, sassafras tea was for a spring tonic, and so on. Herb teas are still used here to some small degree. For example, we sell catnip to a number of people who do not feed it to cats but make tea of it—as they have told us. (Catnip tea is believed good for nervous headache and to ward off a cold.) In Europe, on the other hand, herb teas are still going strong. Perhaps the difference is that Europeans, generally, seem to believe in self-medication, whereas American doctors have quite effectively brainwashed us out of it. For example, the English author, C. Loewenfeld, wrote recently, "Peppermint [tea] will also settle the liver and gall-bladder and still the slight discomfort after too large a meal. Chamomile will settle an upset stomach and also soothe an upset digestion." There is no reason in the world to doubt the truth of these statements; I believe them. I am saying merely that an American would scarcely have dared make them for fear of invading the territory of the American Medical Association.

In any case, here are a dozen herbs which are currently used as teas in the United States and Europe:

anise	marjoram
basil	peppermint
bergamot (Oswego tea)	rosemary
camomile (the blossoms only)	sage
catnip	thyme
lemon balm	woodruff

If you have become fond of herbs, you will want to try one or more of them. Although I'm not a tea drinker, I find some of them—basil and rosemary, for instance—really delightful; interesting and refreshing. To make a herb tea, put into the pot 1 teaspoon of dried herbs (double the amount of fresh herbs) per person and 1 for the pot. Pour in the water as soon as it boils, and let the tea brew for 5 minutes.

It is true these herbs do not contain caffeine as tea does. (As you doubtless know, the caffeine in tea is prettily called theine, but chemically they're identical.) But they may well contain other things of value to people. If the rural folk in England use a lot of sage, as a tea particularly, because their forebears for many generations have said that sage contributes to good health, I would be among the last to laugh it off. It just may do that. It may be something like knocking on wood when one is not superstitious, but I, for one, eat plenty of sage.

POMANDERS

Most people think of pomanders—if indeed they ever think of them at all—as the gold or silver trinkets worn by the upper classes in Elizabethan times. To these people I can make the following trivial announcement: the pomander is back! Yes, it seems that the pomander has reappeared as a sort of minor status symbol for bathroom or dressing room. My wife has just had a communiqué from Bergdorf Goodman, offering a blue and white china pomander, about three inches in diameter, for a modest fifteen dollars. Further: "The fragrance by famed Taylor of London is based on an original Elizabethan formula." A very nice full circle: Elizabethan fragrance in a contemporary Wedgwood ball. I don't know which "Elizabethan formula" is being used—there were many—but here was one favorite: "Cedar wood, orange and lemon peel, rose leaves, cloves, orris root, rosemary, rue, musk, and oil of lily-of-the-valley."

Actually, the pomander was far from a trinket to the people

of past centuries. Its use as an ornament was incidental to its value as a means of counteracting the bad smells of the unwashed and as an antiseptic agent. Its use by the wealthy goes back to ancient Greece. In the first century A.D. the custom was to mix herbs and spices with honey or wine and place in a gold ball which had a few holes in the top to let the fragrance escape. The word comes from *pomme* and *amber* (from the French *pomme d'ambre*) because of the shape, like an apple, and because ambergris was originally used as a fixative for the perfumes. The pouncet box mentioned by Shakespeare is an antique version of the pomander.

Another formula of the sixteenth century was: rosemary, cinnamon, germander, rue, rose, citron, lavender. Note that rue appears in both formulas I have given; people had great faith in its antiseptic powers. Pomanders were also used to help insomnia, but these had to be made of soporific materials—or those thought to be soporific. Francis Bacon's "sleeping apple" was a ball filled with poppy, mandrake, henbane, hemlock, and lettuce, to be placed on the sleepless one's pillow. In the late seventeenth century, and early eighteenth, pomanders became vinaigrettes and contained a sponge saturated with herbs infused in vinegar. One formula which had a powerful reputation for warding off infection—even that of the plague—called for garlic, rosemary, sage, wormwood, lavender, rue, mint, cloves, cinnamon, nutmeg, and camphor. These were to be put in a pot, vinegar added, and left to stand in the sun for several weeks; and then decanted. (Note the rue again.) These "antiseptic" vinegars were also used for washing the face and hands and to sprinkle on one's clothes. Vinaigrettes were used through most of the last century.

Nowadays—aside from the Bergdorf Goodman development—pomanders are and have been the far simpler clove orange which is just what it says—an orange thickly studded with cloves. My first clove orange had a high sentimental value—it was the first present my daughter brought me which she had made in kindergarten. And, I might add, it scented my handkerchiefs with clove for nearly ten years.

It is very simple to make a clove orange; all you need are an unblemished orange, a box of whole cloves, and a lot of patience. The idea is to stick cloves into the orange so that the heads of the cloves barely touch and, when you have finished, you can't see the orange at all. You can make holes with a skewer, or use a thimble for protection. After the orange is covered, roll it around in cinnamon or nutmeg or allspice—or all three together—to which you have added an equal amount of orris root. The spices will adhere to the orange skin, and the orris root acts as a fixative. At this point, you have the option of providing a way to hang it up. You can run a nonrusting wire through a section of it and make a loop to which you can attach a ribbon, or run a ribbon through it on a bodkin. Then put it aside for about ten days until it is dry enough to handle without splitting.

Until about fifty years ago oranges were rather expensive, so people used apples instead, and these work very well. You can also use lemons and limes.

I rush to say that a clove orange is more than an exercise in patience for schoolchildren. One in a bureau drawer and two or three in a closet give very good moth protection. And several of them are very pleasant in a room which gets musty in damp weather. *The Toilet of Flora* of two hundred years ago has the final word on the clove orange: It "will give perfect satisfaction to the most delicate judge."

INSECT REPELLENTS

I remarked many pages back that insects let herbs almost completely alone, and a reasonable guess as to why is that, to insects, herbs smell just terrible.

This occurred to me a couple of years ago when I was being tormented by gnats in the vegetable garden. Would it be possible,

I wondered, for herbs to repel insects from *me?* Accordingly, I made a very strong mint vinegar, using double the amount of the herb I mentioned under *Vinegars. Answer:* It seemed to me it worked considerably better than any druggist's insect repellent I had used. So I tried it again, using another herb with a very strong smell, thyme. Again it seemed to work and perhaps a shade better. In any case it was much more pleasant to rub on my skin than the nasty-smelling "store" repellent. My experimenting stopped there, but I see no reason why it would not also work with rosemary, oregano, or savory.

MOTH REPELLENTS

Moths also are insects and like the biting kinds seem to hate what humans consider fragrant. Before the invention of moth balls and DDT and mothproofing, the ancients coped with moths by using this principle. The Greeks and Romans used chests of perfumed wood—cedar, sandalwood, camphorwood—as many people have done ever since. Herbs have also been used for many centuries. The Elizabethans used lavender and southernwood, for example. Southernwood used to be called *garde-robe* in France, because it was put in chests to guard clothing. Culpeper recommended wormwood: "This herb, wormwood, being laid among cloaths will make a moth scorn to meddle with cloaths as much as a lion scorns to meddle with a mouse or an eagle with a fly." *Banckes' Herbal* pushed rosemary: "Take the flowers of rosemary and put them in thy chest among thy clothes or among thy Bookes and Moths shall not destroy them." In *Godey's Lady's Book* in 1864, this formula was given for keeping away moths: "Cloves, in coarse powder, one ounce; cassia, one ounce; lavender flowers, one ounce; lemon peel, one ounce. Mix them and put them in little bags and place them where the clothes are kept, or wrap the clothes around them. They will keep off insects." The use of cloves and citrus peel gets us close to a clove orange, which is an excellent moth repellent, as we have noted.

The herbs which were used to repel moths included lavender, rosemary, santolina, peppermint, spearmint, wormwood, thyme, tansy, woodruff, southernwood. Also dried orange and lemon peel. You can select whatever ones you wish—and add a teaspoon of ground cloves, cinnamon, or allspice, per quart of dried herbs. Then either put them in little bags or strew them among the clothes.

HERB LIQUEURS

The simplest way to get a herb liqueur is to buy a bottle of chartreuse, which has more than 130 kinds of herbs in it. But if you really like to experiment with herbs, you may want to try making your own.

For example, anisette: Grind 3 tablespoons of anise seed with a mortar and pestle and add to a pint of good brandy. Let stand for at least six weeks, giving the bottle a shake now and then. Strain out the anise seed and add three tablespoons of heavy sugar syrup. If you are pleased with the result, then you may want to go on to . . .

Kummel: Use 3 tablespoons of caraway seed and treat in exactly the same way. You can also try your own crème de menthe, using 2 tablespoons each of dried spearmint and dried peppermint.

If you still want to go further, try a mixture of some of your favorite herbs—basil, thyme, rosemary, marjoram, and so on—and see how close you can come to matching the taste of Benedictine, which also has a great many herbs in it. It won't be easy. On the other hand, don't be too quickly discouraged. I bought a bottle of "Benedictine" at a Benedictine monastery in Rome several years ago. It had been made on the premises, and I will be willing to swear that you or I could do at least as well. This is not arrogance on my part; it was loaded with cinnamon, which doesn't belong in Benedictine at all, and was far too sweet. Anyway, now you're on your own!

RUBBING ALCOHOL

An alcohol rub suggests the medical procedures of the past. However, they are still used in hospitals to refresh the patient and make him feel good (that is, they are used in hospitals if you have a special nurse—the floor nurses are usually too busy). They are, indeed, refreshing if one has been in bed for several days. And the addition of herbs will make them even more so. In the old days the method was to steep herbs in wine for a week and then strain off the liquid. Now it is preferable to use rubbing alcohol—as odorless as possible—as a base. Add the herbs to the alcohol at the rate of a handful to a quart and let steep for two to three weeks. Then strain off the liquid. Herbs which are particularly good for this purpose include rosemary, lavender, lemon balm, spearmint, and peppermint.

HERB BATHS

The use of herbs in the bath water goes back many centuries and was inspired by the therapeutic properties they were thought to have. For instance, Parkinson, who wrote around 1600, said, "Mintes are often times used in Baths with Balm and other herbs as a help to comfort and strengthen the nerves and sinews." In discussing thyme in Chapter 3, I noted that it was a symbol of strength and courage because thyme in the bath renewed the energy of the tired soldier. Since thyme contains an antiseptic component, thymol, this belief might well have been medically valid. In any case, a thyme bath would be most *refreshing* because of the clean fragrance, and thus you would tend to feel that you had recharged your energy.

In past times herbs were not thrown directly into the bath but were steeped in boiling water which was then added to the bath. *The Toilet of Flora* of the eighteenth century gives these instructions for an aromatic bath: "Boil in a sufficient quantity of river water, one or more of the following plants; viz. Laurel, Thyme, Rosemary, Sweet-Marjoram, Bastard-Marjoram [oregano], Lavender, Southernwood, Wormwood, Sage, Pennyroyal, Basil, Balm, Wild Mint, Hyssop, Anise, Fennel or any other herbs that have an agreeable scent. Having strained off the liquor from the herbs, add to it a little Brandy. This is an excellent bath to strengthen the limbs; it removes pains proceeding from cold, and promotes perspiration."

A convenient way to add herbs today is to tie up a couple of tablespoons of the herb you want in a 5-inch square of cheese-cloth—a sort of *bouquet garni* for the bath. About fifteen minutes before you take your bath, drop one herb sac in about a quart of boiling water, and later pour the herb infusion into the tub. The herbs which will give the most refreshing smells include thyme, marjoram, lavender, peppermint, sage, and rosemary—"or any other herbs that have an agreeable scent"!

POTPOURRI

The potpourri, like the pomander, may be defined as the ancient, do-it-yourself version of the aerosol room spray. It started out more as a necessity than a luxury. In past centuries, when bathing was extremely infrequent and fresh air in a house was considered a menace to health, something *had* to be done to make the air breathable. And so evolved the idea of having containers filled with flower petals, herbs, and spices which could bring fragrance indoors.

Although this is the era of the aerosol room spray, the old-time potpourri is still with us or is returning. We have just received a flyer about a pottery jar filled with dried flower petals, "Bendel's potpourri." Note the *Bendel*. Henri Bendel Inc. in New York is undertaking to create trends which will be "the living end" in chic. Because of its limitation in clothing sizes (very, very few of anything over size twelve), it is deliberately appealing to the very young and very chic to whom price is no object.

This scarcely seems the store you would expect to revive a centuries-old custom. But there it is: "Our own English import, ten dollars."

I made my first potpourri quite accidentally years ago, before I had ever heard of such a thing as potpourri. The air in an old farmhouse can become quite musty if it is closed up during the week. So I hit on the idea of filling a gallon jar with the leftovers from herb processing—the stems and bits of leaves of mint, thyme, sage, marjoram, and such. My first act upon arrival on Friday evening was to crunch and stir the contents of the jar to release the wonderful herb smells. And there you have a potpourri at its most primitive.

The term "potpourri" is a most unhappy one, because it comes from the French *pourrir,* "to rot," and thus means literally "rotten pot" or "rotten jar." This name arises from the olden-time moist method of preserving the flower petals, which was to dry them only partially and then to add quantities of salt as a preservative. The dry method is much simpler and calls for drying the petals thoroughly—"chip dry" was one description—and then adding any dried fragrant flowers or leaves one may choose, spices, and a fixative.

The wide latitude one was allowed in the composition of them is shown in *The Toilet of Flora,* which lists as possible ingredients: "Different parts of Aromatic Plants; as Leaves of Southernwood, Balm, Mint, Dittany, Ground-ivy, Bay, Hyssop, Lovage, Sweet Marjoram, Origanum, Pennyroyal, Thyme, Rosemary, Savory. The Flowers of the Orange, Lemon, Lime, and Citron Tree, Saffron, Lavender, Roses, Lily of the Valley, Clove-flower, Wall-flower, Jonquil. Fruits, as Aniseeds, etc. The Rinds of Lemons, Oranges, Juniper-berries, Nutmegs and Cloves. Roots of Angelica, Oriental Costus, Sweet Flag, Orrice etc. Gums, as Frankincense, Myrrh, Storax, Benjamin [benzoin], Ambergrise, and Amber. Barks, as Cannella Alba, Cinnamon etc. Care must be taken that all these ingredients are perfectly dry. To prevent their turning black, add a little common Salt."

There are a vast number of formulas for potpourri which have accumulated over the centuries. Here are a few of them:

ROSE POTPOURRI

2 quarts of rose petals	2 tablespoons ground cloves
1 pint of lavender flowers	2 tablespoons cinnamon
1 pint of rose geranium leaves	25 drops oil of rose
½ pint of marjoram	5 tablespoons powdered orrisroot
½ pint of thyme	
—all the above to be thoroughly dried	

Mix together very thoroughly and store in a closed container for six weeks before using.

Here is another version, also very old:

ROSE POTPOURRI NUMBER 2

2 quarts of rose petals	2 tablespoons crushed dried lemon peel
1 quart of lemon verbena	
1 pint of lemon balm	2 tablespoons allspice
1 pint of lavender flowers	20 drops oil of heliotrope
—all thoroughly dried	5 tablespoons powdered orrisroot

Mix together thoroughly and keep in a tight container for six weeks.

HERB POTPOURRI

½ pint thyme	4 tablespoons powdered orrisroot
½ pint rosemary	8 drops oil of bergamot
½ pint marjoram	
½ pint bergamot	
½ pint sage	
—all thoroughly dried	

Mix together thoroughly.

LAVENDER POTPOURRI

1 quart lavender flowers	8 drops oil of lavender
1 quart rose petals	4 teaspoons powdered orrisroot

Mix together thoroughly.

MINT POTPOURRI

1 quart spearmint
1 quart peppermint
1 quart lemon balm
½ pint thyme
—all thoroughly dried

2 tablespoons crushed dried
   lemon peel
4 tablespoons powdered orrisroot
6 drops oil of thyme

Mix together thoroughly.

Now it seems time for a little experimenting on your part. Why don't you improvise on the formula outlined below, adding any fragrant herb you may have so that it could be called:

A PERSONAL POTPOURRI

To a base of about a quart of rose petals, add a small quantity —about ½ pint—of some of these herbs:

anise seed, ground   marjoram
basil   peppermint
bergamot   rosemary
dill seed, ground   sage
lavender   thyme
lemon balm   woodruff
—or any others you fancy

Add about 4 tablespoons of orrisroot to each 2 quarts of mixture. Add a few drops of oil of bergamot or oil of lavender—or not, as you choose.

The point to keep in mind is that you don't have to follow a formula. When you combine many fragrant leaves and flowers, a wonderful fragrance is bound to result. If you particularly like the fine, clean fragrance of thyme, use a lot of it. If you like spices, add a little clove or cinnamon or allspice. In short, by experiment, you can arrive at a result which you think is just right!

HERB JELLIES

There are a number of herbs which, in the form of a jelly, are excellent with meats of various kinds—roast chicken for one, roast lamb for another. Thyme, rosemary, basil, sage, tarragon, lemon balm, and spearmint are particularly good. They can be made this way:

ROSEMARY JELLY

½ cup dried rosemary   2 cups water
3 cups sugar   ½ bottle of pectin
2 tablespoons lemon juice

Pour the boiling water over the dried rosemary. Cover, let stand for an hour, then strain. Add the sugar and lemon juice. Place over a high flame, and stir until the boiling point is reached. Then add the pectin and boil for another minute. Pour into jelly glasses and seal.

People have been known to make jellies of such exotics as violets, roses, rose geranium, lemon verbena, lavender, and marigolds. However, the ones mentioned above are the most generally satisfactory.

9

A Garden of 234 Herbs

MANY FOR HEALING—A FEW FOR WITCHCRAFT!

Let me rush to say: No, I do *not* expect you, or any other individual, to plant 234 different herbs. But I would feel remiss in my duty of explaining herbs if I did not give you at least a glimpse of the great world of herbs as it was some six hundred years ago, when people's lives literally depended upon them.

We saw in Chapter 7 that the Elizabethans brought flowers into the herb garden and made it a pleasure garden. Before them, the herb garden was, of course, a pleasure to stroll in just as it is today, but growing herbs was a very serious business because herbs provided most of the remedies there were for ill health and misadventure. In other words, to understand what herbs have meant to people for countless centuries, we should take a very quick look at a herb garden of medieval times.

Fortunately it is possible to do this with one's own eyes. There is a superb medieval herb garden growing at The Cloisters in New York City. I might say that The Cloisters is an extension of the Metropolitan Museum of Art and contains treasures from churches, castles, and monasteries of the Middle Ages. Since a herb garden was an indispensable part of every medieval monastery, the museum has wisely provided one here. A photograph

of it is shown following page 122. It is, as you see, a formal garden with a wellhead in the center, of the sort much used in
medieval monastery gardens. (The George Washington Bridge
appears in the background to the south.)

Following is a list of herbs planted in this garden:

1. *Ruta graveolens, L.* Rue
2. *Dianthus*
   a. *D. barbatus, L.* Sweet William
   b. *D. carthusianorum, L.* Carthusian Pink
   c. *D. Caryophyllus, L.* Carnation
   d. *D. deltoides, L.* Maiden Pink
   e. *D. Knappii, Asch.* Yellow Pink
   f. *D. monspessulanus, L.* Montpelier Pink
   g. *D. plumarius, L.* Grass Pink
   h. *D. Seguieri, Chaix* Broad-leaved Pink
   i. Various other Wild Pinks
3. *Cichorium Intybus, L.* Chicory
4. *Melissa officinalis, L.* Lemon Balm
5. *Cheiranthus Cheiri, L.* Wallflower
6. *Malva sylvestris, L.* Purple Mallow
7. *Iris*
   a. *I. florentina, L.* White Iris
   b. *I. foetidissima, L.* Gladwin
   c. *I. germanica, L.* Blue Flag
   d. *I. pallida, Lam.* Lavender Iris
   e. *I. Pseudacorus, L.* Yellow Iris, Water Flag
   f. *I. pumila, L.* Dwarf Iris
8. *Rosa*
   a. *R. alba, L.* White Rose
   b. *R. canina, L.* Dog Rose
   c. *R. centifolia, L.* Cabbage Rose
   d. *R. damascena, Mill.* Damask Rose
   e. *R. damascena* var. *versicolor, West.* York and Lancaster
      Rose
   f. *R. eglanteria, L.* Sweetbrier
   g. *R. gallica, L.* French Rose

    h. *R. gallica* var. *officinalis, Thory*   Apothecary's Rose
    i. *R. gallica* var. *versicolor, Thory*   Rosa Mundi, often called York and Lancaster Rose
    j. *R. pomifera, Herrm.*   Apple Rose

9. *Sedum*
    a. *S. acre, L.*   Love Entangle, Wall Pepper
    b. *S. Telephium, L.*   Orpine, Live-forever

10. *Delphinium*
    a. *D. Consolida, L.*   Field Larkspur
    b. *D. Staphisagria, L.*   Stavesacre

11. *Chrysanthemum*
    a. *C. Balsamita, L.*   Costmary
    b. *C. cinerariaefolium, Vis.*   Dalmatian Pyrethrum
    c. *C. coccineum, Willd.*   Pyrethrum
    d. *C. coronarium, L.*   Crown Daisy
    e. *C. Leucanthemum, L.*   White Marguerite, Oxeye or Field Daisy
    f. *C. Parthenium, Pers.*   Feverfew
    g. *C. uliginosum, Pers.*   Giant Daisy

12. *Sempervivum tectorum, L.*   Houseleek
13. *Anthriscus Cerefolium, Hoffm.*   Chervil
14. *Agrimonia Eupatoria, L.*   Agrimony
15. *Linum usitatissimum, L.*   Flax
16. *Artemisia*
    a. *A. Abrotanum, L.*   Southernwood, Old Man
    b. *A. Absinthium, L.*   Wormwood, Absinthe
    c. *A. Dracunculus, L.*   Tarragon, Estragon
    d. *A. camphorata, Vill.*   Camphor Artemisia

17. *Daphne*
    a. *D. Cneorum, L.*   Garland Flower
    b. *D. Mezereum, L.*   February Daphne

18. *Myrtus Communis*
19. *Juniperus Sabina, L.*   Savin
20. *Lunaria annua, L.*   Satin Flower, Honesty
21. *Muscari*
    a. *M. botryoides, Mill.*   Grape Hyacinth
    b. *M. comosum, Mill.*   Feathered Hyacinth, Purse Tassel

22. *Salvia*
    a. *S. officinalis, L.* Sage
    b. *S. Sclarea, L.* Clary
23. *Origanum; Majorana*
    a. *O. Dictamnus, L.* Cretan Dittany
    b. *M. hortensis, Moench (Origanum Majorana, L.)* Sweet Marjoram
    c. *M. Onites, Benth. (Origanum Onites, L.)* Marjoram
    d. *O. vulgare, L.* Wild Marjoram
24. *Carthamus tinctorius, L.* Safflower, False Saffron
25. *Galium verum, L.* Yellow Bedstraw
26. *Santolina*
    a. *S. Chamaecyparissus, L.* Lavender Cotton
    b. *S. virens, Mill.* Green Santolina
27. *Hyoscyamus niger, L.* Henbane
28. *Anthemis*
    a. *A. nobilis, L.* Camomile
    b. *A. tinctoria, L.* Golden Marguerite
29. *Myosotis*
    a. *M. alpestris, Schmidt* Forget-me-not, Scorpion Grass
    b. *M. scorpioides, L.* True Forget-me-not
30. *Matthiola bicornis, DC.* Evening Stock, Gillyflower
31. *Hespéris matronalis, L.* Dame's Rocket
32. *Allium*
    a. *A. ascalonicum, L.* Shallot
    b. *A. Schoenopresum, L.* Chives
33. *Citrullus Colocynthis, Schrad.* Bitter Apple
34. *Anchusa azurea, Mill.* Flowering Alkanet
35. *Saponaria officinalis, L.* Bouncing Bet, Soapwort
36. *Bellis perennis, L.* English Daisy
37. *Physalis Alkekengi, L.* Winter Cherry
38. *Trigonella Foenum-Graecum, L.* Fenugreek
39. *Asphodeline lutea, Reichenb.* Asphodel
40. *Symphytum officinale, L.* Comfrey
41. *Sanguisorba minor, Scop.* Burnet
42. *Cornus mas. L.* Cornelian Cherry
43. *Lavandula officinalis, Lois.* Lavender

44. *Valeriana officinalis, L.*   Valerian, Garden Heliotrope
45. *Lychnis*
    a. *L. alba, Mill.*   White Campion
    b. *L. Coronaria, Desr.*   Mullein Pink, Rose Campion
    c. *L. Flos-cuculi, L.*   Cuckoo Flower, Ragged Robin
    d. *L. Fos-Jovis, Desr.*   Flower of Love
    e. *L. Githago, L.*   Corn Cockle
46. *Levisticum officinale, Koch*   Lovage
47. *Anagallis*
    a. *A. arvensis, L.*   Common Pimpernel
    b. *A. linifolia, L.*   Large Pimpernel
48. *Alkanna tinctoria, Tausch.*   Dyer's Bugloss, Alkanet
49. *Rubia tinctorum, L.*   Madder
50. *Isatis tinctoria, L.*   Woad
51. *Tussilago Farfara, L.*   Coltsfoot
52. *Rumex*
    a. *R. Acetosa, L.*   Garden Sorrel
    b. *R. Patientia, L.*   Herb Patience
    c. *R. scutatus, L.*   French Sorrel
53. *Portulaca oleracea, L.*   Purslane, Pigweed
54. *Chenopodium*
    a. *C. Bonus-Henricus, L.*   Good-King-Henry
    b. *C. Botrys, L.*   Jerusalem Oak, Botrys
    c. *C. capitatum, Asch.*   Strawberry Blite
55. *Bryonia dioica, Jacq.*   Bryony
56. *Coriandrum sativum, L.*   Coriander
57. *Ocimum*
    a. *O. Basilicum, L.*   Sweet Basil
    b. *O. minimum, L.*   Bush or Small-leaved Basil
58. *Dipsacus fullonum, L.*   Fuller's Teasel
59. *Achillea*
    a. *A. Millefolium var. rosea, L.*   Yarrow, Milfoil
    b. *A. nan, L.*   Dwarf Yarrow
60. *Althaea*
    a. *A. ficifolia, Cav.*   Antwerp Hollyhock
    b. *A. officinalis, L.*   Marshmallow
61. *Inula Helenium, L.*   Elecampane

62. *Cirsium monspessulanum, All.* Plumed Thistle
63. *Euphorbia lathyrus, L.* Caper Spurge
64. *Centaurea*
    a. *C. Cyanus, L.* Bluebottle, Cornflower
    b. *C. Jacea, L.* Common Centaury, Knapweed
    c. *C. montana, L.* Hardy Cornflower, Mountain Bluet
65. *Tanacetum*
    a. *T. vulgare, L.* Common Tansy
    b. *T. vulgare* var. *crispum, DC.* Curly Tansy
66. *Marrubium vulgare, L.* Horehound
67. *Carum Carvi, L.* Caraway
68. *Foeniculum vulgare, Mill.* Fennel
69. *Pimpinella Anisum, L.* Anise
70. *Anethum graveolens, L.* Dill
71. *Nigella*
    a. *N. damascena, L.* Love-in-a-Mist
    b. *N. sativa, L.* Black Cumin, Git Flower
72. *Dracunculus vulgaris, Schott.* Dragon Plant
73. *Viola*
    a. *V. calcarata, L.* Alpine Pansy
    b. *V. cornuta, L.* Horned Violet
    c. *V. odorata, L.* Sweet Violet
    d. *V. tricolor, L.* Heartsease, Wild Pansy
74. *Nepeta*
    a. *N. cataria, L.* Catnip
    b. *N. hederacea, Trev.* Ground Ivy, Alehoof
    c. *N. Mussinii, Spreng.* Flowering Catnip
75. *Angelica Archangelica, L.* Angelica
76. *Lilium candidum, L.* Annunciation, Madonna, or Bourbon Lily
77. *Digitalis purpurea, L.* Foxglove
78. *Aconitum Napellus, L.* Monkshood
79. *Helleborus*
    a. *H. foetidus, L.* Setterwort, Bear's Foot
    b. *H. orientalis, Lam.* Lenten Rose
    c. *H. niger, L.* Christmas Rose, Black Hellebore
80. *Borago officinalis, L.* Borage

81. *Mentha*
    a. *M. crispa, Ter.*   Curled Mint
    b. *M. piperita, L.*   Peppermint
    c. *M. Pulegium, L.*   Pennyroyal
    d. *M. rotundifolia, Huds.*   Applemint
    e. *M. spicata, L.*   Spearmint
82. *Chelidonium, majus, L.*   Celandine
83. *Campanula*
    a. *C. rotundifolia, L.*   Bluebells-of-Scotland
    b. *C. Trachelium, L.*   Throatwort
84. *Hyssopus officinalis, L.*   Hyssop
85. *Acanthus*
    a. *A. mollis, L.*   Acanthus, Bear's-Breech
    b. *A. spinosus, L.*   Acanthus
86. *Onopordun Acanthium, L.*   Scotch Thistle
87. *Cynara Cardunculus, L.*   Cardoon
88. *Papaver*
    a. *P. Rhoeas, L.*   Corn Poppy
    b. *P. somniferum, L.*   Opium Poppy
89. *Paeonia officinalis, L.*   Peony
90. *Verbena officinalis, L.*   Vervain
91. *Dictamnus*
    a. *D. albus, L.*   Fraxinella, Dittany, Gas Plant
    b. *D. albus* var. *rubra, L.*   Fraxinella, Dittany, Gas Plant
92. *Convallaria majalis, L.*   Lily of the Valley
93. *Stachys*
    a. *S. grandiflora, Benth.*   Large-flowered Betony
    b. *S. lanata, Jacq.*   Lamb's-Ears, Woolly Woundwort
    c. *S. officinalis, Franch.*   Betony
94. *Carlina acaulis, L.*   Charlemagne's Thistle
95. *Cytissus scoparius, Link.*   Scotch Broom, Planta Genista
96. *Rosmarinus officinalis, L.*   Rosemary
97. *Satureja*
    a. *S. hortensis, L.*   Summer Savory
    b. *S. montana, L.*   Winter Savory
98. *Calendula officinalis, L.*   Pot Marigold

99. *Petroselinum*
    a. *P. crispum, Nym.* Common or Italian Parsley
    b. *P. crispum, Nym.* Curled Parsley
100. *Cuminum Cyminum, L.* Cumin
101. *Thymus*
    a. *T. Serpyllum, L.* Mother-of-Thyme
    b. *T. Serpyllum* var. *vulgaris, Benth.* Lemon Thyme
    c. *T. vulgaris, L.* Common Thyme
    d. *T. Herba-barona, Loisel.* Herba-barona
    e. *T. micans, Lowe.* Creeping Thyme
102. *Teucrium Chamaedrys, L.* Wall Germander
103. *Fragaria vesca, L.* Wild Strawberry
104. *Reseda Luteola, L.* Dyer's Weed
105. *Narcissus*
    a. *N. Bulbocodium, L.* Hoop-Petticoat Daffodil
    b. *N. Jonquilla, L.* Jonquil
    c. *N. Pseudo-Narcissus, L.* Daffodil
    d. *N. triandrus, L.* Angel's-Tear Daffodil
106. *Scilla hispanica, Mill.* Spanish Jacinth
107. *Colchicum autumnale, L.* Meadow Saffron, Colchicum
108. *Crocus*
    a. *C. sativus, L.* Saffron Crocus, Autumn Crocus
    b. *C. speciosus, Bieb.* Autumn Crocus
    c. *C. zonatus, Gay.* Autumn Crocus
109. *Leucojum vernum, L.* Spring Snowflake
110. *Geranium Robertianum, L.* Herb Robert
111. *Linaria vulgaris, Mill.* Toadflax
112. *Centranthus ruber, DC.* Red Valerian
113. *Primula*
    a. *P. acaulis, Hill.* Primrose
    b. *P. Auricula, L.* Auricula, Bear's Ears
    c. *P. polyantha, Hort.* Polyanthus
    d. *P. polyantha* (hybrid). Hose-in-Hose
    e. *P. veris, L.* Cowslip, Saint-Peter's Wort
114. *Aquilegia vulgaris, L.* Columbine
115. *Anthericum ramosum, L.* Spiderwort
116. *Catananche caerulea, L.* Blue Cupidone, Cupid's Dart

117. *Pulmonaria angustifolia, L.* Lungwort
118. *Anemone Pulsatilla, L.* Pasqueflower
119. *Taraxacum officinale, Weber.* Dandelion
120. *Mespilus germanica, L.* Medlar
121. *Asperula odorata, L.* Sweet Woodruff
122. *Tunica Saxifraga, Scop.* Coat Flower
123. *Stellaria media, Cyrill.* Chickweed
124. *Ornithogalum umbellatum, L.* Star-of-Bethlehem
125. *Datura Stramonium, L.* Stramonium
126. *Arum*
    a. *A. italicum, Mill.* Arum
    b. *A. maculatum, L.* Cuckoo-Pint
127. *Mandragora officinarum, L.* Mandrake
128. *Ranunculus Ficaria, L.* Lesser Celandine, Buttercup
129. *Cnicus benedictus, L.* Blessed Thistle
130. *Silybum Marianum, Gaertn.* Milk or Saint Mary's Thistle
131. *Capsicum annuum, L.* Pepper
132. *Atropa Belladonna, L.* Belladonna, Deadly Nightshade
133. *Urginea Scilla, Steinh.* Sea Onion, Squill
134. *Pancratium maritimum, L.* Mediterranean Lily, Sea Daffodil
135. *Galega officinalis, L.* Goat's Rue
136. *Cydonia oblonga, Mill.* Quince
137. *Conium maculatum, L.* Poison Hemlock
138. *Alchemilla vulgaris, L.* Lady's Mantle
139. *Ceratonia Siliqua, L.* Carob. Saint John's Bread
140. *Laurus nobilis, L.* Sweet Bay

The source of this garden is the Abbey of Bonnefont-en-Comminges which flourished in the fourteenth century. However, it is not intended as a replica but rather a composite of monastery and castle gardens of the era, based on old records and herbals, including Charlemagne's garden of seventy-some herbs. One thing that leaps to the eye from this list is that so many of the herbs are what we call flowers. But don't forget that our flowers were valuable medicinal herbs to the people of the Middle Ages. If they were pleasant to the eye, all well and good, but the main thing was they were good for health. For instance, the majestic mallows (Number 60), which we plant, of course, for beauty—centuries ago mallows were planted because Pliny had written long before, "Whosoever take a spoonful of any of the Mallows shall that day be free from all diseases that may come unto him; and it is specially good for the falling sickness." Also Dioscorides had said, "The decoction of the roots and leaves helps all sorts of poison, so as the poison be presently voided by vomit." So never mind what mallows looked like—they were dependable and effective medicines (they thought). This was of vital importance because in the Middle Ages monasteries were the closest things there were to hospitals.

You will recognize in this Bonnefont garden most of the herbs we have discussed before but not all, because some came from the New World which had not yet been discovered. And many will seem strange and "outlandish," as Parkinson liked to say. To give you a better idea of the purpose of a herb garden of long ago, it might be useful to select at random a few of these strange ones and explain very quickly why they were grown. I have already promised to mention agrimony.

Agrimony (14). This was thought to be very beneficial for the gout, either as an ointment or swallowed in an infusion. Also it was believed good for jaundice and "is very beneficial to the bowels, healing all inward wounds, bruises, hurts and other distempers." It is still used in Europe as a tonic.

Comfrey (40). Used in lung ailments and thought extremely effective for whooping cough. Also thought good as a healing poultice when roots and leaves were crushed to a pulp.

Yellow Bedstraw (25). Sometimes called Our-Lady's-bedstraw from the legend that it padded the manger in Bethlehem. This was used to stuff mattresses as late as the eighteenth century. It was once used by women as a blond hair coloring, but of course this has nothing to do with monasteries. It was also used as a rennet in making cheese, and the roots yield an excellent red dye for wool.

Valerian (44). Also called allheal because it was thought it could cure anything. Pliny said that a decoction of it "helps all stoppings and stranglings in any part of the body, whether they proceed of pains in the chest or sides, and takes them away." It was also thought a good diuretic and helpful in hysteria. N. Coon says currently, "When properly used it has an anti-spasmodic effect which gave it a considerable reputation as a treatment for epilepsy."

Centaury (64b). Its primary use was for wounds: "Singularly good for both green and fresh wounds, to close up the one and cleanse the other, and perfectly to cure them both."

Fuller's Teasel (58). Also called fuller's thistle. Dioscorides thought that the root, crushed and boiled with wine, applied as a salve, would heal "cankers and fistulas, also take away warts and wens."

Betony (93c). A cousin of the lamb's-ear we looked at earlier. This herb was thought to have buckshot virtues. Antonius Musa, physician to Augustus Caesar, wrote that it cured no fewer than forty-seven diseases. These ranged from wounds and "the stinging of venomous serpents" to jaundice, epilepsy, palsy, convulsions, gout, and colic. Culpeper summed it up neatly: "It is a very precious herb, that is certain, and most fitting to be kept in a man's house."

Peony (89). The root was thought to be effective for epilepsy, and the seeds, crushed and taken in wine, for nightmares. The seeds were also useful against "the hauntings of fairies and witches."

Soapwort (35). Its name comes from the foam, suggesting soap bubbles, on top of an infusion of the leaves or roots. Its principal use was for skin diseases, and it was taken internally as well as applied to the skin.

Heartsease (73d). Its principal uses appear to have been as a laxative and for skin ailments. However, Culpeper recommends it primarily for venereal disease, but adds, "It is excellently good for the convulsions in children, as also for the falling sickness and a gallant remedy for the inflammation of the lungs." He points out that the plant is also called "Three Faces in a Hood, Live in Idleness, Cull Me to You; and in Sussex we call them Pancies."

Lungwort (117). As you know by now, lungwort meant "lung plant"—so, as you would expect, this was grown "to help diseases of the lungs, and for coughs, wheezings, and shortness of breath, which it cures both in man and beast," according to Culpeper.

Orpine (9b). The crushed root, mixed with oil, was used to ease inflamed wounds and burns; "and being bound to the throat, much helps the quinsy."

Columbine (114). An infusion of the leaves was used "with good success for sore mouths and throats."

Celandine (82). In Roman times the juice of the roots was used to remove corneal cataracts—and Culpeper, incidentally, protests violently against this dangerous practice because it may "be a readier way to extinguish the sight than to restore it." In later times it was used as a purgative and to heal eczema, ringworm, and other skin ailments, hence its common names of "felonwort" and "tetterwort." ("Tetter" was a blanket term for various skin ailments, ringworm, eczema, herpes, etc.)

Vervain (90). The Romans used vervain, and its reputation for healing was passed along through the centuries, snowballing as it went, until by the Middle Ages it was believed capable of curing almost anything. It was thought to be especially effective against the plague and to ward off the spells of witches, a virtue extremely important in those days.

Gladwin Iris (7b). Culpeper listed it as "Stinking Gladwin" and said it had "a strong ill-scent." It was used for a variety of ailments but particularly for skin diseases: "The root boiled in vinegar, and laid upon any tumor or swelling, doth very effectually dissolve and consume them; yea, even the swellings of the throat called the king's evil [scrofula]; the juice of the leaves or roots heals the itch, and all running or spreading scabs, sores, blemishes, or scars in the skin, wheresoever they be."

Purslane (53). Its primary use was as a salad herb, but it was also used as an antiseptic and a diuretic. Also, "the seed bruised and boiled in wine, and given to children, expels the worms."

Bryony (55). Used as a violent purgative and understandably, since both root and berries are poisonous. But its primary use was for a variety of skin diseases, hence "the berries are by some country people called tetter-berries."

Cowslip (113e). "For wounds, spots, wrinkles, freckles and sunburnings, an ointment is made of the leaves, and hog's grease." The flowers were thought to be more effective than the leaves, and an infusion of them was used as a nerve tonic—"they take away trembling" along with "vertigo, false apparitions, convulsions, pains in the nerves."

Chickweed (123). Used particularly for skin ailments. Also, as an ointment for "cramps, convulsions and palsy." Further, "it helps the sinews when they are shrunk by cramps or otherwise, and to extend and make them pliable again." Hence the common name "stitchwort."

You have noticed, I'm sure, how numerous were the remedies for skin ailments. This was the price medieval men paid for being prevailingly unwashed and, let's face it, verminous. It was not a comfortable time in which to live, physically. Nor mentally— witchcraft was a pervasive fact of life.

HERBS FOR WITCHCRAFT

The twenty herbs in the Bonnefont garden we have looked at so far have all been healing and benign. But some of the herbs in this garden are just the opposite—deadly poisons, seldom, if ever, used in ancient medicine. Therefore they wouldn't have been in a monastery garden at all but in the garden of a mischief-maker —in short, of a witch, whether she lived in a castle or a cottage. To round out our knowledge of herbs in ancient times, we should take a glance at some of the herbs used for witchcraft and some of those for protection against it.

What was witchcraft all about, anyway? This is no place for a real discussion of it, because its lore is tremendous. But to simplify (or oversimplify), it was a determined effort to continue the fertility-rite religions of the pre-Christian era. As such, of course, it collided head-on with the Church, which finally won. In the beginning, its adherents were sincerely religious, according to their beliefs. However, as the centuries passed, many charlatans joined the ranks, people willing to cause mischief and commit crimes—for a price.

It should be clearly understood that witches were not phonies. They knew herbs thoroughly. They used as a basis for their nostrums powerful herbs which we now know have definite physiological effects—to produce sleep, excitement, hallucinations, delirium, coma, death. The fantastic ingredients such as the Macbeth witches used:

> Eye of newt, and toe of frog,
> Wool of bat, and tongue of dog.

—and such—were put in simply for mystery. It was the herbs which gave results.

In any case, the menace of witches and the evil eye was a very real and pervading fear in the Middle Ages. There were many witches, and their power was believed very great. A man never knew when an enemy had hired a witch to do him harm. D. Jacob * says that a witch's clients, usually neither very bright nor very moral, most often came to her (or him) for certain standard results: "A cure for impotence or sterility; a charm to steal the affections of, or seduce, some reluctant man or woman; a spell to blight a neighbor's herd or crops; infanticide and abortion; frequently an avaricious hope of illicit wealth; perhaps less often, murder."

* Dorothy Jacob, *A Witch's Guide to Gardening.*

To give you an idea of the combination of reality and illusion with which witches worked, I quote two medieval formulas for a witch's "flying ointment," which they used on themselves, from M. A. Murray, *The Witch-Cult in Western Europe:*

1. Water hemlock, sweet flag, cinquefoil, bat's blood, deadly nightshade and oil.
2. Baby's fat, water hemlock, aconite, cinquefoil, deadly nightshade and soot.

She adds that irregular action of the heart (caused by aconite) in a person falling asleep produces the sensation of falling through space, and that the combination of this with a delirium-producing herb, deadly nightshade, might produce the sensation of flying. In other words, the witch had the illusion she was flying to her coven, or congregation, because she had administered poisonous herbs which do, in reality, produce a flight from normal consciousness. Let's glance at these herbs and others used by witches:

Monkshood or Aconite (78). Also called wolfsbane because the tips of hunters' arrows were dipped in an infusion of the root. However, it poisoned more than wolves—it was so popular with professional poisoners during the Roman Empire that a law was passed prescribing the death penalty for growing it. Its action is to produce a slowing-down, then an irregularity, and then a cessation of the heart. So much for aconite!

Belladonna or Deadly Nightshade (132). According to legend, this plant is the personal property of the devil, who watches over it constantly. This was one of the deadliest of witches' poisons. A dozen berries can cause death; a small dose can cause hysteria and delirium. And yet, interestingly, modern medicine has tamed it to usefulness—to dilate the pupils for eye examinations, for instance.

Henbane (27). It was known as far back as Dioscorides and was probably the drug used to poison Hamlet's father. It is a two-faced herb. Hyoscine, pain-reliever and anodyne, is derived from it, and a generation or two ago came into great popularity as "twilight sleep" to alleviate the pains of childbirth. On the other hand, it can cause hallucinations and death, and a modern "witch," Dr. Crippen, used it some sixty years ago to poison his wife.

Stramonium (125). Also called Jimson (for Jamestown) weed, stinkweed, devil's trumpet, and thorn apple. Dioscorides said of it, "The root being drunk with wine in the quantity of a dram has the power to effect not unpleasant fantasies. But two being drunk, make one beside himself for three days, and four being drunk kill him." In short, this herb is poisonous, narcotic, antispasmodic, hallucinogenic—and medicinal. It has sometimes been substituted for belladonna. Perhaps its greatest usefulness in later centuries was to treat the spasms of asthma by inhaling the fumes of the burning leaves.

Mandrake (127). No herb had as great a reputation for magic properties as the mandrake. It could work every spell or curse. The solid basis for this was that it contains a strong alkaloid resembling that of belladonna and could produce sleep or delirium. Both Pliny and Dioscorides spoke of its value as an anaesthetic. The superstitious basis probably stemmed from the fact that some roots are divided and thus—with the help of imagination—look like a man with long legs. From this, it was thought a sovereign means of producing pregnancy. It was also thought a powerful aphrodisiac and therefore also called love apple by some early writers. This was a thoroughly evil plant and the devil's own; indeed the Arabs forthrightly called it the devil's testicles. The lore is that it sprang from the seed of a man hanged for murder and therefore grew at the foot of the gallows. And it was no easy thing to gather—if you pulled it up (while it shrieked), as you did you would either die or go mad. Therefore you somehow got a dog to pull it up for you—and presumably the dog went mad. I find it pleasant to note that charlatans in "the witch trade" were quite willing to cut through this evil and awesome aura—when mandrake was in short supply, which was often, they calmly substituted the root of bryony!

Honesty (20). Called moonwort from the silvery moon-shaped disks which are its seed pods. This is a somewhat less sinister herb than the five foregoing ones. It apparently has astringent properties and thus was thought good for wounds and bruises. For witches, it had the virtue of "opening locks and unshoeing such horses as tread upon it"—relatively harmless sport. Culpeper disclaims this superstition but then goes on to say that country people he knows call it unshoe-the-horse and offers "proof" of its unshoeing power.

Other herbs used in witchcraft included hemlock (the Macbeth witches' brew included "root of hemlock, digg'd i' the dark"), dill, dyer's alkanet; cudweed; foxglove (digitalis, a heart stimulant but poisonous if used often), yarrow, feverfew, plantain, sesame, and opium poppy (for obvious reasons). Also elder, alder, poplar, and hawthorn.

Now, how does one protect himself against witchcraft? Obviously by employing herbs which witches hate or fear! Here are some of them: Angelica heads the list, probably because of its name. This was the only herb Gerard, contemptuous of superstitions, admitted was effective. Marigold is a powerful protector because its orange and yellow flowers suggest the sun—and if there's anything a witch hates, it's sunlight! Sage is very good, and even better if planted with rue. Mullein is extremely offensive to witches. So is clover—trefoil—because its three leaves evoke the Holy Trinity. Remember:

> Trefoil, Johnswort, vervain, dill,
> Hinder witches of their will.

Beans are a powerful emergency measure; you are supposed to spit one at the witch, and she will be off.

Mugwort, one of the artemisias, is a splendid herb to have in your corner. It will ward off witches and practically anything else, including sunstroke and the plague. Bay is excellent: "Neither witch nor devil, thunder nor lightning will hurt a man in the place where a bay-tree is"—a good thing to keep in mind. Having juniper around is a powerful protection; the witches feel the compulsion to count every tiny leaf, and if they make a mistake, they must start all over again. Thus they become so engrossed that before you know it, it's dawn, and they must flee. This is sneaky but effective. (Parenthetically, this compulsion of witches to count objects is the basis of an old Pennsylvania Dutch charm to protect your livestock. You put a bucket of shelled corn just inside the door of your barn; the witch can't prevent herself from counting every kernel—and so spends a harmless night.) Also remember that no witch will enter your house if you have rubbed rue on the floors.

Certain herbs were considered effective, time out of mind, in protecting a house from lightning—often caused by witches! Bay was one, as we have seen. Others were stonecrop, mugwort (in addition to its other virtues), thistle, and peony. Also coral— yes, coral was considered a plant! Culpeper wrote as late as 1684, "These plants, though their hard substance makes them seem rather to be stones, yet they are vegetables." Coral also protected against fire and shipwreck.

The usual way these herbs were used as protectors was to hang a few sprigs of them above one's doorway. Alternatively, one could wear a sprig around his neck. In addition to the herbs I have mentioned, you can rely on these as being strong and dependable: tansy, purslane, elder, pennyroyal, garlic, rosemary, hyssop, alyssum—and, above all, mistletoe, which William Coles ranked even above angelica.

And now I trust you will feel secure!

10

Rose-Petal Pudding, Violet Wine, and Other Old Herb Formulas

To me, a rose-petal pudding has always seemed an enchanting idea. So, for that matter, has a Roman recipe for roast wild boar. In the belief that they will interest you also, in this chapter I shall share with you some of the herb recipes, hints, and formulas from past centuries I have been collecting over the years. Some are usable, some surprising, some merely amusing—but, to me at least, none is dull. And, taken together, they give a good insight into the importance of herbs in the lives of our ancestors. Indeed, they throw a great deal of light on how people lived. First, the pudding, from the eighteenth century:

A PUDDING OF ROSE PETALS

Collect two quarts of rose petals, mix them well with one quarter pound of grated Naples Biscuit (lady fingers) and one quart of cream, and boil a short time. Beat eight eggs with a little cream and add sugar to taste. Mix all together very well, pour into buttered dish and bake. When done, sprinkle with powdered sugar and serve forth.

From *The Art of Cookery,* 1760

EOWTES OF FLESSH (*Herb Soup*)

Take borage, colewort [cabbage], lang-debuf [bugloss], persel [parsley], betes [beets], orach, violet, savory and fenkel [fennel], cut into small pieces and cast them in gode broth, seeth [boil] them and serve them forth.

From *The Forme of Cury,* 1390

Incidentally, this cookbook recognized that the color of food can contribute to its enjoyment and recommended "to make the potage of sangwayne [red] colour for wyntur season," using beets or alkanet root.

BEST ORDINARY POTAGE (*Another Herb Soup*)

Violet petals, succory [chicory], strawberry leaves, spinach, bugloss, marigold flowers, scallions, parsley, and oatmeal.

From *The English Hus-wife,* 1623

ROAST BOAR

Boar is prepared in the following manner: Sponge it and sprinkle with salt and grilled cumin and leave it like that. The next day put it in the oven. When it is cooked, pour over it a sauce made of pepper, lovage, celery seed, mint, thyme, toasted pine kernels, wine, vinegar, liquamen [see note below], and a little oil. When the liquid in which the boar is roasting has boiled, put the pounded mixture in and stir with a bunch of onions and rue. If you wish to make it thicker, bind the juice with white of eggs, stir slowly, sprinkle with ground pepper, and serve.

From *Apicius,** fourth or fifth century A.D.

Note: To give you a feeling of the original, it begins: *Aper ita conditur: Spongiatur, et sic aspergitur ei sal et cuminum frictum.*

* *Apicius, The Roman Cookery Book,* translated by Barbara Flower and Elizabeth Rosenbaum, London, George G. Harrap & Co. Ltd., 1958. Quotations on pages 169, 171, 173, 177, 178, 179, and 180 used by permission of the publishers.

... The translation by Barbara Flower and Elizabeth Rosenbaum is by long odds the best to date. Additionally, they have tried most of the recipes and rationalized them where necessary. *Note on liquamen:* They suggest substituting salt. However, they point out that liquamen was made from salt fish. Therefore my personal thought is to use salt plus a few dashes of Lea & Perrins sauce, since it is heavy on anchovies. Incidentally, I have had excellent roast wild boar at the Fontanella Restaurant in Rome.

PREVENTING DRUNKENNESS

If you would not be drunk, take the powder of Betony & Coleworts [cabbage] mixt together; and eat it every morning fasting, as much as will lye upon a six-pence, and it will preserve a man from drunkenness.

From a seventeenth-century herbal

TO MAKE AN APPLE HASH

Take ye largest Apples you can get, pare ym and cut ym in round slices. Dip ym in wheat meal and fry ym until they begin to brown. Be carful in the turning for fear they break. So lay ym up on your dish. Melt butter and Sack [white wine] and Sugar wt a sprig of rosemary. So put it upon ym and Sinimond upon them. Serve ym up for the second [main] course.

From a recipe book of 1711

PYKES IN BRASEY (*Roast Fish*)

Take pykes and clene them, and waisshe them clene, and lay them on a roost irne [roasting iron]. Thenne take gode wyne and powdorgynger and sugar, a good deal, and salt, and boil it in an erthen panne, and messe forth the pyke, and lay the sewe [liquor] onoward.

From *The Forme of Cury,* 1390

FLOWER SALAD, PICKLED

To each Pound of Flowers, allow one Pound of Loaf Sugar, and one Pint of White-Wine Vinegar, which boil to a Syrup and cover it scalding hot. Thus you may pickle clove-gilly flowers, Elder, Orange, Cowslip, Rosemary, Sage, Nasturtium, and other Flowers, which being eatn alone, make a very agreeable Salletine.

From *Acetaria,* 1699

A REMARKABLE APHRODISIAC

The brain of Sparrows being eaten provokes lust exceedingly.

From *Complete Herbal,* 1684

VIOLET WINE

Violet wine you will make like this: Thread together violet petals and steep as many as possible in wine for 7 days. After 7 days take the violet petals out of the wine, and in the same way put in other fresh violet petals threaded together to rest 7 days in the wine, then take them out. Repeat a third time, take out the violet petals, strain the wine, and when you want to use it for drinking, add honey to make violet wine.

From *Apicius,* fourth or fifth century A.D.

A LINIMENT TO DESTROY NITS

Take oil of Bays, Oil of Sweet Almonds, and old Hogs Lard, of each two ounces, powdered Stavesacre, and Tansy Juice, of each half an ounce; Aloes, and Myrrh, of each a quarter of an ounce, the smaller Centaury and Salt of Sulphur, of each a drachm; mix the whole into a liniment. Before you use it, wash the hair with Vinegar.

From *The Toilet of Flora,* 1779

A CERTAIN METHOD OF DESTROYING FLEAS

Put Tansy Leaves about different parts of the bed, viz. under the matrass, or between the blankets.

Or

Rub the bed posts well with a strong decoction of Elder Leaves.

From *The Toilet of Flora,* 1779

TO MAKE HAIR GROW

Take the leaves of Willow, and boyle them well in oyl, and therewith anoint the place where you would have hair to grow.

From *The English Hus-wife,* 1623

TO MAKE HAIR GROW—ANOTHER

Take one quart of white wine, put in one handful of Rosemary flowers, half a pound of honey, distil them together; then add a quarter of a pint of oil of sweet almonds, shake it very well together, put a little of it into a cup, warm it blood-warm, rub it well on your head, and comb dry.

A recipe from 1760

TO QUICKEN THE GROWTH OF HAIR—ANOTHER

Dip the teeth of your comb every morning in the expressed Juice of nettles, and comb the hair the wrong way. This expedient will surprisingly quicken the growth of the hair.

Some, after having shaved the head, foment it with a decoction of Wormwood, Southernwood, Sage, Betony, Vervain, Marjoram, Myrtle, Roses, Dill, Rosemary, or Mistletoe.

From *The Toilet of Flora,* 1779

PUDDING OF CARROT

Pare off some of the Crust of Manchet-Bread, and grate off half as much of the rest as there is of the Root, which must also be grated: then take half a Pint of fresh Cream or New Milk, half a Pound of fresh Butter, six new laid Eggs (taking out three of the Whites) mash and mingle them well with the Cream and Butter: Then put in the grated Bread and Carrot, with near half a Pound of Sugar; and a little Salt; some grated Nutmeg and beaten Spices; and pour all into a convenient Dish or Pan, butter'd, to keep the Ingredients from sticking and burning; set it in a quick Oven for about an Hour, and so have you a Composition for any ROOT-PUDDING.

From *Acetaria,* 1699

PUREE OF LETTUCE-LEAVES WITH ONIONS

Boil in water with cooking-soda; chop finely. Pound in the mortar pepper, lovage, celery seed, dried mint, and onions, add liquamen, oil, and wine. Mix with the lettuce and onions and serve.

From *Apicius,* fourth or fifth century A.D.

BUKKENADE (*Chicken Stew*)

Take hennes or rabbits, or veal, or other flessh, and hewe them to gobbetts; waische [wash] it, and hit [braise] well. Grynde almondes unblanched, and draw them up with a broth. Caste thereinne currants, sugar, powdor gynger, erbes ystewed in grees, oynonns [onions] and salt. If it is too thynne, alye [mix] it up with floer of ryse [rice] or with other thyng and color it with safronn.

From *The Forme of Cury,* 1390

GEES IN HOGGEPOT (*Goose Ragout*)

Take gees and smyte them in pecys [pieces]. Cast them in a pot; do thereto half wine and half water; and do thereto a gode quantite of oynons and erbest [herbs]. Set it over the fyre and cover it fast. Take a layor [mixture] of brede and blode and lay it therewith. Do [put] thereto powdor-fort [hot spices—pepper, ginger, etc.] and serve it forth.

From *The Forme of Cury,* 1390

GYNGERBREDE

Take a quart of hony, & seethe it, and skeme it clene; take Safroun, pouder Pepir, & throw ther-on; take gratyd Brede, & make it so stiff that it wol be cut into strips; then take pouder Cinnamon, & Strew ther-on y-now [enough]; then make yt square, lyke as thou wolt slice yt; take when slicest hyt, an caste Box leves above y-stykyd ther-on on cloves. And if thou wolt have it Red, coloure it with Saunderys y-now. ("Saunderys"—red sandalwood).

From a manuscript *ca.* 1430

AN EXCELLENT RECEIPT TO CLEAR A TANNED COMPLEXION

At night going to rest, bathe the face with the Juice of Strawberries, and let it lie on the part all night, and in the morning wash yourself with Chervil Water. The skin will soon become fair and smooth.

From *The Toilet of Flora,* 1779

HONEY OF MULBERRIES

It is vulgarly known to be good for sore mouths, as also to cool inflammations there.

Take of the juice of Mulberries & Blackberries before they be ripe, gathered before the sun be up, of each a pound & a half, Honey two pounds, boil them to their due thickness.

From *The English Physician Enlarged,* 1684

BENES Y-FRYED

Take benes and seethe hem almost til they bersten [burst]. Take and wryng out the water clene. Do [add] thereto oynons ysode [boiled] and y-mynced, and garlic therewith. Frye hem in oile, other [or] in grece; and do thereto powder-douce [allspice], and serve it forth.

From *The Forme of Cury,* 1390

TART OF HERBS

An Herb-Tart is made thus: Boil fresh Cream or Milk, with a little grated Bread or Naples-Biscuit (which is better) to thicken it; a pretty Quantity of Cervile, Spinach, Beete (or what other Herb you please) being first par-boil'd and chop'd. Then add Macaron, or Almonds beaten to a Paste, a little Sweet Butter, the Yolk of five eggs, three of the Whites rejected. To these some add Corinths [currants] plump'd in Milk, or boil' therein, Sugar, Spice at Discretion, and stirring it all together over the Fire, bake it in the Tart-Pan.

From *Aceteria,* 1699

TO MAKE ONE SLENDER

Take Fennell, & seeth it in Water, a very good quantity, & wringing out the juice thereof when it is sodde [boiled], drink it first & last & it shall swage either man or woman.

From *The Good Huswifes Jewell,* 1587

TO QUICKEN THE WIT

To quicken a man's wits, spirit & memory let him take Langdebeet [bugloss], which is gathered in June or July, & beating it in clean mortar, let him drink the juice thereof with warm water, & he shall find the benefit.

From *The English Hus-wife,* 1623

A POWDER TO CLEANSE THE TEETH

Take of Cuttlefish-bone, and the finest prepared Chalk, each half an ounce; Peruvian Bark, and Florentine Iris Root, each two drachms; reduce the whole into a fine Powder, and mix them. This may be coloured with a little Rose Pink and scented with a few drops of Oil of Cinnamon.

From *The Toilet of Flora,* 1779

A SKIN LOTION

The juice of the flowers of Primroses and Cowslips is commended to cleanse the spots or marks of the face, whereof some Gentlewomen have found good experience.

From *Paradisi in sole paradisus terrestris,* 1629

A FINE LIP SALVE

Take two ounces of Virgin's wax, two ounces of hog's lard, half an ounce of spermacetti, one ounce of oil of sweet almonds, two ounces of balsam of Peru, two drams of alkanet root cut small, six new raisins shred small, a little fine sugar, simmer them all together a little while; then strain it off into little pots. It is the finest lip salve in the world.

From *The Art of Cookery,* 1760

QUEEN ELIZABETH'S PERFUME

Take eight spoonfuls of compound water, the weight of twopence in fine powder of sugar, & boil it on hot embers & Coals softly, & half an ounce of sweet marjoram dried in the sun, the weight of two-pence of the powder of Benjamin [benzoin]. This perfume is very sweet & good for the time.

From a sixteenth-century manuscript

TO SWEETEN THE BREATH

At night, going to bed, chew about the quantity of a small nut of fine Myrrh.

Or

Chew every night and morning a Clove, a piece of Florentine Orrice-Root, about the size of a small bean, or the same quantity of Burnt Alum.

From *The Toilet of Flora,* 1779

MUSHROOM SOUP

Takes funges [mushrooms] and pare them clene and dyce them; take leke [leeks], and shred thym small, and do thym to seethe in gode broth; color it with safronn, and do thereinne powdor-fort [pepper, ginger, etc.].

From *The Forme of Cury*, 1390

CUMIN SAUCE FOR OYSTERS AND SHELLFISH

Pepper, lovage, parsley, dry mint, plenty of cumin, honey, vinegar, liquamen.

From *Apicius*, fourth or fifth century A.D.

VIRGIN'S MILK, A SAFE AND APPROVED COSMETIC

Beat a quantity of Houseleek [stonecrop] in a marble mortar, squeeze out the Juice and clarify it. When you want to use it, pour a few drops of rectified Spirit on the Juice, and it will instantly turn milky. It is a very efficacious remedy for a pimpled face, and preserves the skin soft and smooth.

From *The Toilet of Flora*, 1779

TO TAKE AWAY SPOTS & FRECKLES

The sappe that issueth out of a Birch tree in great abundance, being opened in March or Aprill, with a receiver of glasse set under the boring thereof to receive the same, doth perform the same most excellently & maketh the skin very cleare. This sap will dissolve pearl, a secret not known unto many.

From *Delights for Ladies*, 1609

TO SWEETEN THE BREATH

After having eat Garlic or Onions, chew a little raw Parsley. It will infallibly take away their offensive smell.

From *The Toilet of Flora*, 1779

PEAS OR BEANS À LA VITELLIUS

Boil the peas (or beans), stir until smooth. Pound pepper, lovage, ginger; and over the spices put yolks of hard-boiled eggs, three ounces honey, liquamen, wine, and vinegar. Put all this, including the spices which you have pounded, in the saucepan. Add oil, and bring to the boil. Season the peas with this. Stir until smooth if lumpy. Add honey and serve.

From *Apicius,* fourth or fifth century A.D.

CONNYNGES IN GRAVEY (*Rabbit Stew*)

Take connynges [rabbits], smyte them to pecyş. Parboile and drawe them with a gode broth, with almandes blanched and braised. Do [put] thereinne sugar and powdor gynger and boyle it, and the flessh therewith. Floer it with sugar, and with powdor gynger, and serve forth.

Also:

Take chykens, and serve in the same manner, and serve forth.

From *The Forme of Cury,* 1390

CHICKEN IN THE NUMIDIAN WAY

Prepare the chicken, boil, take out of the water, sprinkle with asafoetida and pepper, and roast. Pound pepper, cumin, coriander seed, asafoetida root, rue, Jericho date, pine-kernels; moisten with vinegar, honey, liquamen, and oil. Mix well. When it boils thicken with cornflour, pour over the chicken, sprinkle with pepper, and serve.

From *Apicius,* fourth or fifth century A.D.

THE QUEEN'S ORDINARY BOUILLON

A Hen, a handful of Parsley, a sprig of Thyme, three of Spearmint, a little Baum, half a great Onion, a little Pepper & Salt, & a Clove;

as much water as would cover the Hen; & this boyled to less than a pinte, for one good pottinger ful.

From *Choice and Experimental Receipts in Physick and Chirurgery,* 1682

BAGS TO SCENT LINEN

Take Rose Leaves dried in the shade, Cloves beat to a gross powder, and Mace scraped; mix them together, and put the composition into little bags.

From *The Toilet of Flora,* 1779

SAUCE FOR ROAST CRANE OR DUCK

Make the following sauce and pour over the roast bird: pound pepper, lovage, origan, liquamen, honey, a little vinegar, and a little oil. Cook well. Add cornflower to bind and put into the sauces slices of boiled cucumber or taro. Boil. If available, add also cooked pig's trotters and chicken livers. Sprinkle in the serving-dish with ground pepper, and serve.

From *Apicius,* fourth or fifth century A.D.

A POWDER TO PREVENT BALDNESS

Powder your head with powdered Parsley Seed, at night, once in three or four months, and the hair will never fall off.

From *The Toilet of Flora,* 1779

PATINA WITH MILK

Soak pine-kernels and let them dry. Have ready fresh, unprepared sea-urchins. Take a shallow pan and arrange in it the following ingredients: hearts of mallows and beets; fully grown leeks; celery sticks; vegetable puree; boiled greens; pieces of chicken cooked in broth; boiled brains; Lucanian sausages; hard-boiled eggs cut in halves; pork sausage stuffed with Terentian sauce (pound pepper, laurel berry, rue; moisten with best liquamen and a few drops of best oil) cooked and chopped; chicken liver; fried fillets of hake; jellyfish; oysters without their shells; fresh cheese. Arrange all this in layers. Add the pine-kernels and peppercorns on top and pour over the following sauce: pepper, lovage, celery-seed, asafoetida. Cook. When it is done strain milk into which you mix raw eggs to a smooth mixture. Pour it over the dish. When it has set garnish with the fresh sea-urchins, sprinkle with pepper, and serve.

From *Apicius,* fourth or fifth century A.D.

TO PERFUME A HOUSE, AND PURIFY THE AIR

Take a root of Angelica, dry it in an oven, or before the fire, then bruise it well and infuse it four or five days in White Wine Vinegar. When you use it, lay it upon a brick made red hot, and repeat the operation several times.

From *The Toilet of Flora,* 1779

FOR BRUISES

The roote of Solomon's Seal—stamped while it is fresh and greene, and applied, taketh away in one night or two at the most, any bruse, blacke or blew spots gotten by fals or women's wilfulness, in stumbling upon their hasty husband's fists or such like.

From *Gerard's Herball,* 1597

OYSTRYS IN GRAVY BASTARD

Take grete Oystrys, an schale hem; an take the water of the Oystrys & ale, an brede y-straynid, an the water also, an put it on a potte, an Gyngere, Sugre, Saffron, powder pepir, and Salt, and let it boyle wyl; then put yn the Oystrys there-to, and dresse it forth.
("Bastard" was a sweet Spanish wine.)

From a manuscript *ca.* 1430

FOR COLIC

Grass-hoppers, being eaten, ease the colic.

From *The English Physician Enlarged,* 1684

REMEDIES FROM THE PHYSICIANS OF MYDDRAI

In Chapter 4, I mentioned the fabulous Physicians of Myddrai, who maintained a hereditary doctors' guild in Wales for six hundred years; and I quoted some of their medical applications of rosemary. Here are a few more of their formulas, also quoted from Mrs. Leyel's *The Magic of Herbs:* *

TO PREVENT SPEAKING DURING SLEEP

Take the seed or leaves of rue and pound with vinegar till it becomes a mass, then mix it well in old ale, strain through a clean linen, and let the patient drink it.

A GOOD GARGLE

Take sage, rue, mallows and elder flowers, either fresh or dry, boil them well in water, then when you have done so for a while add a spoonful of vinegar, and as much of honey, continuing the boiling some time longer, then strain carefully through a linen cloth and keep. When required for use, warm from two to four spoonfuls, take a mouthful thereof and gargle well as long as you can, taking care not to swallow any, then finally eject it; do this from twice to four times with a spoonful at a time.

FOR A COUGH

Take mustard seed coarsely powdered, boil with stewing figs in strong ale, and drink.

FOR A DANGEROUS WOUND

Take sage, rue, cummin, and pound them like pepper, then boil them together in honey, and make into a confection. Take a spoonful thereof night and morning and by the help of God you will obtain benefit.

* Hilda W. Leyel, *The Magic of Herbs*, New York, Harcourt, Brace & Company, 1926. Copyright Hilda Leyel. Used by permission.

TO KNOW WHETHER A MAN WHO HAS BEEN SEVERELY BEATEN WILL RECOVER OR NOT

Take the violet, bruise and bind about the forefinger; if he sleep he will live, if not he will die. You should ascertain this before you interfere with the case.

TO PREVENT DREAMING

Take the vervain and hang about a man's neck, or let him drink some of the juices in going to bed; certainly he will not dream if he does so.

APHORISMS

The bread of yesterday, the meat of to-day, and the wine of last year, will produce health.

Do not ask for milk after fish.

He who sees fennel and gathers it not is not a man, but a devil.

In pottage without herbs there is neither goodness nor nourishment.

THINGS THAT ARE HURTFUL TO THE BRAIN

For all brains the following things are hurtful: gluttony, drunkenness, late eating, much sleeping after food, tainted air, anger, depressed spirits, much standing bareheaded, eating much or hastily, too much warmth, excessive watching, too much cold, curds, all kinds of nuts, frequent bathing, onions, garlic, yawning, smelling a white rose, excess of venery, too much music, singing and reading, strong drink before sleeping, restless sleep, too frequent fasting, wet feet.

The good doctors of Myddrai were undoubtedly gifted or they couldn't have survived for six hundred years, and undoubtedly they accomplished much for the health of their patients. But the concept that frequent bathing is "Hurtful to the Brain" must have resulted in a great many formulas for skin ailments.

THE HERBS OF HIPPOCRATES

The great Hippocrates, a contemporary of Plato and Socrates, was the first doctor of medicine, as we understand the word. That is, he was the first to separate medicine from magic and superstitious rites (the witch-doctor approach). He used some four hundred simples, specific treatments for specific diseases. According to Mrs. Leyel, half of them are in use in the twentieth century, and some of these are given below. I thought you might be interested, as I have been, to see some of the herbs with a twenty-five-hundred-year medical history behind them.

absinthium	fig
almond	garlic
alum	hawthorn
anchusa	heather
anemone	hellebore
anise	hemlock
asphodel	henbane
balm	horehound
basil	ivy
brier	juniper
bryony	laurel
burdock	lettuce
cabbage	mallow
caper	mandragora
cardamom	mint
carrot	mugwort
cinnamon	myrrh
clove	myrtle
coriander	narcissus
cress	oak
cucumber (wild)	olive
cyclamen	onion
elder	pennyroyal
fennel	peony

pomegranate   sesame
poppy   squill
quince   tarragon
rose   thistle
rosemary   thyme
rue   verbena
saffron   violet
sage   willow

11

Sources of Herb Seeds and Plants

EAST OF THE MISSISSIPPI

Connecticut:
Caprilands Herb Farm
Coventry, Conn.

Laurel Hill Herb Farm
Falls Village, Conn.

Hemlock Hill Herb Farm
Litchfield, Conn.

The Charles C. Hart Seed Co.
Main and Hart Sts.
Wethersfield, Conn. 06109

Max Schling Seedsmen, Inc.
199 Hamilton Ave.
Greenwich, Conn. 06830

White Flower Farm
Litchfield, Conn. 06759

District of Columbia:
F. W. Bolgiano & Co.
411 New York Ave., N.E.
Washington, D.C. 20002

The Herb Cottage
The Washington Cathedral
Mount St. Alban
Washington, D.C. 20016

Georgia:
Fruitlands Nurseries
Augusta, Ga.

Pine Hill Herb Farm
Box 307
Roswell, Ga.

Louisiana:
Kiskatom Farm
7425 Dominican St.
New Orleans, La. 70118

Maine:
Merry Gardens
1 Simonton Rd.
Camden, Maine

Maryland:

Carroll Gardens
Box 310
Westminster, Md.

Massachusetts:

Thomas J. Grey Co.
217 Center Ave.
Abington, Mass.

Breck's of Boston
200 Breck Building
Boston, Mass. 02210

Perry Seed Co.
12 Faneuil Hall Sq.
Boston, Mass. 02109

The Cape Cod Nurseries
Falmouth, Mass.

Hardy Herbs
80 Hill St.
Lexington, Mass.

Bay State Nurseries
North Abington, Mass.

Stony Hills Gardens
North Chatham, Mass.

May H. Sargent
The Crossroads Herbary
Orleans, Mass.

William B. Olney
Lincoln St.
Seekonk, Mass.

Village Hill Nursery
Williamsburg, Mass.

Michigan:

Hav'alook Gardens
10045 Grand River Ave.
Fowlerville, Mich.

New Jersey:

Rex D. Pearce
Moorestown, N.J.

Vaughan's Seed Co.
Chimney Rock Rd.
Bound Brook, New Jersey

New York:

Cottage Herb Farm Shop
311 State St.
Albany, N.Y.

Farm & Garden Nursery
85 Vesey Street
New York, N.Y. 10008

Mohonk Gardens
Mohonk Lake, N.Y.

The Tool Shed Herb Nursery
Turkey Hill Rd., Salem Center
Purdy's Station, N.Y.

Ohio:

Charles J. McCullough Seed Co.
230 E. 4th St.
Cincinnati, Ohio 45201

Wayside Gardens
Mentor, Ohio

H. Kohankie & Sons
Painesville, Ohio

Fragrant Herb Farm
Silverton, Ohio 45236

Pennsylvania:
W. Atlee Burpee Co.
Philadelphia, Pa. 19132

Rhode Island:
Greene Herb Gardens, Inc.
Narrow Lane
Greene, R.I. 02827

Little Compton Herb Nurseries
Box 526 W. Main Rd.
Little Compton, R.I.

South Carolina:
The George W. Park Seed Co.
122 Cokesbury Rd.
Greenwood, S.C. 29647

Vermont:
Evergreen Nurseries
Shelburne, Vt.

Virginia:
Plantation Gardens
Rte. 2, Box 223
Lynchburg, Va.

T. W. Wood & Sons
11 S. 14th St.
Richmond, Va. 23216

Wisconsin:
John A. Salzer Seed Co.
LaCrosse, Wis.

L. L. Olds Seed Co.
Madison, Wis. 53701

WEST OF THE MISSISSIPPI

California:
Mail Box Seeds
2042 Encinal Ave.
Alameda, Calif. 94501

Aggeler & Musser Seed Co.
Los Angeles, Calif.

Germain Seed & Plant Co.
747 Terminal St.
Los Angeles, Calif. 90021

Schmidt Nursery
355 Lambert Ave.
Palo Alto, Calif.

Lagomarsino & Sons
1223 Alhambra Blvd.
Sacramento, Calif. 95816

Hallawell Seed Co.
510 Market St.
San Francisco, Calif. 94105

Taylor's Garden
2649 Stingle Ave.
South San Gabriel, Calif.

Carl Purdy Gardens
Ukiah, Calif.

Road Runner Ranch
2458 Catalina Ave.
Vista, Calif.

Idaho:

    Garden of Memories
    Box 107
    Hagerman, Idaho

Iowa:

    W. Atlee Burpee
    Clinton, Iowa

    Di Giorgi Brothers Co.
    Council Bluffs, Iowa

Minnesota:

    Farmer Seed & Nursery Co.
    Faribault, Minn.

Texas:

    Hilltop Farm
    Rte. 3, Box 216
    Cleveland, Tex.

II

COOKING WITH HERBS

12

How We Cook with Herbs
at Anderson Farm

The recipes which follow were worked out by my wife Lois,
who is (in addition to her other attributes) an accomplished
gourmet cook. This is most fortunate, because the author can't
cook at all. I can claim no more than being a sort of "executive
cook" whose function is to say, "I think it needs a little more sugar
and a little more vinegar," or whatever.

Under no circumstances does this section set out to be a definitive book of herb cookery. There are thousands of ways of combining herbs with food. These are simply some of our special
favorites which we have collected in our travels in the United
States and abroad. Many of them we have sent out to our mail-
order customers to help them enjoy the herb products they have
bought from us. But most of them are seeing print for the first
time. They represent notes we made in Italy, say, and then worked
on here until they were perfected recipes.

"Worked on" is the operative phrase, because it is only rarely
one can get a complete recipe from a restaurant abroad—the chef
often feels it is his secret. The usual procedure is that which we
followed with the Ponte Vecchio Chicken. The *maître* was
friendly and cooperative, and told us exactly what the ingredients

were, so when we got home we were able to match the taste on about the third try. (Yes, one *can* remember tastes if one is intensely interested.) Sometimes the owner or *maître* is not cooperative, so there is nothing for it but to go back a second time and try to "taste-read" what is in the dish. Once in a while one hits a bonanza, as with our recipe for *gazpacho*. The *maître* in the Hotel Christina in Sevilla was sympathetic to the eager faces eating the best *gazpacho* in Spain—and brought us the recipe neatly typed!

"How we cook with herbs at Anderson Farm" is, naturally, to use our own herb products—and wouldn't it be a scandal if we didn't! But I can't ask you to do that, of course, so we have adapted the seasonings and show individual herbs in most of the recipes. Also, we give you approximations of taste. For example, if a recipe calls for Mixed Herbs, you can use one of these mixtures which you have made yourself. They were given in Chapter 5, but are repeated here for your convenience:

FOR FRESH OR DRIED HERBS

Mixture A: Equal parts of basil, thyme, oregano
Mixture B: Equal parts of thyme, savory, basil, dill, fennel
Mixture C: 3 parts basil
           1 part thyme
           ½ part sage
           ½ part savory
           ½ part lovage
           ½ part oregano

Always remember to use twice as much of fresh herbs as you would use of dried. So whenever the recipe calls for Mixed Herbs you can substitute, with safety, Mixtures A, B, or C, as you prefer

Two of our meat sauces are called for in a few of the recipes and they are very difficult to approximate:

DAMASCUS MEAT SAUCE

The closest I can approximate this is to say: Use the amount called for of Houses of Parliament Sauce plus one teaspoon of minced onions.

WINE-HERB MEAT SAUCE

Use ¼ each of port, sherry, Mixture A, and bland mustard.

Other approximations are given with each recipe.
So now let's start with a few hors d'oeuvres . . .

HORS D'OEUVRES

HUMMUS (*Jordan*)
An exotic cocktail dip

All through Jordan, Syria, Lebanon, we found the traditional *mezze* (pronounced "mazzah"): the table laden with thirty-one saucers, each containing what we would call an hors d'oeuvre (carrot sticks, cheeses, baloney, celery, olives, deviled eggs, radishes, etc.). *Hummus* was always part of this spread, always eaten on a piece of pancake-shaped Middle Eastern bread. We have adapted this *hummus* recipe, but the taste is identical.

for 8 people

1½ cups canned chick peas, thoroughly drained
½ cup plain yogurt
juice of one lemon

1 teaspoon Mixed Herbs (or basil, thyme, and oregano)
1 clove garlic, crushed
1 teaspoon salt

Place lemon juice, yogurt, herbs, and salt in an electric blender. Slowly add the chick peas, a few at a time. Blend until very smooth. Remove to bowl and chill in refrigerator. *Hummus* is excellent served on sesame crackers or pumpernickel bread, and it may be kept in the refrigerator for several days.

CHICKEN LIVER PÂTÉ (Israel)

We enjoyed this excellent pâté at the Jerusalem home of Israeli friends. On being questioned about it, they said they used a meat grinder in preference to an electric blender, in the making of the pâté. We agreed we preferred the texture to that of a blender paste. Our own additions—the herbs and the brandy.

for 8 people

1 pound chicken livers	1 teaspoon Mixed Herbs (or
2 small onions, chopped fine	thyme and oregano)
2 tablespoons butter	¼ cup brandy
¼ pound butter, melted	½ teaspoon salt

Cut the livers into ½-inch pieces. Sauté them with the onions in 2 tablespoons of hot butter until they are rosy inside, about 2 or 3 minutes. Grind them in a meat grinder, then place ground liver and onions in large bowl. Add the melted butter, herbs, brandy, and salt, and blend thoroughly. Check the seasoning. Pack the pâté into a bowl or jar, cover with waxed paper and chill for 2 to 3 hours. (If you are using an electric blender, add the brandy, melted butter, and seasonings to the liver and onions before blending. Cover and blend at top speed until liver is a smooth paste.)

HERBED CHEESE BUBBLES

24 hot canapes

6 slices white bread	2 beaten egg yolks
3 ounces Kraft Smokelle cheese	1 tablespoon Mixed Herbs (or
roll (or approximately ½ roll)	basil, savory, and thyme)
1 3-ounce package cream cheese	1 clove garlic, crushed

Preheat broiler. Place the two cheeses in a bowl, and let stand at room temperature until soft enough to mash. Mash thoroughly with a fork, then add the garlic, herbs, and egg yolks, and beat lightly until mixture is well blended. This can be refrigerated, then brought to room temperature before spreading. Cut twenty-four 1½-inch rounds from the bread and place them on a baking sheet under a preheated broiler until one side is lightly toasted. Remove toast rounds and spread untoasted sides with the cheese mixture. Place canapes on baking sheet again and return to broiler, broiling 2 inches from heat until they are bubbly and brown.

HERBED SARDINE SPREAD (*Portugal*)

This was served to us by friends in Lisbon.

for 4 people

1 3¼-ounce can Portuguese sardines
1 teaspoon lemon juice
3 tablespoons mayonnaise
2 hard-boiled eggs
1 teaspoon mustard

1 teaspoon Mixed Herbs (or 2 teaspoons fresh chopped tarragon, chives, thyme)
1 teaspoon chopped chives and parsley
3 green onions, minced

Drain the oil from the sardines and place in mixing bowl. Mash fish with fork, then blend in other ingredients. Pack contents in bowl and chill in refrigerator. At serving time, you can invert the bowl onto a large serving plate and mold will slip out. Garnish with minced parsley. Surround with melba rounds, crackers, or bread rounds.

HOT CHEESE AND SHRIMP CANAPÉS (*Hawaii*)

16 canapes

4 slices white bread
16 large cooked shrimp
2 teaspoons chopped thyme, tarragon, chives
1 cup mayonnaise
2 tablespoons soy sauce

8 or 10 water chestnuts, finely chopped
½ cup shredded American cheese
½ cup heavy cream
parsley sprigs

Preheat broiler. Combine mayonnaise, herbs, soy sauce, water chestnuts, cheese, and cream, and blend thoroughly. Cut four 1½-inch rounds from each slice of bread. Top each round with one shrimp. Spread the mayonnaise mixture completely over and around each shrimp. Place canapes on a baking sheet, and broil 4 inches from the heat in a hot broiler until bubbly and brown. Top each canapé with a parsley sprig before serving.

CHICKEN LIVERS WITH HERB MUSTARD SAUCE DIP

for 8 people

1 pound fresh chicken livers	*Sauce:*
1 cup bread crumbs	2 tablespoons mustard
2 teaspoons Mixed Herbs (or thyme and savory)	1 tablespoon chopped thyme, tarragon, oregano
½ teaspoon salt	2 tablespoons minced chives
¼ cup butter	¼ cup milk
	½ cup tartar sauce or sandwich spread

Preheat oven to 350°. Melt the butter, add to it the bread crumbs, salt, and herbs. Blend well with your fingertips; add more butter if mixture is not moist enough. Cut each chicken liver in half. Roll each half in the moistened crumbs until thoroughly coated and place on a baking sheet or in a shallow baking pan. Bake in the oven for 30 minutes.

The sauce. Combine all the ingredients and chill in the refrigerator. Serve the hot livers on toothpicks, with sauce used as a dip.

COLD SHRIMP HORCHER (*Spain*)

Horcher's in Madrid is one of the great restaurants of Europe, and this is their particular specialty of the house. We have often served it as a first course. But because our friends have been so enthusiastic about the sauce, we use this sauce when we make shrimp salad (or any fish or poultry salad), and we also often serve the sauce as a dip with cooked shrimp. In short, the sauce is astonishingly good!

for 4 people

24 to 32 cooked shrimp	*Sauce:*
4 slices canned pineapple	½ cup light cream
	1 cup mayonnaise
	3 tablespoons ketchup
	3 teaspoons Mixed Herbs (or 2 teaspoons basil, 1 teaspoon thyme)
	1 clove garlic, crushed
	½ teaspoon salt

Chill the shrimp and pineapple. To make sauce, blend sauce ingredients in a bowl or an electric blender until smooth. Place in jar and chill (sauce keeps for several days in the refrigerator). Just before serving, place one slice of pineapple on a salad plate, cover with 6 or 8 shrimp. Pour the sauce over the pineapple and shrimp. Serve as a first course with sesame crackers.

SOUPS

GAZPACHO (*Spain*)
A salad in a soup

This recipe is from the Hotel Christina in Sevilla, remarkably delicious and completely authentic. This point is important, because we have seen many recipes for *gazpacho* which have had no more than four or five ingredients and which thus degrade this classic soup, we think.

for 6 people

4 slices wet bread, broken into small pieces	3 large pieces pimientos
1 pound canned tomatoes	2 cloves garlic, crushed
¼ cup white vinegar	2 hard-boiled eggs
¼ cup olive oil	½ onion, chopped
1 teaspoon thyme and oregano	½ cucumber, chopped

Place all the above ingredients into an electric blender and blend thoroughly. Then add sufficient water (about 2½ to 3 cups) to make enough soup for six persons. However, you will find it impossible to do this, and blend in the water, in one blending.or blender.. Therefore, we use a mixing-bowl technique: We put all the above ingredients into our largest mixing bowl. We pour them into the blender, until it's three quarters full, and blend thoroughly, then pour them from the blender into a second mixing bowl. When all the ingredients are blended, we pour part of the blended mixture back into the blender and add some water, continuing this process until all the soup and all the water have been thoroughly blended together.

Garnitures for Gazpacho. Gazpacho is not *gazpacho* unless the soup is thickened at the table with these four garnitures. We have a four-sectioned dish which we use; otherwise four little saucers on a tray or plate, each with a spoon for serving, work beautifully. For 6 people use:

2 cucumbers, in small cubes	2 tomatoes, in small cubes
2 onions, in small cubes	2 hard-boiled eggs, in small cubes

SOPA MEXICANA (Mexico)

for 2 or 3 people

1 10½-ounce can cream of chicken soup	6 tablespoons tomato puree
	½ teaspoon Mixed Herbs (or basil and tarragon)
1 3-ounce can boned chicken	
1 can of milk (measured from soup can)	½ avocado
	grated American cheese
½ onion, grated	salt, pepper to taste

Heat the soup and milk slowly, stirring constantly until well blended and smooth. Add the chicken, onion, tomato puree, herbs, and seasonings. Heat thoroughly but do not boil. Meanwhile, peel and slice the avocado into bite-size strips. Pour the soup into individual soup plates, garnish with the avocado strips, and sprinkle with the grated cheese.

GRANADA BEEF SOUP (*Spain*)

A noodle soup with a piquant difference, from Andalusia, the
flamenco country. So easy to fix! Serve it in winter piping hot;
in summer it is delicious jellied.

for 2 or 3 people

1 10½-ounce can condensed beef consommé	1 tablespoon mustard
2 tablespoons chopped pimientos	1 tablespoon horseradish
1 teaspoon Mixed Herbs (or ½ teaspoon thyme)	1 7-ounce can artichoke hearts ¼ cup sherry
½ clove garlic, crushed	½ cup cooked fine noodles salt, pepper to taste

Pour the soup into a saucepan, and stir in one soup can of water.
Heat to boiling and simmer a few minutes. Add the balance of ingredients and serve immediately.

Jellied. Pour the condensed soup into a large bowl. Add the
pimientos, herbs, garlic blended with the mustard, sherry, artichoke
hearts and salt. Stir well. Refrigerate for 3 to 4 hours or until jellied.

APFELSUPPE COLOGNE (*Germany*)

We have tried this apple soup hot and chilled. It is delicious
either way.

for 6 people

5 large cooking apples	1 tablespoon seedless raisins
½ cup sugar	1 cup white wine
1 teaspoon dried rosemary	2 cups milk
4 whole cloves	2 tablespoons flour
½ teaspoon cinnamon	½ cup heavy cream
grated rind and juice of 1 lemon	

Peel, core, and slice apples into a large saucepan. Add water to
cover, together with the cloves, cinnamon, and herbs. Simmer until

apples are tender. Put all through a sieve. Return the puree to the saucepan and add the raisins, sugar, lemon rind, and lemon juice. Slowly reheat the mixture, simmer for about 5 minutes. Add the wine and milk, stirring constantly, then remove from heat. Blend the cream and flour into the soup. Return soup to a boil and simmer 5 minutes.

POTAGE DE FLANDRES (Belgium)

Cream of vegetable soup

for 6 people

4 potatoes, peeled	½ teaspoon thyme and fennel
2 stalks celery	½ bay leaf
3 carrots	1 clove garlic, crushed
3 leeks	1 tablespoon butter
1 onion	salt, pepper to taste
4 ounces tomato puree	2 tablespoons croutons
3 sprigs parsley	

Chop up the vegetables, add the herbs, and put them in a large saucepan of water. Add the garlic and tomato puree and stir well. Bring to a boil, then simmer over low heat for about 3 hours, stirring occasionally. Strain through a sieve and retain liquid in a large mixing bowl. Mash the strained vegetables to a smooth pulp. Add enough of the soup liquid to the vegetables to make a thick, creamy mixture. Reheat the creamed soup. Add the butter and the croutons before serving.

To make the croutons. Dice buttered bread into ½-inch cubes and bake until toasted.

KALAKAUA OXTAIL SOUP AND STEW (Fiji)

This recipe is from the Club Hotel in Suva. Enjoying food in the South Pacific is as easy as enjoying the exotically beautiful and serene surroundings. So one wonders, Will the food taste as magnificent when the surroundings are not there? Our answer is *yes!* This recipe, with its herbs and spices, the novel texture and flavor of the peanuts, is as exciting during a Pennsylvania winter as when eaten under palm trees.

for 4 people

3 pounds oxtails, joints separated	1 tablespoon Mixed Herbs (or
4 cups water	thyme and basil)
3 tablespoons oil	1 7-ounce package salted peanuts
1 tablespoon powdered ginger	2 tablespoons flour
½ cup soy sauce	½ cup sherry

In a pressure cooker, brown the oxtails in hot oil. Add the water, ginger, soy sauce, herbs, sherry, and peanuts. Pressure cook at 15 pounds pressure for 45 minutes. Reduce heat quickly. Strain the soup and remove 1½ cups of soup, to use for the stew. Chill remaining soup and skim off the fat. Cut the meat from the joints. Before heating the skimmed soup, add a small amount of the meat and peanuts. (If regular pot is used to make soup, cook soup 2½ to 3 hours, or until meat is completely tender.)

To fix the stew. Chill the reserved 1½ cups of soup and skim off fat. Melt 2 tablespoons of this fat in a pan, add to it the flour and reserved soup. Stir until smooth and boiling and slightly thickened. Add the balance of the meat and peanuts. (Cooked carrots and celery can be added, if desired.) Serve with mashed potatoes or cooked noodles.

EGG DISHES

HUEVOS EXQUISITOS (Mexico)

This is a grand brunch recipe for guests. Both the eggs and the sauce can be prepared a day ahead, then the sauce heated just before serving.

for 4 people

8 hard-boiled eggs	2 cups canned tomato sauce
2 tablespoons butter	½ cup heavy cream
1 onion, minced	8 ripe pitted olives, sliced
1 green pepper, chopped	2 ounces grated Swiss cheese
⅛ teaspoon chili powder *	
1 teaspoon Mixed Herbs (or	
thyme and oregano)	

* If you like your Mexican foods really hot, you may add a bit more chili powder.

Melt the butter in a pan. When the foam subsides, add the onion and green pepper and sauté until soft. Add the spices, herbs, tomato sauce, cream, olives, and cheese, then simmer gently until the sauce is well blended and hot. Cut each egg in half, allowing four halves per serving, and place on hot plates. Pour the sauce over the eggs.

BAKED EGGS EL FUERTE (*Spain*)

During the winter of 1963 we spent a month at the Hotel El Fuerte in Marbella, a delightful resort on the Costa del Sol. One of our favorite luncheon dishes was this individual casserole. We keep it in mind whenever preparing vegetables and prepare enough extra for this recipe. You can use practically any number or variety of cooked vegetables.

for 2 people

2 tablespoons butter
1 tablespoon oil
½ onion, chopped
4 tablespoons cooked peas
1 boiled potato, diced
4 tablespoons cooked beets, diced
½ teaspoon Mixed Herbs (or thyme)

4 eggs
⅓ cup Anderson Farm Wine Herb Meat Sauce
(see introductory note to this chapter)

Heat oven to 375°. Heat butter and oil until foam subsides, and sauté onions until soft. Add the potatoes, beets, peas, and herbs. Reduce heat, and cook gently about 3 minutes. Divide this mixture into two small flat baking dishes, previously buttered. Break 2 eggs into each dish and bake in the oven for about 15 minutes, or until eggs are nicely done. Heat Wine Herb Meat Sauce and spoon over eggs before serving.

HUEVOS RANCHEROS (Mexico)
Ranch-style fried eggs

This is a hearty entree we serve for Sunday brunches or for luncheons on cold days.

for 4 people

8 eggs
8 canned tortillas
2 tablespoons butter
1 avocado, thinly sliced
grated American cheese

Sauce:
1 large onion, chopped
1 green pepper, chopped
2 cups canned tomato sauce
2 tablespoons butter
½ cup heavy cream
⅛ to ½ teaspoon chili powder (depending on whether you like your foods hot or mild)
1 teaspoon Mixed Herbs (or oregano and thyme)

Prepare the sauce by sautéing the onion and green pepper in the butter until they're soft. Add the balance of sauce ingredients, and heat thoroughly, stirring until smooth. Melt 2 tablespoons of butter in a large skillet. When foam subsides, add the tortillas, and sauté quickly on each side, allowing them to cook for about 5 minutes altogether. Place 2 tortillas each on four heated plates. Fry the eight eggs. Place one egg on each tortilla, spoon a little of the hot sauce over each egg, then garnish with a few slices of avocado and grated cheese.

OEUFS BRUXELLES (Belgium)

Eggs Belgian style

for 4 people

8 eggs
2 tablespoons butter
½ pound large cooked shrimp
1 4-ounce can mushrooms
1 cup heavy cream

2 teaspoons Mixed Herbs (or
   chopped thyme, fennel, and
   parsley)
2 tablespoons mustard
salt, pepper to taste
grated cheese

Preheat oven to 425°. Hard-boil the eggs, shell them, cut them into strips, and put them in a large mixing bowl. Cut the shrimp into bite-size pieces and add them to the eggs, together with 1 tablespoon of butter (melted or softened), the mushrooms, thoroughly drained, the cream, herbs, mustard, and seasonings. Mix thoroughly. Butter a casserole or four individual baking dishes. Pour the mixture in, sprinkle with grated cheese, and dot with butter. Bake in the oven until brown on top, approximately 15 minutes.

EGG SURPRISE ANDERSON

To us, this is one of the most satisfying of all egg dishes for a weekend breakfast.

for 2 people

4 eggs
3 strips bacon
1 teaspoon Mixed Herbs (or
   basil and thyme)
½ tomato or 2 tablespoons
   canned tomatoes

2 teaspoons Kraft Smokelle
   Cheese blend
1 teaspoon mustard
1 clove garlic, crushed
salt, pepper to taste

Fry bacon until crisp and drain on paper toweling. Melt the cheese with the tomatoes in a double boiler over simmering water. Add the eggs, herbs, mustard, garlic, and seasonings, and beat well. Cook, stirring frequently, until eggs are scrambled. Just before serving add the bacon, broken into small bits with a fork.

SUVA VEGETABLE OMELETTE (*Fiji*)

This was our luncheon dish in the Grand Pacific Hotel in Suva.

for 2 people

4 eggs
½ cup diced cooked ham
½ cup finely sliced bamboo shoots
4 scallions or ½ yellow onion, minced
½ cup cooked peas (or string beans)

2 tablespoons butter
1 teaspoon Mixed Herbs (or thyme and oregano)
salt, pepper to taste
soy sauce

Sauté ham, bamboo shoots, onions in 1 tablespoon of butter until onions are soft. Add the peas, and heat thoroughly. Beat the eggs, herbs, and seasonings in a bowl. Heat 1 tablespoon of butter in an 8-inch skillet until foam subsides. Add the eggs and let them set for 2 or 3 seconds. Add the sautéed mixture and finish the omelette. Serve with soy sauce.

SCRAMBLED EGGS DELUXE

for 2 people

5 eggs
1 4-ounce can sliced mushrooms, drained
1 tablespoon sour cream
½ cup diced cooked ham, chicken, or shrimp

½ teaspoon salt
½ teaspoon Mixed Herbs (or chopped dill)
1 tablespoon butter

Beat the eggs lightly in a mixing bowl. Add the mushrooms, sour cream, salt, herbs, and ham, chicken, or shrimp. In the top of a double boiler, over simmering water, melt the butter. Add the egg mixture and stir frequently, until eggs are well scrambled.

FRITTATA FIRENZE (*Italy*)

We found this recipe in Florence several years ago but have modified it considerably.

for 2 people

6 slices bacon	1 teaspoon Mixed Herbs (or
1 medium onion, chopped	basil, thyme, and tarragon)
10 pimiento-stuffed olives, sliced	1 generous pinch of allspice
4 eggs	salt, pepper to taste

Fry the bacon in an 8-inch skillet until crisp enough to crumble. Remove and drain on paper toweling. Sauté the onion until soft in the bacon drippings. Combine the crumbled bacon, onion, and sliced olives in a small bowl. Beat the eggs lightly until just mixed. Stir the bacon mixture into the eggs, add the herbs and seasonings. Pour out the remaining fat from the skillet, leaving just enough to coat the bottom. Heat the skillet and pour in the egg mixture. Slide the pan back and forth so the eggs keep moving. When they coagulate, lift them away from the edges with a spatula so the undone eggs run toward the center. Eggs are done when bottom is firm and the top the consistency of scrambled eggs.

PENNSYLVANIA DUTCH EGG CASSEROLE

for 2 or 3

5 hard-boiled eggs	1 teaspoon Mixed Herbs (or
2 teaspoons mayonnaise	basil, thyme, and oregano)
2 teaspoons mustard	salt, pepper to taste
¼ teaspoon curry powder	½ pint sour cream
a pinch of garlic powder	paprika

Preheat oven to 375°. Make highly seasoned deviled eggs by mixing the yolks with the mayonnaise, mustard (curry powder if desired), garlic, herbs, seasonings. Place the 10 egg halves in a baking dish, cover them with sour cream, sprinkle liberally with paprika, and bake, uncovered, about 20 minutes.

MEAT

STEAK COLOMBO (*Ceylon*)

This recipe is from the Galle Face Hotel in Colombo, one of those wonderful old outposts-of-Empire hotels with twenty-foot ceilings and the guests, largely British, in impeccable dinner clothes although the temperature was 105 degrees! It is the only steak recipe we've ever found which we enjoy as much as a good steak served rare and plain. The marinade and sauce give a remarkably delicate and exotic accent. You'll find it an interesting change.

for 3 or 4 people

2 pounds sirloin steak, ¾-inch thick

2 teaspoons meat tenderizer

3 tablespoons soy sauce

2 tablespoons sherry

1 teaspoon Mixed Herbs (or basil and oregano)

1 clove garlic, crushed

⅓ teaspoon black pepper

1 tablespoon sugar

2 tablespoons chopped dry-roasted peanuts

Sprinkle the meat tenderizer on both sides of the steak, rub in, and let stand in refrigerator at least 2 hours. Meanwhile, make a sauce of remaining ingredients (except the peanuts). Place steak on a platter, cover with marinade, return to refrigerator for another hour or so. Turn steak frequently so that both sides will be well seasoned. Preheat broiler, grease broiler rack. Take steak out of marinade but save the sauce. Place steak on rack about 2 inches from heat. Broil according to your taste: about 8 minutes each side for well done; 6 minutes for medium; 5 minutes for rare. Place steak on hot platter. Pour marinade and peanuts into a small saucepan, add meat juices from broiler. Heat marinade and pour over steak.

BITTERBALLEN (Holland)

Dutch meat balls

for 3 or 4 people

1 pound lean ground beef
6 scallions, minced
1 egg
½ teaspoon thyme (or Mixed Herbs)
1 tablespoon bread crumbs

3 tablespoons butter
1 tablespoon oil
2 tablespoons tomato puree
½ cup sour cream
1 cup beef stock or bouillon
salt, pepper to taste

Cook the minced onion in 1 tablespoon of butter until transparent. Place the ground beef in a large mixing bowl, add the onions, egg, thyme, bread crumbs, salt, pepper, and mix well. Form this mixture into small balls (about 16). Heat the balance of the butter with the oil in a large skillet until the foam subsides. Sauté the meat balls quickly until all color disappears. Add the tomato puree and stock, and simmer for 25 minutes. (This may be all done in advance; the meat gains flavor if left to stand for an hour or so.) Reheat and stir in the cream just before serving.

BEEF AND FRUIT STEW HORCHER (Spain)

This is a delicious summer casserole, making use of ripe pears, apples, and yellow squash.

for 4 people

2 tablespoons olive oil
2 tablespoons butter
1½ pounds beef, cut into ¾-inch cubes
1 cup chopped onions
½ cup sherry
1 tablespoon tomato paste
1 teaspoon Mixed Herbs (or basil, thyme, and oregano)

pinch of allspice
2 cups canned beef broth
2 cups cubed potatoes
2 cups cubed yellow squash
2 pears, cubed
2 apples, sliced
3 tablespoons seedless raisins
1 teaspoon minced parsley

Heat the oil and butter in a Dutch oven or heavy casserole. Brown the beef thoroughly. Remove the meat and brown the onions in the remaining fat. Return the meat to the casserole and stir in the sherry, tomato paste, herbs, seasonings, and broth. Cover the casserole and cook over low heat for one hour. Add the potatoes and squash, re-cover, and cook another 30 minutes. Gently mix in the pears, apples, and raisins, and cook for 10 minutes. Sprinkle with parsley before serving.

PICADILLO (Mexico)

Ground beef casserole

In the 1930's I had occasion to spend a month in and around Mexico City and stayed much of the time in the house of a friend at 140 Cipres. I shiver to think of what may be covering 140 Cipres now—perhaps a skyscraper—but then it was the perfect example of an upper-middle-class Mexican house of the olden times. A patio in the center was filled with lush tropical plants; the bedrooms gave on a balcony overlooking the patio; and on the roof were the huts of the five servants—and several chicken coops! I was so wide-eyed over the marvelous food that, when I left, my friend's mother was so kind as to give me an old Mexican cookbook. This recipe, and the other Mexican ones in this book, are from the old cookbook—exotic cooking of the olden times.

Picadillo is an ideal dish for a simple buffet party. Add a green salad, a crusty herb bread, dessert, and your menu is perfect. You can prepare *picadillo* the day before and heat it up just before serving. (*Note:* If you double or triple the recipe, use proportionately less tomato sauce and juice.)

for 6 people

1½ pounds lean ground beef
2 tablespoons butter
1 tablespoon oil
1 large onion, chopped
1 large green pepper, finely diced
2 cups tomato sauce
1 cup tomato juice
1½ teaspoons chili powder
½ teaspoon powdered cloves
½ teaspoon powdered cinnamon

1 teaspoon minced oregano
1 clove garlic, crushed
18 ripe black olives, sliced
⅓ cup raisins
⅓ cup candied orange peel (or any citrus fruit)
1 tablespoon sugar
¾ teaspoon salt
⅓ cup slivered almonds
1 large banana, sliced

Heat the butter and oil in a large skillet or Dutch oven. When foam subsides, add the ground beef, separating with a fork as it cooks. Add the onion, green pepper, and sauté these ingredients until the meat is colorless and starting to brown. Add the balance of the ingredients, except for the banana, and simmer covered for one hour, stirring frequently. (If liquid absorbs too quickly, add more tomato juice. Recipe should be very thick and juicy, not running.) Add the sliced banana the last fifteen minutes of cooking.

BOEUF LUXEMBOURG (Luxembourg)

for 4 people

2 pounds lean beef, cut in 1-inch cubes
1 small onion, sliced
1 cup dry white wine
1 teaspoon Mixed Herbs (or oregano, savory, and thyme)
¼ pound beef suet

2 teaspoons salt
½ cup flour
¼ teaspoon pepper
1 cup water
1½ cups diced carrots
½ pound small white onions

Place the beef, onion slices, herbs, and wine in a large bowl. Marinate in the refrigerator for 2 days, turning meat occasionally. Render the suet in a large skillet or Dutch oven, then discard the solid pieces.

Drain the meat, saving the marinating wine. Discard the onions. Place meat, flour, salt, pepper in paper bag and shake vigorously until meat is well coated. Brown the meat in the hot rendered fat, making sure all sides are well browned. Add the water and marinating wine, cover, and cook over low heat for 2 to 2½ hours, or until meat is almost tender. Add the diced carrots and onions and continue cooking for another half hour, or until meat and vegetables are tender. (If desired, potatoes may be added with the carrots and onions.) Without the potatoes, this dish is delicious served with egg noodles and spiced fruit slices.

VEAL CHOPS PONTE VECCHIO (*Italy*)

Florentine veal in foil wrap

Walk from Via Lungarno across the Ponte Vecchio, turn left at the first little street, and you are at the Ponte Vecchio Restaurant, which we love both for its excellent cooking and for the fact that one can eat at a table actually overlooking the Arno River. Our veal chops were *not* served to us in aluminum foil but in a paper bag. However, we find the aluminum foil way of cooking them easier—and even more delicious.

for 4 people

4 loin veal chops, about 1-inch thick
8 tablespoons butter
1 tablespoon oil
¼ pound mushrooms, sliced
8 chicken livers

4 tablespoons Marsala wine or dry vermouth
2 tablespoons chopped parsley
1 teaspoon tarragon, or mixed basil and thyme
salt, pepper to taste

Preheat oven to 325°. Cut aluminum foil into four large pieces, each piece large enough to hold one chop and to seal tightly. Heat 2 tablespoons of the butter with 1 tablespoon of oil. When foam subsides, add the chops, and sauté them until nicely browned on each side. While the chops are cooking, sauté the mushrooms and chicken livers in 2 tablespoons of butter until tender. Chicken livers can then be diced. Season the mushrooms and chicken livers with the herbs, salt, and pepper. Place each chop on a piece of foil. On top of each chop place a spoonful of the mushroom-chicken liver mixture, a tablespoon of the wine, some chopped parsley, and a dab of butter. Fold the foil over each chop and seal tightly. Place the foil packages on a baking sheet and bake in oven for 15 to 20 minutes.

SALTIMBOCCA ROMANA (Italy)

Veal scallops with prosciutto and sage leaves

This dish is as Roman as the Trevi Fountain! We first enthused over it on the *Leonardo da Vinci* on our way to Italy, then found it in almost every good restaurant throughout Rome and northern Italy. It's quick to prepare and its success is assured—the subtle taste of sage makes it a conversation piece. (*Note:* It is easy to get the sage taste too strong; for us, 3 leaves per scallop is a maximum.)

for 4 people

8 veal scallops, about 4 inches in diameter
4 tablespoons butter
2 tablespoons oil
¼ cup dry vermouth, Marsala wine, or cognac

24 fresh sage leaves
8 slices prosciutto (or thinly sliced boiled ham)
salt, pepper to taste
chopped parsley

Pound scallops and trim each one to about 4 inches diameter. Place a slice of prosciutto on each scallop and 3 sage leaves between scallop and prosciutto. Fasten together with toothpicks. Heat 2 tablespoons of butter with 1 tablespoon of oil in a large skillet. When foam has almost subsided, sauté the scallops quickly until the veal is tender, or until juices run yellow when meat is pierced with a fork. Remove to a hot platter. Rinse the skillet with the wine or cognac, and pour the juices over the scallops. If there is not enough juice, add a little beef broth or beef bouillon. Garnish with chopped parsley.

CHARCOAL-BROILED VEAL CHOPS *EN PAPILLOTTES*
(*France*)

Here's an exciting main course for your outdoor grill—veal chops cooked in aluminum foil. If you're a kitchen cook, you can get the same result by doing them in the oven. The chops get their tender, delicious flavor by marinating them for 24 hours before cooking them.

for 4 people

4 loin veal chops, about 1-inch thick, well trimmed	*Marinade:*
2 teaspoons fresh basil, tarragon, and chervil, minced	1 tablespoon vinegar
	1 clove garlic, crushed
4 tablespoons butter	2 tablespoons olive oil
1 tablespoon oil	1 tablespoon chopped parsley
salt, pepper to taste	2 tablespoons minced scallions
	6 peppercorns

If cooking in kitchen, heat oven to 325°. Place the raw chops in a Pyrex bowl, pour the marinade over them, making sure each chop is well coated. Cover the bowl and refrigerate 24 hours, turning the chops occasionally. Let the chops come to room temperature before cooking. Remove the chops from the marinade, making sure they have a good coating of oil. Brown them on both sides over hot coals (or in 2 tablespoons of butter and 1 tablespoon of oil in a large skillet). Prepare four large sheets of baking foil, large enough to hold one chop with room to seal tightly. Lay each sheet of foil out flat. Sprinkle each sheet with ¼ teaspoon of the herbs. Put a chop on each sheet of foil, sprinkle with another ¼ teaspoon of herbs, place a small pat of butter on each chop, sprinkle with salt and pepper. Seal foil tightly. Place chops on grill and continue grilling for 15 to 20 minutes, turning foil packages frequently. Or place foil packages on a baking sheet and bake in the oven for about 30 minutes.

GOSHT TARKARI (India)

Meat curry

This delicious confection is from the Taj Mahal Hotel in Bombay, another stately outpost of Empire, except that here the ceiling on the ground floor is thirty feet high.

for 4 people

1½ pounds boneless veal cut into 2-inch cubes
flour
salt, pepper
1 teaspoon Mixed Herbs (or thyme)
2 tablespoons butter
1 tablespoon oil
1 large onion, chopped

1 apple, peeled and chopped
4 teaspoons curry powder
2 cups chicken stock or 4 chicken bouillon cubes dissolved in 2 cups water
1 teaspoon lemon juice
1 teaspoon sugar
2 ounces golden raisins
2 ounces chutney

Season the flour with salt and pepper and coat the veal thoroughly. (We like to place the seasoned flour in a clean paper bag, drop in the veal pieces, and shake the bag until all pieces are well coated.) Heat the butter and oil in a large skillet or casserole until almost smoking. Brown the veal, a few pieces at a time, and remove to a plate. Add more butter and oil if necessary until all pieces are browned. Add the curry powder, chopped apple, and onion to the skillet, adding more butter and oil if needed, and sauté them until they're golden brown. Replace the veal in the skillet, and add the stock and herbs. Cover and simmer slowly for about 45 minutes or until the veal is tender. Add the lemon juice, raisins, and chutney, and continue cooking slowly for additional 15 minutes. Serve over boiled rice, with chutneys, coconut, and other Indian side dishes.

OSSO BUCO (*Italy*)

Milanese veal knuckle with marrow

for 4 people

2½ pounds young veal knuckle or shanks sawed into 2-inch pieces, with marrow remaining inside bone
flour
½ teaspoon salt
¼ teaspoon pepper
½ cup oil
3 small carrots, chopped
2 small celery stalks, chopped
1 medium onion, chopped
1 teaspoon flour

1 tablespoon butter, creamed
1 1-pound can tomatoes
½ cup dry white wine
½ cup beef stock or broth
2 strips lemon peel
2 teaspoons Mixed Herbs (or basil and oregano)
Garnish:
2 tablespoons grated lemon peel
½ cup chopped parsley
4 anchovies

Heat ¼ cup oil in a large skillet. Coat the veal chunks with flour, seasoned with salt and pepper. Add a few pieces of veal at a time to the hot oil and brown them on all sides, until they're dark and crusty. While veal is browning, heat balance of oil in a large casserole or Dutch oven and sauté the carrots, celery, and onion, until soft and tender. Add the veal, the butter and flour creamed together, and continue cooking for 5 minutes longer. Stir in the tomatoes, wine, beef broth, add the lemon peel and Mixed Herbs, and gradually bring to a boil. Cover and let simmer gently for 1 to 1½ hours, stirring occasionally. Transfer the meat to a hot platter, strain the sauce over it, first tasting it for seasoning. Combine the garnish ingredients well. Pass them separately. Serve oyster forks to get at the marrow. (Spaghetti is a wonderful accompaniment for this dish.)

VEAL TRE SCALINI (*Italy*)

Two of the greatest joys in Rome are its sightseeing and its food. Both are combined when one visits the Restaurant Tre Scalini, on the Piazza Navona, one of Rome's most beautiful squares. In the summer, while dining in the piazza, one can enjoy the breathtaking Bernini fountain. It was at Tre Scalini that we enjoyed this superb veal dish, served to us accompanied by sautéed mushrooms.

for 4 people

8 veal scallops, pounded ¼-inch thin

2 tablespoons butter

1 tablespoon oil

1 large bunch asparagus or 2 packages frozen asparagus

½ teaspoon oregano or thyme

4 slices prosciutto or thinly sliced cooked ham

½ cup white wine or dry vermouth

4 slices Provolone or Bel Paese cheese

grated Parmesan cheese

Have asparagus cooked and ready to serve. Dry the scallops thoroughly between paper towels. Heat the butter and oil in a large skillet. When foam subsides, sauté the scallops, 3 or 4 at a time, for 4 or 5 minutes on each side, until they're lightly browned and juices turned to yellow. Add more butter and oil to skillet as needed. Remove them to a hot platter. Add the herbs, wine to the skillet, scraping up remaining butter and oil, and boil for 2 or 3 minutes. Place the scallops in a shallow baking pan or dish and pour the wine sauce over them. Top each scallop with a half slice of cheese. Sprinkle the Parmesan cheese generously over the 8 scallops and place under a hot broiler until cheese melts. Place a helping of asparagus on each plate, and cover with 2 scallops and the cheese sauce.

ANDERSON FARM VEAL PAPRIKA

This is known to us as "slithery veal" and is one of our favorites.

for 3 or 4 people

1½ pounds boneless veal, cut into 1-inch pieces

2 teaspoons meat tenderizer

3 strips bacon

flour

1 large onion, diced

1 cup sour cream

2 cups water

2 tablespoons paprika

½ teaspoon oregano

2 cups shell macaroni

salt, pepper to taste

Sprinkle the veal with the tenderizer and let stand for an hour or two in the refrigerator. Sauté the bacon in a large skillet until crisp, then drain on paper towels, using the remaining bacon fat to sauté the veal. Flour the veal pieces lightly and add them to the bacon fat, along with the onion and the bacon, crumbled. Sauté the veal and onion until veal starts to brown. Add the water, herbs, paprika, and seasonings, cover skillet tightly, and simmer for one hour. Meanwhile, cook the macaroni and drain well. When veal is fork-tender, add the cooked macaroni and sour cream. Stir well and cook for a few minutes to thicken the sauce.

ROMAN VEAL (*Italy*)

for 4 people

8 veal scallops pounded ¼-inch thin

flour

½ teaspoon thyme

2 tablespoons grated Parmesan cheese

juice of 2 lemons

2 tablespoons butter

1 tablespoon oil

salt, pepper to taste

Dry the scallops thoroughly. Season the flour with the herbs and cheese. Coat each scallop lightly with the seasoned flour, then dip it in the lemon juice, then into the flour again. Heat the butter and oil in a large skillet until the foam subsides. Sauté the scallops, 3 or 4 at a time, for about 8 to 10 minutes, turning them once. They are done when they are golden brown and juices have turned to yellow. Remove them to a heated platter. Add the remaining lemon juice to the skillet and let come to a boil, scraping up all the coagulated cooking juices, then pour this sauce over the scallops.

VEAU AU VIN LUCULLUS (*Lebanon*)

We not only discovered an elegant French cuisine at the Restaurant Lucullus in Beirut but also one of the most delightful settings. The restaurant is on the street bordering the harbor, up a steep flight of narrow stairs—a large room with big windows that look out over the palm trees to the blue Mediterranean. At

both noon and evening hours the immense dining room is loud
and crowded with affluent Lebanese and good-food-loving tourists. There are specials every day—a bouillabaisse, a special
chicken in wine, or a marvelous fish filet in a rich sauce. *Veau
au vin* is such a special. Served with tiny browned potatoes and
a salad, it is a dish for gourmet eating.

for 4 people

2 pounds veal cutlets, in 1-inch
  cubes
2 tablespoons butter
1 tablespoon oil
4 carrots, sliced
2 onions, cubed
½ pound fresh mushrooms,
  sliced
2 tablespoons flour

1 cup beef stock (or 2 beef cubes
  dissolved in 1 cup boiling
  water)
¼ cup sherry
1 tablespoon Mixed Herbs (or
  basil and thyme)
1 clove garlic, crushed
salt, pepper to taste

Heat oven to 350°. Heat the butter and oil in a large skillet until
foam subsides, then add the veal, and brown quickly on all sides.
Remove the veal to a casserole. Add the mushrooms, carrots, and
onions to the skillet, and sauté them until onions are soft and golden
(adding more butter and oil if needed). Sprinkle the flour over these
vegetables, and gradually add the beef stock, stirring constantly with
a wire whisk until sauce is smooth and blended. Add the herbs, seasonings, and sherry, and stir well. Pour this mixture over the veal, cover,
and bake for 45 minutes or until veal is fork-tender.

MIRACLE QUICK VEAL ROAST

Almost effortless!

for 6 people

4- or 5-pound veal roast
1 cup sherry
⅔ cup tomato paste
⅓ cup Wine Herb Meat Sauce

1 teaspoon Mixed Herbs (or
  thyme and basil)
1 clove garlic, crushed
1 package dry onion soup
salt, pepper to taste

Heat oven to 375°. Mix the sherry, meat sauce, herbs, garlic, and tomato paste until smooth. Lay meat on sheet of heavy broiling foil large enough to seal meat in completely. Sprinkle roast with the dried onion soup, pour the herb sauce over the roast. Fold the foil around roast, sealing tight. Place foil package in baking pan or on baking sheet. Place in oven for 2 to 3 hours (allowing 30 to 40 minutes per pound of roast).

VEAL STROGANOFF, ANDERSON STYLE

for 2 people

6 veal scallops, pounded to ¼-inch thickness	1 tablespoon oil
½ cup white vinegar	¼ pound fresh mushrooms sliced
1 clove garlic, crushed	1 cup sour cream
1 large onion, chopped	½ teaspoon oregano
3 tablespoons butter	salt, pepper to taste

In a large bowl, mix the vinegar and garlic. Use this as a marinade for the veal scallops, and marinate them for about 2 or 3 hours. Dry them thoroughly before sautéing. Heat 2 tablespoons butter and 1 tablespoon oil in a large skillet until foam disappears. Arrange the scallops in the skillet, 2 or 3 at a time, and sauté them on one side 4 or 5 minutes, turning them and sautéing them on the other side. Scallops are cooked when juices have turned yellow and meat is almost colorless. Remove scallops to a hot platter. Add remaining butter to skillet and sauté onions and mushrooms for about 5 minutes. Return scallops to skillet, add the sour cream, herbs, and seasonings, and cook slowly for 5 additional minutes.

CÔTELETTES DE VEAU LE TRIANON (*Australia*)

Veal cutlets in herb mustard sauce

One doesn't travel all the way to Sydney to find an excellent French restaurant (the Sydney specialties are very small, sweet oysters and very strong beer) but it was a pleasure to find one anyway. Le Trianon has French cooking at its best.

for 2 or 3 people

1 pound thin veal cutlets, cut into serving pieces	3 teaspoons mustard
2 tablespoons flour	1 teaspoon horseradish
4 tablespoons butter	½ teaspoon Mixed Herbs (or savory and thyme)
2 tablespoons oil	½ cup heavy cream
1 large onion, chopped	salt, pepper to taste
1 10½-ounce can beef broth	

Preheat oven to 325°. In a large skillet, melt half the butter and oil, and cook the onions slowly until they're transparent. Remove them to a casserole. Wipe the cutlets, and flour them lightly. Heat remaining butter and oil in the skillet until foam has subsided, then add the cutlets, and sauté them quickly until they're golden and juices have turned yellow. Place them in the casserole, along with the beef broth, mustard, horseradish, and herbs. Cover the casserole, and bake in the oven for 1¾ hours, basting five or six times. When veal is fork-tender, remove it to a hot platter. Add the cream to the sauce in the casserole, and heat quickly. Spoon sauce over the cutlets.

DOLMADES (Greece)

Lamb rolls in lettuce leaves

The Flocca Restaurant in Athens is a combination tearoom, café, and elegant dining room. Early in the afternoon women gather for tea; around six o'clock men gather for coffee and talk; and around eight thirty or nine P.M., the dining room opens—one of the loveliest places in Athens to eat. On our first visit, we asked the headwaiter to suggest a menu. He insisted we try the *dolmades* for a first course, then proceed to a chicken dish as our main entree. As you will see after you try it, the *dolmades* was quite sufficient—a fascinating main dish. Since it is served with a generous helping of hollandaise sauce, we usually accompany *dol-*

mades with asparagus or broccoli, either of which is piqued by hollandaise. In Athens, *dolmades* is served in grape leaves, but since this delicacy is not always available in the United States, we have adapted the recipe to lettuce leaves. If you have young grape leaves, by all means use them, making small, bite-size stuffed leaves.

for 4 people

1 pound ground lamb
8 large, unbroken iceberg lettuce leaves
grated rind of 4 lemons
½ teaspoon thyme
1 teaspoon chopped parsley or fennel
1 clove garlic, crushed
4 tablespoons butter
½ cup lemon juice
½ cup beef broth (or 1 beef bouillon cube dissolved in ½ cup boiling water)
2 teaspoons sugar

Hollandaise Sauce:

6 tablespoons butter
6 egg yolks
2 teaspoons cornstarch
6 tablespoons lemon juice
1 cup boiling water
1 teaspoon salt

Heat oven to 375°. Pick large, firm lettuce leaves (we find the tough outside leaves of iceberg work well) and drop them into a large pot of boiling water. Let them boil for 2 or 3 minutes until they're wilted, then spread them out tenderly on paper toweling to drain thoroughly. Handle them carefully so that they do not break. Cut off the heavy part at the base of each leaf if it is too thick to roll up easily. Combine the lamb, lemon rind, herbs, garlic, and knead well until thoroughly mixed. Divide mixture into 8 sausagelike rolls. Place one roll on each lettuce leaf, fold in the sides over the lamb and roll up, making sure the leaf completely covers the lamb roll. Secure the leaf with two or three toothpicks. Place the rolls close together in a greased baking pan or dish, and dot each with butter. Combine the sugar and lemon juice with the beef broth, and pour over the rolls. Bake, uncovered, one hour.

Hollandaise sauce. Melt the butter slowly in the top of a double boiler over simmering water. Remove pan from water and add the egg yolks, beating them well with a wire whisk. Add the cornstarch and lemon juice. Return the pan to the double boiler and, over simmering water, add the water slowly, stirring constantly until sauce thickens. You can leave the sauce until ready to use it. To reheat it, place it over a low flame and stir constantly until hot enough to serve.

DEVILED LAMB CHOPS

for 4 people

4 shoulder lamb chops	2 tablespoons butter
2 tablespoons mustard	1 tablespoon oil
1 teaspoon Mixed Herbs (or oregano)	1 green pepper, sliced
	2 medium onions, sliced
1 clove garlic, crushed	¼ cup water
flour	grated rind of 1 lemon
½ teaspoon salt	

Mix the mustard with the herbs and garlic. Spread this mixture on both sides of the lamb chops. Season the flour with the salt, and flour the lamb chops on both sides. Heat the butter and oil in a skillet or casserole until the foam subsides, and brown the lamb chops quickly on both sides. Arrange the sliced pepper and onions over the lamb chops, add the water and lemon rind, cover the skillet or casserole, and simmer for 45 minutes.

ROAST LEG OF LAMB (*Sweden*)

We found this in the Grand Hotel in Stockholm. For a variation on the traditional roast leg of lamb, this recipe is a treasure. The sauce is an ambrosia with a faint flavor of coffee and red currants—a perfect complement to succulent lamb! We have based our roasting time on 30 minutes to the pound, which results in medium-rare lamb of a faint pink color. If you prefer it well done, count on 35 minutes per pound.

for 6 people

4-pound leg of lamb, boned and rolled
½ lemon
⅓ cup mustard
1 teaspoon Mixed Herbs (or rosemary)

1 cup cooked coffee
1 teaspoon sugar
1 tablespoon heavy cream
2 tablespoons flour
1 cup milk
3 tablespoons red currant jelly
slivers of garlic

Preheat oven to 300°. Insert slivers of garlic under the lamb's skin. Rub the lamb with the lemon, mix the herbs with the mustard, and brush this mixture all over the lamb. Place in a roasting pan, and roast for one hour. Add the sugar and cream to the coffee, mix well and pour over the roast. Continue to roast the lamb, basting from time to time, for another hour, or until meat is done to your liking. Remove roast to a serving dish, and keep warm. Pour the liquid from the pan, and let cool until you can skim off the fat. After skimming the fat, add the milk to the liquid to make about 1 pint in all. Put 2 tablespoons of the skimmed fat back into the roasting pan or a small pan, and place on low heat. Stir in the flour, and add the stock gradually, stirring until thick and smooth. Add the jelly, and stir until the jelly melts. Pour into saucebowl and serve with the roasted lamb.

LAMB STEAKS WITH MINTED APRICOT SAUCE

for 4 people

4 lamb steaks
2 tablespoons butter
1 tablespoon oil
1 onion, finely chopped
½ cup chicken stock (or 1 chicken bouillon cube dissolved in ½ cup boiling water)
¼ cup apricot preserves

1½ teaspoons fresh mint, chopped
1 teaspoon Mixed Herbs (or ½ teaspoon savory)
1 clove garlic, crushed
1 tablespoon cornstarch
¼ cup sherry
salt, pepper to taste

Heat butter and oil in skillet until foam has subsided. Brown the steaks quickly on both sides. Remove from skillet. Sauté the onion in remaining butter and oil (or add as much as is needed) until soft and golden. Stir in herbs, seasonings, chicken stock, preserves, and bring to boil. Add the lamb steaks, cover, and simmer until tender, about 30 minutes. Remove the steaks to a heated platter. Combine the sherry with the cornstarch and stir into the sauce. Cook until mixture thickens slightly. Serve this sauce over the steaks.

DAMASCUS LAMB CASSEROLE (*Syria*)

We found this in L'Oasis Restaurant, probably the best in Damascus. The *mezze,* mentioned under hors d'oeuvres, was a standard first course here.

for 3 or 4 people

2 pounds lamb shoulder, cut into 2-inch cubes
2 tablespoons butter
1 tablespoon oil
2 medium onions, finely chopped
1½ tablespoons flour
1½ teaspoons salt
1 clove garlic, crushed
1 teaspoon Mixed Herbs (or oregano or thyme)

1½ cups canned tomatoes
1 cup canned beef bouillon
1½ cups raw rice
4 tablespoons Anderson Farm Damascus Meat Sauce (or 4 tablespoons Houses of Parliament Sauce plus 1 tablespoon minced onion)

Preheat oven to 375°. Heat butter and oil in heavy skillet or casserole. When foam subsides, add the meat and onions, and brown meat. Sprinkle meat with flour, and toss until flour browns slightly. Add the seasonings, tomatoes, and bouillon, cover tightly, and simmer for one hour. Remove from stove, add the rice and a little more bouillon if desired, and the Damascus Meat Sauce. Stir until rice is moistened, cover, and bake in oven for 35 minutes.

SPICED LAMB (*Ceylon*)

for 4 people

1½ pounds boneless lamb cut into ½-inch cubes
2 tablespoons butter
1 tablespoon oil
2 sticks cinnamon
1 onion, grated
¼ teaspoon nutmeg
½ teaspoon pepper
1 teaspoon salt

1½ teaspoons Mixed Herbs (or thyme, oregano, and savory)
2 cups beef stock (or 4 beef bouillon cubes in 2 cups boiling water)
1 cup water
¼ cup sherry
¼ cup heavy cream

Heat butter and oil in a large skillet until foam subsides. Brown the lamb pieces on all sides. Drain off the remaining oil, and add the herbs, spices, and seasonings together with the onion and beef stock. Simmer, covered, until lamb is tender—about 50 minutes. Add the water, if mixture gets too thick. Remove the lamb to a hot platter. Discard cinnamon sticks. Add the sherry and cream to remaining liquid in skillet, and boil down until slightly thickened. Pour over lamb, and serve immediately over cooked rice.

MOUSSAKA (*Greece*)

Lamb and eggplant casserole

There are many variations on this classic Greek dish. This one we've adapted from the *moussaka* served to us in a small *taverna* in the old section of Athens, near the Parthenon. We usually accompany this *moussaka* with the Greek salad with which it was served at this *taverna;* you will find the recipe in the salad section.

for 3 or 4 people

1 pound lamb, ground	2 teaspoons Mixed Herbs (or
1 medium-sized eggplant	thyme, oregano, and savory)
flour	½ cup sherry
6 tablespoons oil	2 tablespoons chopped parsley
1 large onion, chopped	¼ pound mushrooms, sliced
1 clove garlic, crushed	4 small potatoes
3 tablespoons butter	¼ cup milk
1 cup tomato sauce	¼ pound sharp cheese, crumbled
1 bay leaf	salt, pepper to taste

Preheat oven to 375°. Boil the potatoes, mash them with the heated milk and set aside. Pare the eggplant, and cut it into ¼-inch round slices. Dredge the slices in flour. Heat 4 or more tablespoons of oil in a large skillet until foam subsides, add the eggplant slices a few at a time, and brown them well on both sides. Drain them on paper toweling. Pour off remaining oil in skillet, and add 2 tablespoons of butter with 1 tablespoon of oil. Heat until foam subsides, then cook the onion and garlic until soft. Add the ground lamb, and cook, separating meat with fork, for 10 minutes or until lamb is colorless. Add to the skillet the tomato sauce, bay leaf, herbs, seasonings, wine, and parsley, and blend well. Cook until almost all the liquid is absorbed. In the meantime, sauté the mushrooms in 1 tablespoon of butter in a separate skillet, and add them to the cooked lamb mixture. Grease a casserole. Put a layer of eggplant in the bottom, cover with a layer of lamb mixture. Continue alternating eggplant and lamb mixture (approximately 3 layers each) ending with top layer of lamb. Cover with the mashed potatoes, spread out like a top crust. Cover casserole and bake for one half hour. Add the crumbled cheese, and continue baking, uncovered, an additional 15 minutes.

PAPEETE PORK STEW (*Tahiti*)

Considering that we had this ambrosial stew at the Tahitian Village Hotel one evening in Papeete, sitting on an outdoor terrace surrounded by palm trees and frangipani blossoms, with Tahitian dancers and singers performing their hypnotically beautiful dances to the accompaniment of low voices and drums, we wondered whether it was solely the recipe that we thought so marvelous or the combination of the food and the surroundings and the music. Since returning home we have served this recipe many times—and it's great in Pennsylvania, too!

for 4 to 6 people

3 pounds boneless pork shoulder butt
2 teaspoons meat tenderizer
2 tablespoons olive oil
2 tablespoons cornstarch
3 tablespoons soy sauce
1 cup water
2 tablespoons brown sugar
2 tablespoons honey

2 tablespoons sherry
1 teaspoon Mixed Herbs (or sage and thyme)
½ teaspoon each of powdered cloves, ginger, nutmeg
juice of 1½ lemons
½ cup dry roasted peanuts, chopped

Cut meat into 1-inch cubes. Sprinkle it with meat tenderizer, and let stand in refrigerator for 2 hours. Heat the olive oil in a heavy skillet or Dutch oven. Add the pork cubes, and brown them thoroughly on all sides. Combine the cornstarch with the soy sauce, sherry, and water, add to it the sugar, honey, herbs, spices, and lemon juice. Add this sauce to the pork. Cover tightly, and simmer for 2 to 2½ hours, or until pork is fork-tender. Just before serving, add the peanuts, and stir them through the stew.

HUNGARIAN PORK CHOPS

for 2 people

4 loin pork chops
1 small onion, chopped
2 tablespoons butter
1 tablespoon oil
1 cup chicken stock (or 2 bouillon cubes dissolved in 1 cup boiling water)

1 cup white wine
¾ teaspoons flour
1 teaspoon butter
1 teaspoon mustard
1 teaspoon Mixed Herbs (or sage and thyme)
2 sliced sweet pickles

In heavy skillet or casserole, brown the onion and the chops in the butter and oil. Add the wine and chicken stock, cover, and simmer for one hour. Cream together the flour and softened butter, and stir them into the sauce, cooking until smooth. Add the mustard, herbs, and pickles, and heat thoroughly.

PENNSYLVANIA DUTCH PORK CHOPS

for 4 people

4 large loin pork chops	1 teaspoon Mixed Herbs (or sage
1 medium onion, chopped	and thyme)
2 6-ounce cans tomato sauce	6 tablespoons sherry
1 cup sour cream	1 dill pickle, chopped
	salt, pepper to taste

Heat a large skillet, and brown the pork chops quickly on both sides (do not add fat to skillet). Cover and cook over low flame for 20 minutes. Add the chopped onion, cover, and cook slowly for about 10 minutes or until onion is soft. Pour off *all* fat, add the tomato sauce and sour cream, and bring to simmer. Stir in the sherry, pickle, herbs, and seasonings.

ALABAMA HAM

for 2 people

1 1-pound slice tenderized ham	1 cup milk
2 tablespoons mustard	1 cup light cream
½ teaspoon Mixed Herbs (or	½ of a 1-pound can white whole
basil and thyme)	hominy
	butter

Preheat oven to 350°. Butter a baking dish or shallow casserole. Slash the fat on the ham. Combine the mustard with the Mixed Herbs, and spread this mixture thickly on the ham. Place the ham in the baking dish or casserole, and pour the milk over it. Bake, covered, in the oven for ¾ hour. Pour off any remaining milk, drain the hominy, and add it to the ham. Cover with the cream, and return to the oven, covered, for 15 minutes. Uncover, and bake additional 5 minutes.

PENNSYLVANIA DUTCH HAM CASSEROLE

for 4 people

1 pound sliced cooked ham	1 teaspoon Mixed Herbs (or
1 pound canned sweet potatoes	basil and savory)
1 pound and 1 4-ounce can	¼ cup white vinegar
sliced apples	¼ cup pineapple juice
2 tablespoons mustard	½ cup brown sugar

Preheat oven to 375°. Slice the sweet potatoes, and place them in a greased baking dish. Cover them with the ham slice. Combine in a saucepan the apples, mustard, herbs, vinegar, pineapple juice, and sugar. Bring to a boil, and simmer 10 minutes. Pour this sauce over the ham and sweet potatoes, and bake in the oven for 30 minutes.

CALVES LIVER TAVARES (*Portugal*)

The Tavares is an excellent restaurant in Lisbon, perhaps the best in town.

for 2 people

½ pound calves liver	¼ cup heavy cream
2 tablespoons butter	1 tablespoon mustard
1 tablespoon oil	½ teaspoon Mixed Herbs (or
2 onions, sliced thin	thyme and savory)
¼ cup canned beef bouillon	salt, pepper to taste

Cut the liver into bite-size pieces. Heat the butter and oil in a heavy skillet until foam subsides. Sauté the liver for 2 to 3 minutes until tender. Remove to a hot platter. Add the onions to the skillet, and sauté them until brown, using more butter and oil if necessary. Remove the onions to the hot platter, and pour the bouillon into the skillet, letting it boil down for a minute or two. Add the cream, mustard, herbs, and seasonings. Simmer until sauce thickens. Pour over the liver, and serve.

INDIAN CURRY AUCKLAND (*New Zealand*)

A festive dish for leftover meat or fowl

During a South Seas cruise from San Francisco, we met a pleasant couple who were returning to their home in Auckland. They insisted we spend a day and evening in Auckland with them, including sightseeing and a home-cooked dinner. Their housekeeper had most thoughtfully prepared a leg of mutton for their return. But—"No!" said our hostess, "I'll fix you our special Indian curry—Auckland style." She used the cooked mutton for this dish. In experimenting at home, we have found that cooked lamb, veal, or chicken is equally good in this fine curry.

for 4 people

3 cups cooked meat or fowl, cut into 1-inch cubes
2 tablespoons butter
1 tablespoon oil
1 onion, chopped
1 large apple, peeled and cut into ½-inch cubes
2 tablespoons golden raisins
1 clove garlic, crushed
1½ tablespoons shredded coconut

¼ teaspoon chili powder
4 teaspoons curry powder
2 teaspoons Mixed Herbs (or thyme and savory)
½ teaspoon salt
¼ teaspoon pepper
1½ cups beef or chicken stock made with bouillon cubes
1 large banana, sliced

Preheat oven to 250°. Melt the butter and oil in a large casserole, and sauté the onion until transparent. Add the apple, raisins, coconut, and mix well. Add the curry powder, herbs, salt, and pepper, and cook for 5 minutes, stirring until well blended. Add the stock and the meat or fowl. Cover tightly, and bake for 1½ hours. Uncover, and add a little water if curry has become dry. Add the banana, stir, cover, and bake another half hour. Serve over cooked rice.

PENNSYLVANIA DUTCH SAUSAGE CASSEROLE

for 3 people

1 pound bulk sausage	2 teaspoons mustard
¾ cup uncooked wild rice	1 teaspoon curry powder
1 pound canned tomatoes	½ teaspoon thyme
1 medium onion, chopped	salt, pepper to taste

Preheat oven to 350°. In 2-quart casserole mix all the ingredients until rice is well moistened. Cover casserole, and bake in oven for one hour. Uncover, and continue baking an additional half hour, or until recipe is moist, not running.

CHICKEN BREASTS ALFREDO ALLA SCROFA (*Italy*)

Of the two most famous Alfredo restaurants in Rome, this one on Via della Scrofa is the lesser known to tourists. On a short stay in Rome one usually rushes to Alfredo all'Augusteo for *fettucini*, where Mr. Alfredo, "the noodle king," stirs his celebrated egg noodles for you with the golden spoon presented to him by Douglas Fairbanks and Mary Pickford. However, we have had the time to eat also at his former restaurant, Alfredo alla Scrofa, where we found this unusually good chicken dish—and it's very easy to prepare!

for 4 people

2 whole chicken breasts, boned, skinned, and halved	½ teaspoon Mixed Herbs (or 1 teaspoon fresh tarragon and basil)
3 to 4 tablespoons butter	
4 slices prosciutto (or boiled ham sliced paper-thin)	1 clove garlic, crushed
	grated Parmesan cheese
1 cup tomato sauce	salt, pepper to taste
½ cup heavy cream	

Preheat oven to 400°. Dry the 4 chicken pieces thoroughly, and sprinkle them with salt and pepper. Melt the butter in a large skillet.

When foam subsides, add the chicken breasts, and cook them for 5 minutes, turning them once or twice, or until they turn white and juices turn yellow. Remove them to a shallow baking pan or dish, and pour the remaining butter over them. Cover them with baking foil, and bake for 15 minutes. Remove them from oven and uncover. In a small pan, heat the tomato sauce, add the cream, herbs, and garlic. Cover each chicken piece with a slice of prosciutto, pour the tomato sauce over the four pieces, then sprinkle with Parmesan cheese. Place baking pan under a hot broiler until cheese melts, bubbles, and browns. Serve immediately.

MOLE POBLANO (Mexico)

Chicken in nut sauce

for 4 people

8 to 10 chicken parts	1 teaspoon oregano or thyme
4 tablespoons butter	1 onion, chopped
2 tablespoons oil	1 green pepper, chopped
1 cup chicken stock or bouillon	1 clove garlic, crushed
2 sticks cinnamon	¼ cup dry roasted peanuts, ground
1 10-ounce can tomatoes	
½ cup golden raisins	¼ cup almonds, ground
2 teaspoons chili powder	½ ounce melted unsweetened chocolate
½ teaspoon cloves	

Melt 2 tablespoons of butter with 1 tablespoon of oil in a large skillet or casserole. When foam subsides, sauté the chicken pieces until they're golden brown. Add the chicken stock, tomatoes, cinnamon, raisins, chili powder, herbs, and cloves. Simmer, covered, for one hour. While chicken is cooking, melt remaining butter and oil in a skillet, add the onions, green pepper, and garlic. Sauté until soft. Grind the peanuts and almonds, and add this to the onion mixture, stirring until thick. Meantime, melt the chocolate in a small pan placed in a warm oven or over hot water. When chicken is tender, remove it from its sauce, discard the cinnamon sticks. Add the nut mixture to the sauce, and mix in the melted chocolate. Chicken can then be placed in sauce and served from the casserole.

SIEM REAP CHICKEN (*Cambodia*)

The only possible reason I can think of for going to Siem Reap (pronounced as in Italian) is that it is the airport for Angkor Wat. But this is a very compelling reason, because Angkor is one of the most fabulous ancient ruins in the world, surpassing even Persepolis, to our eyes. Luckily there is a rather good small hotel in this meager little town, Siem Reap, the source of this delicious oriental way to prepare chicken.

for 4 people

1 frying chicken, cut into serving pieces or 8 to 10 chicken parts	½ teaspoon turmeric
	¼ teaspoon cloves
¼ pound butter	1 tablespoon powdered ginger
1 large onion, chopped	1 teaspoon curry powder
1 clove garlic, crushed	1 teaspoon salt
1 10-ounce can tomatoes	½ teaspoon Mixed Herbs (or 1
1 cup chicken stock or bouillon	teaspoon minced fresh savory)

optional: ¼ cup shredded coconut

Melt the butter in a heavy casserole or Dutch oven. Add the onion and garlic, and sauté until soft. Add the chicken pieces and brown slowly, turning them frequently, until chicken is golden. Add the balance of the ingredients, and simmer, covered, for one hour. An excellent way to serve this dish is with pilau (Indian peas and rice), recipe for which is given in this section. As accompaniment, any or all of the Indian condiments, chutney, coconut, etc.

POLLO EN NOGADA (*Mexico*)

Spiced chicken

The good old Mexican standbys, spices and nuts, give a most interesting flavor to this chicken dish. We've used a gentle touch of chili (just enough to taste), but if you like your Mexican dishes really hot, the addition of more chili powder is up to you.

for 6 people

12 to 16 serving pieces of chicken	1 clove garlic, crushed
flour	½ cup ground almonds
4 to 6 tablespoons butter	¼ cup dried peanuts
2 to 4 tablespoons oil	2 cups chicken broth, or 4
2 green peppers, diced	chicken cubes dissolved in 2
1 large onion, diced	cups of water
½ teaspoon cinnamon	1 teaspoon oregano
½ teaspoon ground cloves	4 tablespoons cornstarch
¼ teaspoon chili powder	salt, pepper to taste

Dry the chicken parts well, and flour them lightly. Heat 2 tablespoons of the butter and 1 tablespoon of oil in a large skillet or casserole. When foam subsides, add the chicken pieces, a few at a time, and sauté them until they're golden brown. Add more butter and oil to skillet as needed. Remove the browned chicken pieces to a platter. Add the diced onion and green pepper to the remaining butter and oil (or add more if needed), and sauté them until soft. Add all the remaining ingredients, except the cornstarch, and heat to boiling. Remove ½ cup of this sauce, and blend it with the cornstarch. Then add this to the sauce in the casserole, and simmer until the sauce thickens. Add the chicken pieces, cover, and simmer for 45 minutes or until the chicken pieces are fork-tender.

CHICKEN AND SHRIMP (*Japan*)

This recipe is from a modest little restaurant in Tokyo, under the elevated railroad near the Imperial Hotel. It has an unusual and delicious taste.

for 4 people

12-ounce package frozen shrimp	2 carrots
½ pound fresh or canned	1 cup water
mushrooms	¼ teaspoon salt
2 chicken breasts, boned and	4 tablespoons soy sauce
skinned	1 teaspoon sherry
1 large onion, sliced thin	3 tablespoons cornstarch
1½ cups bamboo shoots	1½ tablespoons cold water
1 cup tiny canned peas or young	1½ teaspoons Mixed Herbs (or
peas in pods	thyme, oregano, and parsley)
1 10½-ounce can beef broth	

Cook shrimp according to directions on package. Drain and set aside. Slice the chicken breasts very thin lengthwise, then cut each strip into halves or thirds. Cut the bamboo shoots the same way—into thin strips, then each strip into two or three pieces. (Make sure canned bamboo shoots are thoroughly drained.) Cut the carrots also into thin slivers. Scald the peas and pods, or heat the canned green peas. Combine the chicken, mushrooms, shrimp, bamboo shoots, and carrots in a large pot. Add the beef broth and a cup of water, salt, herbs, and soy sauce, and cook 4 or 5 minutes. If desired, more soy sauce can be added (be careful—it's salty). Add the sherry at this time, too. Mix the cornstarch with 1½ tablespoons cold water, and add to the pot, along with the drained peas. Let mixture come to a boil, and cook for 1 or 2 minutes until sauce is thickened.

OAHU CHICKEN (*Hawaii*)

This chicken dish was served to us at the Royal Hawaiian Hotel in Honolulu. We thought it was superb. When we returned home, we spent many hours adapting and correcting our recipe until we knew it was as good—or perhaps even better—than the dish we were served. Our guests have confirmed our opinion, which is always reassuring. In fact, our recipe has made the rounds of Bucks County, and we are often introduced to people who say to us, "Aren't you the Andersons who have that wonderful Hawaiian chicken recipe?"

for 4 to 6 people

6 chicken legs halved
1 8-ounce jar guava jelly
3 tablespoons cornstarch
¼ cup lime juice
¼ cup Anderson Farm Damascus Meat Sauce (or ¼ cup Houses of Parliament Sauce plus 1 teaspoon grated onion)

1 cup chicken stock or consommé
2 ounces sherry
⅛ teaspoon powdered ginger
1½ teaspoons allspice
1 teaspoon Mixed Herbs (or basil and tarragon)
3 teaspoons salt

Preheat oven to 450°. Place chicken parts in oven dish or roasting pan. Do not overlap. Melt the guava jelly over low heat in a large saucepan. Mix the lime juice with the cornstarch until smooth. Add this to the melted jelly, together with balance of ingredients. Bring to a boil and simmer 5 minutes, or until sauce thickens. Pour the sauce over the chicken and bake uncovered 15 minutes. Reduce heat to 350°, continue baking for 45 minutes, basting frequently. (We serve Oahu Chicken over Pepitas Rice—boiled rice blended with ½ cup canned salted pumpkin seeds [*pepitas*] just before serving.)

CHICKEN WITH CINNAMON TEHERAN (*Iran*)

We were fortunate enough to stay in a lovely pension in Teheran, run by a most sophisticated and young (thirty-nine) grandmother, who spoke English fluently and was delighted to make us Iranian specialties and to give us the recipes as precisely as she could (their quantities and products are quite different from ours). This chicken recipe was one of our favorites.

for 4 people

1 frying chicken, cut in pieces	2 teaspoons Mixed Herbs (or
4 tablespoons butter	basil and thyme)
2 tablespoons oil	1 clove garlic, crushed
2 cups canned tomatoes	1½ teaspoons salt
1 tablespoon tomato paste	2 sticks cinnamon
1 cup water	grated Parmesan cheese
2 chicken bouillon cubes	

Heat 2 tablespoons of butter with 1 tablespoon of oil in a large skillet or casserole. Brown the chicken pieces, a few at a time (adding more butter and oil if necessary), until they are golden. Add tomatoes, tomato paste, water, bouillon cubes, spices, and herbs. Cover, and simmer about 45 minutes or until chicken is tender. Remove the cinnamon sticks before serving.

We like to serve this dish Middle Eastern style: Shape cooked rice into a round mold on a large platter. Arrange chicken pieces on rice. Sprinkle with grated cheese. Serve the sauce in a separate bowl.

CHICKEN EMPEROR

This recipe lives up to its name—the brandy in the sauce gives the whole dish a regal, majestic taste. It has been a favorite at Anderson Farm for many years.

for 4 people

4-pound frying chicken, cut up as for fricassee	1 teaspoon Mixed Herbs (or basil and savory)
flour	½ clove garlic, crushed
4 tablespoons butter	20 fresh mushroom caps (or enough to cover top of casserole)
2 tablespoons oil	
2 cups heavy cream	
¼ teaspoon salt	½ cup French brandy
pinch of black pepper	

Preheat oven to 300°. Melt half the butter and oil in a large skillet, and heat until foam subsides. Flour chicken pieces lightly, and brown them on all sides, adding balance of butter and oil as needed. Remove chicken pieces, as they are browned, to a large casserole. Heat the cream, salt, pepper, herbs, and garlic in a small pan until the boiling point, but do not let them boil. Pour the cream mixture over the chicken, cover the casserole, and bake for about 45 minutes or until chicken is tender. Remove casserole from oven, place mushroom caps (inside up) over top of chicken. Put a little dab of butter into each cap. Place casserole, uncovered, under broiler until mushrooms are cooked—about 10 minutes—watching that they don't burn. Heat the brandy slightly, pour it over the chicken, stir, and serve.

SUPRÊMES DE VOLAILLE CANNES (*France*)

Chicken breasts in champagne

for 4 people

2 large chicken breasts, halved, boned, and skinned	pinch of black pepper
6 tablespoons butter	2 teaspoons Mixed Herbs (or fresh tarragon and basil)
2½ teaspoons lemon juice	4 tablespoons heavy cream
¼ teaspoon salt	2 cups champagne

Preheat oven to 400°. Rub the 4 supremes (boned breasts halved) with ½ teaspoon lemon juice, salt, and pepper. Heat the butter in a large skillet until it is foaming. Poach the chicken breasts on both sides, until flesh is white and juices run clear yellow. Remove them to covered casserole or shallow baking pan covered with aluminum foil. Bake, covered, in oven for 15 minutes. Meanwhile, to the butter remaining in the skillet, add the champagne, mixed herbs, 2 teaspoons lemon juice, and the cream. Bring to boil, stirring constantly, and boil until slightly thickened. Pour over chicken.

ORANGE CHICKEN (*Hawaii*)

for 4 people

1 fryer, cut into serving pieces
2 tablespoons butter
1 tablespoon oil
2 tablespoons flour
1½ cups orange juice
1 orange, separated into sections

½ cup sliced almonds
dash each of ground cinnamon, cloves, ginger
½ teaspoon Mixed Herbs (or thyme)
salt to taste

Heat the butter and oil in a large casserole until foam disappears. Add the chicken pieces, and brown them well. Remove them, and to the drippings in the casserole add the flour and spices, stirring well. Gradually pour in the orange juice, and bring to boil, stirring constantly, until sauce thickens. Add the herbs, spices, and almonds, return chicken to casserole. Cover tightly, and simmer about 45 minutes. Just before serving, add the orange sections, and simmer for 5 minutes.

PONTE VECCHIO CHICKEN BREASTS (*Italy*)

This is another of the great recipes we have adapted from those served to us at the Ponte Vecchio Restaurant in Florence. This recipe was served to us with diced tongue and truffles under melted Bel Paese cheese. Because these ingredients are not always available, we suggest boiled ham and Swiss cheese as an alternative. However, the result is noticeably better with Bel Paese cheese. If you can get truffles and you find them tasty (we don't), you should include them.

for 4 people

2 boned chicken breasts, skinned and halved
4 tablespoons butter
2 tablespoons oil
2 teaspoons Mixed Herbs (or thyme and basil)
¾ cup diced cooked tongue, or ham

4 thin slices Bel Paese, or Swiss, cheese
2 teaspoons chopped truffles
1 cup heavy cream
grated Parmesan cheese
salt, pepper to taste

Preheat oven to 400°. Rub 1 teaspoon of herbs into the breasts. Heat 2 tablespoons butter and 1 tablespoon oil in a skillet. Add the chicken breasts, and cook over moderate heat for 4 or 5 minutes until breasts are whitish and resilient to the touch. Add more butter and oil if necessary. Remove breasts to a shallow baking dish, pour remaining butter and oil over them, cover with baking foil, and place baking dish in oven for 15 minutes. Remove from oven, and discard baking foil. Sprinkle remaining herbs over all four pieces. Spread tongue or ham (and truffles) over each piece; cover with a slice of cheese; pour cream over all, and sprinkle each chicken breast with grated cheese. Place under a hot broiler until cheese melts and is bubbling and brown. Serve each chicken portion covered with sauce.

CHICKEN ROQUEFORT

for 4 people

8 to 10 chicken parts cut into serving pieces
2 tablespoons butter
2 tablespoons oil
3 ounces crumbled Roquefort cheese

½ teaspoon Mixed Herbs (or thyme)
½ pint sour cream
½ teaspoon salt

Preheat oven to 375°. Heat 2 tablespoons of butter with 1 table-spoon oil in a large skillet until foam disappears. Add the chicken parts, and brown slowly on all sides, adding more butter and oil if necessary. Arrange in a baking dish. Mix the sour cream with the Roquefort cheese, mixed herbs, and salt until well blended. Spoon this over the chicken, cover, and bake for 45 minutes.

FRIED CHICKEN ANDERSON

for 4 people

8 to 10 chicken parts	1 clove garlic, crushed
4 tablespoons butter	1 cup chicken stock (or 2 chicken
2 tablespoons oil	bouillon cubes dissolved in 1
flour	cup boiling water)
1 teaspoon Mixed Herbs (or	5 tablespoons sour cream
basil and thyme)	salt, pepper to taste

optional: 1 jigger of whiskey

Season chicken parts with salt and pepper, and coat lightly with flour. Heat half the butter and oil in a large skillet until foam subsides, and brown the chicken parts, a few at a time. Remove each piece, as it is done, to a large casserole. When all pieces are browned, add the chicken stock, herbs, garlic, seasonings to the remaining fat in skillet, and let boil for a minute or two, scraping up coagulated juices. Add the sour cream to the chicken stock, and boil for a minute longer, then pour this sauce over the chicken. Cover chicken, and simmer slowly for about 45 minutes, or until chicken is fork-tender. For something special, add the jigger of whiskey to the sauce right before serving.

PAELLA ANDALUSIA (*Spain*)

From the Hotel El Fuerte in Marbella

for 6 people

12 to 16 chicken parts
½ cup olive oil
3 cloves garlic, peeled and slivered
1 large green pepper, cut into strips
1 jar whole clams (7½ ounces)
½ teaspoon pepper
1½ teaspoons salt
2 teaspoons Mixed Herbs (or thyme and oregano)

2½ to 3 cups chicken stock or bouillon
1¼ cups raw long-grain white rice
1 can artichoke hearts (8 ounces) or 2 boxes frozen artichoke hearts
1 can tomatoes (1 pound), drained, or 2 large tomatoes, chopped
1 pound cooked shrimp
1 can tiny peas

Preheat oven to 350°. Heat oil in large skillet. Slowly brown chicken parts, a few pieces at a time, removing them to a large oven-proof casserole as they are browned. Sauté the garlic and green pepper in remaining oil for about 5 minutes. Drain the clams, and set them aside, adding the clam juice to the chicken stock, to make 3 cups in total. Add the stock to the skillet, and bring to boil over medium heat. Pour over the chicken in casserole. Stir in the rice, herbs, salt, and pepper, and bring to boil again. Cover and bake for 40 minutes, stirring the rice frequently. Meanwhile, cook the frozen artichoke hearts according to directions, or drain canned artichoke hearts and rinse them well. Cut artichoke hearts and clams in half; combine them in a large bowl with the tomatoes. When chicken has baked 40 minutes, add this mixture to the chicken, together with the cooked shrimp and canned peas. Bake 10 minutes longer. Serve immediately, as rice should be oily not dry.

BAKED CHICKEN RAFFLES (*Singapore*)

For years I had read in British fiction about the famous Raffles Hotel in Singapore. Thus I felt rather smug in the early 1960's when I found myself in the cocktail lounge of the Raffles, sipping an authentic Singapore Gin Sling (this was where it originated) —even though the temperature was 104 degrees and the only air-conditioning those slow wooden ceiling fans of yesteryear. I felt so lucky that I had outraced "progress" and had got to see this delightful rambling old vestige of empire before it was replaced by a concrete-and-glass cube called Hilton-Raffles or Sheraton-East or some such. Fortunately, the dining room had proper air-conditioning—and it was here we enjoyed this slightly tropical chicken dish.

for 4 people

8 to 10 chicken parts
flour
2 teaspoons Mixed Herbs (or savory and basil)
6 tablespoons butter
½ teaspoon curry powder
⅛ teaspoon cumin
¾ cup chicken broth (or 2 chicken bouillon cubes dissolved in ¾ cup boiling water)

½ cup sherry
½ cup chopped scallions
½ pound fresh mushrooms
1 package frozen artichoke hearts
salt, pepper to taste

Preheat oven to 350°. Combine flour, salt, and pepper in a large clean paper bag, and shake well. Add chicken pieces, and shake until all pieces are coated with flour. Melt 4 tablespoons butter in a shallow baking pan. Place chicken pieces in pan, skin side down, making sure they don't overlap. Bake, uncovered, for 45 minutes or until almost tender. Meanwhile, melt remaining butter in saucepan. Stir in 2 tablespoons flour, add the broth and wine, and cook, stirring, until thickened and smooth. Add the herbs, curry, and cumin to the sauce.

Cook the artichoke hearts according to package directions. Sauté the onions and mushrooms in butter until soft. Remove baking pan from oven after 45 minutes. Turn chicken parts over. Sprinkle them with the onions and mushrooms, cover with the cooked artichokes, and pour the sauce over all. Return chicken to oven, reduce heat to 325°, and bake 30 minutes longer. (Chicken may be baked for 45 minutes, then refrigerated, well in advance. An hour before serving, remove it from refrigerator, let it come to room temperature, return it to the 325° oven, covered with the vegetables and sauce, ½ hour before serving.)

CHICKEN LIVERS IN WINE SAUCE OVER RICE

for 2 people

¾ pound chicken livers, cut in halves
¼ pound mushrooms, diced
2 tablespoons butter
2 tablespoons flour
1½ cups heavy cream

1 teaspoon Mixed Herbs (or basil and thyme)
1 teaspoon salt
4 tablespoons sherry
1½ cups cooked rice

Heat the butter in a skillet until it foams. Add the chicken livers, and sauté over a very low flame for about 4 minutes, stirring frequently. Remove to a hot dish, and sauté the mushrooms. Replace the chicken livers in skillet, add the flour, cream, herbs, and salt, and sherry. Simmer until thickened. Pour over cooked rice.

PENNSYLVANIA DUTCH CHICKEN LIVERS

for 2 or 3 people

6 slices bacon
1 pound chicken livers
2 tablespoons flour
1 can onion soup
2 4-ounce cans mushrooms

1 teaspoon Mixed Herbs (or thyme and basil)
¼ teaspoon allspice
¾ cup white wine
1 tablespoon chopped parsley

In a large skillet, cook the bacon until well done. Remove it, drain, and crumble it. Brown the chicken livers in the bacon fat. Remove them and cut each in half. Stir the flour into the hot fat, add the soup, and stir until thickened. Add the mushrooms, herbs, allspice, wine, and parsley. Mix well, and cook 10 minutes. Pour this sauce over the chicken livers.

ANDERSON FARM TURKEY CASSEROLE

for 4 people

3 to 4 cups diced cooked turkey
1 cup wild rice
3 tablespoons butter
½ pound sliced mushrooms
1 onion, chopped
1 teaspoon Mixed Herbs (or thyme and sage)

1 garlic clove, crushed
1 teaspoon salt
1½ cups heavy cream
½ cup slivered almonds
grated Parmesan cheese

Preheat oven to 350°. Wash the rice, cover it with boiling water, and let it soak 1 hour. Drain. Melt 2 tablespoons of the butter in a skillet, and sauté the onions and mushrooms. Combine the turkey, rice, onions, mushrooms, cream, herbs, seasonings, and almonds, and mix well. Pour mixture into a greased casserole, cover, and bake for 1½ hours. Remove the cover, sprinkle thickly with the grated cheese, dot with remaining butter. Turn oven to 450°, and bake 5 minutes more or until cheese is melted and bubbling.

FISH

Since imported sole—real sole—is most difficult to get, it is the custom that fish filets sold under the name "sole" are usually those of flounder or of some other white-fleshed fish. The following recipes for "filets of sole" actually mean flounder filets prepared in the sole manner. Fresh flounder filets or defrosted frozen filets may be used.

NEW ORLEANS FILETS OF SOLE

Sole baked in sour cream

for 3 or 4 people

1 pound filets of sole	1 garlic clove, crushed
2 large onions, chopped	2 teaspoons Mixed Herbs (or
½ pound fresh mushrooms,	dill and thyme)
sliced	1½ cups sour cream
4 tablespoons butter	

Preheat oven to 350°. Melt the butter in a skillet, add the garlic, and sauté the onions and mushrooms. Put half this mixture on the bottom of a baking dish. Put the filets in next, then top the filets with the balance of onions and mushrooms. Cover the whole mixture with the sour cream. Sprinkle the herbs over the top. Bake, uncovered, for one half hour.

FILETS DE SOLE BRETONNE (France)

Sole, grapes, and mushrooms baked in a wine sauce

for 2 or 3 people

1 pound filets of sole	1 teaspoon Mixed Herbs (or
2 tablespoons flour	fennel)
3 tablespoons butter	½ pound seedless white grapes
⅓ cup milk	¼ pound sliced fresh mushrooms
⅓ cup white wine	salt, pepper to taste

Preheat oven to 325°. Make the sauce for this dish by melting 2 tablespoons of butter over low heat in a saucepan. Blend in the flour, stirring constantly until flour and butter froth. Add the milk slowly, stirring, then add the wine and herbs. Over moderately high heat, stir the sauce until it comes to a boil, and boil for 1 minute or until thick. Add salt and pepper to taste. Place the filets in a shallow baking dish. Cover with the sauce, add the grapes and mushrooms, dot with butter, and bake for 30 minutes.

FILET OF SOLE GAMBRINUS (*Portugal*)

The Gambrinus is a popular luncheon spot for Lisbon business-men. It has a modest appearance but a most excellent kitchen.

for 2 or 3 people

1 pound filets of sole	1 teaspoon Mixed Herbs (or dill
1 banana	and fennel)
¼ pound butter	2 tablespoons sherry
flour	salt, pepper to taste
¼ cup lemon juice	

Slice banana lengthwise, then in half, making four long strips. Sauté the strips slowly in butter in a small skillet until golden and just starting to get brown. Sprinkle the filets with salt and pepper, dust them lightly with flour. Melt 6 tablespoons of butter in a large skillet, add the fish, and sauté the filets for about 4 or 5 minutes, turning them once. When done, fish should be white and fork should go through easily. Remove filets to a hot platter, cover them with the sautéed banana slices, pour the lemon juice over the fish. Add the sherry, herbs, and remaining butter to the skillet and boil quickly, scraping up coagulated juices, and thickening sauce slightly. Pour the sauce over the filets, and serve immediately.

ANDERSON FARM FISH SOUFFLÉ

for 2 or 3 people

	Sauce:
1 pound filets of sole	3 tablespoons flour
1 tablespoon vinegar	3 tablespoons butter
1 garlic clove, crushed	1 cup milk
2 teaspoons salt	4 eggs
½ teaspoon chopped dill	¾ cup grated Parmesan cheese
	1 teaspoon Wine Herb Meat Sauce *

* See introductory note to this chapter.

Preheat oven to 350°. Cook fish gently in water to cover, to which you have added the vinegar, garlic, and dill. Let the fish cool in the water. Meanwhile, make a smooth cream sauce of the flour, butter, and milk, by melting the butter, blending in the flour slowly, then adding the milk, stirring constantly. Add the Wine Herb Meat Sauce or its equivalent. Separate the eggs, beat the yolks, and add them to the sauce, beating with a wire whisk. Add the grated cheese to the sauce. Beat the egg whites until stiff, and fold them into the sauce. Drain the fish, and place it in a greased baking dish. Pour the sauce over the fish. Place the baking dish in a shallow pan of water, and bake for about 45 minutes, or until top of soufflé is golden brown.

ADOBO FISH (*Mexico*)

for 2 or 3 people

1 pound filets of sole	pinch of cumin
2 tablespoons butter	pinch of chili powder
1 onion, minced	½ cup orange juice
1 clove garlic, crushed	grated rind of one orange
1 cup tomatoes	salt, pepper to taste
1 teaspoon oregano	

Heat oven to 375°. Melt the butter in a large skillet. Dry the fish thoroughly, and sauté it in the butter for 3 or 4 minutes, turning it once, until a fork goes through fish easily. Remove the fish to a hot platter. Add to the skillet the onion, garlic, tomatoes, chili powder, cumin, oregano, salt, pepper, and orange rind. Simmer for about 20 minutes, or until sauce is thickened. Add the orange juice. Put ½ the fish in the bottom of a buttered casserole, cover with half of the sauce; add the balance of the fish, and top with the remainder of the sauce. Cover and bake for ½ hour.

COD AND DILL PUDDING (*Finland*)

for 4 people

1 pound frozen cod filets	3 anchovies, finely chopped
4 medium potatoes, peeled and boiled	3 tablespoons butter, melted
2 eggs	2 teaspoons ground dill
1 cup milk	2 cups cooked peas
1 onion, grated	1 teaspoon salt
	bread crumbs

Preheat oven to 350°. Simmer defrosted cod filets, in just enough water to cover, until tender, about 10 minutes. Strain the cod, rinse it, and shred it by cutting it into thin strips. Mash the cooked potatoes, add the eggs, well beaten, 2 tablespoons of the butter, milk, onion, salt, anchovies, and dill. Mix thoroughly. Add the cod and the peas. Butter a baking dish, and sprinkle it inside with bread crumbs. Pour in the fish pudding, and sprinkle a layer of bread crumbs on top. Dot with butter, and bake for 30 minutes.

WAIKIKI SHRIMP (*Hawaii*)

for 4 people

1½ pounds fresh or frozen shrimp, cleaned, deveined	¾ cup soy sauce
1 9-ounce can pineapple rings	2½ cups water
1 cup brown sugar	6 tablespoons cornstarch
1 cup vinegar	2 green peppers, cut in strips
1 teaspoon Mixed Herbs (or dill and basil)	2 peeled tomatoes, diced
	4 cups cooked rice
	1 cup *pepitas*

Cook shrimp, and set aside. Drain the syrup from the pineapple, and pour into a saucepan. Cut the pineapple slices in half, and reserve. Add the brown sugar, vinegar, herbs, soy sauce, and 2 cups water to the pineapple syrup, and bring to a boil. Combine the cornstarch with ½ cup water, and stir until smooth. Add this mixture to the saucepan, and cook, stirring constantly until sauce is thickened. Add the green peppers, pineapple slices, and tomatoes. Cook 2 minutes, then add the shrimp. Add the *pepitas* to the cooked rice. Serve the shrimp over the rice.

SHRIMP ST. TROPEZ (*France*)

for 4 people

1½ pounds frozen shrimp	¼ teaspoon allspice
1 can quick-frozen cream of shrimp soup	1 teaspoon mustard
½ can milk (measured from soup can)	½ teaspoon curry powder
	2 egg yolks
1 teaspoon Mixed Herbs (or dill and fennel)	a flick of nutmeg
	3 tablespoons sherry

Heat the soup and milk slowly, stirring constantly, until well blended. Add the herbs, mustard, curry, nutmeg, and 2 tablespoons of the sherry. When sauce is hot, add the shrimp. Bring to a boil, and cook slowly about 2 minutes, until shrimp are pink and tender. Meanwhile, beat the egg yolks with 1 tablespoon sherry. Stir several spoonfuls of the hot sauce into the egg yolk mixture, then add it to the sauce. Serve over rice.

SHRIMP AND BLACK-EYED PEAS (*Morocco*)

This makes an excellent main course, served with a green vegetable and salad. The recipe is from Tangier.

for 3 or 4 people

1 pound cooked shrimp	1 clove garlic, crushed
1 package frozen black-eyed peas	½ teaspoon salt
1 cup onion, chopped	2 tablespoons tomato paste
1 large tomato, skinned and chopped	3 bananas, cut in ¼-inch slices
½ teaspoon cayenne pepper	½ cup slivered almonds
2 teaspoons Mixed Herbs (or thyme and oregano)	½ cup water

Cook black-eyed peas according to directions on package until they are tender. To the peas and remaining liquid in saucepan, add the chopped onion, tomato, cayenne, herbs, garlic, salt, and water. Cover and simmer for 15 minutes. Add the shrimp, tomato paste, bananas, and almonds. Cover, and simmer additional 10 minutes. Serve immediately.

VEGETABLES

The following recipes are *not* the answer to "how to cook vegetables with herbs." That answer is simple: Any fresh or frozen vegetable is made more delicious by the addition of a teaspoon or so of herbs sprinkled on and tossed well just before serving. The herb or herbs you use should be the ones *you* like! .

These recipes are our favorites—imaginative ways of serving vegetables which we have discovered both in our travels and in experimenting ourselves. We are convinced that one good recipe leads to another. Perhaps these recipes will lead you to create some exciting ones yourself.

One little P.S.: You will notice that some of these recipes (for string beans, peas, carrots, etc.) call for "frozen vegetables." These frozen vegetable recipes are our winter favorites. In summer, we prefer fresh-picked vegetables from our garden served *au naturel*—cooked with a minimum of liquid, tossed in butter and herbs, then served immediately.

ITALIAN BEANS CAPRI (*Italy*)

We were served this wonderful vegetable in a small seafood restaurant near the Piazzetta in the center of Capri. The sauce is excellent, also, over asparagus, broccoli, or other vegetables.

for 4 people

2 boxes frozen Italian-style beans

Capri Sauce:

2 tablespoons butter
1 tablespoon chopped scallions
1 clove garlic, crushed
1½ tablespoons flour
⅔ cup water
⅓ cup Marsala wine
1 tablespoon anchovy paste
1 teaspoon Mixed Herbs (or basil and oregano)
8 pitted black olives, sliced
1 cup shredded Parmesan cheese

Cook Italian-style beans according to package directions. In a skillet, melt the butter, add the scallions and garlic, and cook slowly until soft and golden. Sprinkle them with the flour, water, and wine, stirring constantly, until mixture is thickened. Simmer for 5 minutes, add the anchovy paste, the herbs, olives, and cheese. Stir until cheese is completely melted. Serve this sauce over the string beans.

GLAZED CARROTS

for 4 people

1 pound carrots, scraped and sliced
1 cup water
3 tablespoons butter

2 teaspoons Mint Mixture (or dried spearmint)
4 tablespoons sugar
salt to taste

In a saucepan, bring carrots to boil with 1 tablespoon of the butter, the water, and salt. Cover and boil slowly for 20 to 30 minutes, or until carrots are tender and liquid has evaporated. Melt remaining 2 tablespoons of butter in the saucepan, cover the carrots with the sugar, sprinkle with the mint mixture or spearmint. Cook over a low flame, shaking the pan several times, until carrots are glazed.

CORDOBA CARROTS (*Spain*)

for 4 people

2 bunches carrots
4 tablespoons butter
1 4-ounce can pimientos or
roasted sweet peppers
1 teaspoon Mixed Herbs (or
fennel)

1 pinch garlic powder
3 tablespoons Damascus Meat
Sauce
salt, pepper to taste

Scrape the carrots, wash them, and cook them in salted water until tender, about 45 minutes. Drain and chop them. Drain and chop the sweet peppers. Melt the butter in a skillet, add the carrots, sweet peppers, herbs, seasonings. Stir in the Damascus Meat Sauce and serve.

BAKED EGGPLANT ANDERSON

You wouldn't believe eggplant could taste so sweet yet so piquant!

for 2 to 4 people

1 medium eggplant, peeled and
cut into 1-inch slices
1 can frozen orange juice,
undiluted
2 medium yellow onions, sliced

1 teaspoon salt
1 teaspoon Mixed Herbs (or
thyme and basil)
1 teaspoon chopped fresh dill

Preheat oven to 350°. Place eggplant in a deep baking dish, cover with the onions, and sprinkle with the salt, herbs, and chopped dill. Pour orange juice over the top, and bake, covered, for about 1 hour.

BATINJAAN (*Iran*)

Baked eggplant

Batinjaan is the Iranian word for eggplant, a vegetable that is used extensively in Iran. True, the average Iranian cannot afford the imported anchovy paste called for in this recipe. But there is a large supermarket now in Teheran that stocks these foreign delicacies, and this is where our hostess in Teheran bought her anchovy paste.

for 2 or 3 people

1 medium eggplant	1 tablespoon Mixed Herbs (or
1 cup herb French dressing	basil, thyme, and oregano)
2 tablespoons anchovy paste	grated Parmesan cheese

Preheat oven to 400°. Pare the eggplant, and cut it crosswise into ½-inch slices. Marinate the slices for 2 hours in the herb French dressing. Place the slices on a baking sheet, spread each slice with the anchovy paste mixed with the herbs. Sprinkle grated cheese over each slice. Bake for about 12 minutes, or until tender, turning the slices once. (If they become dry, baste them with additional dressing.)

RATATOUILLE MARSEILLE (*France*)

This is our version of this classic South of France dish, served to us at the Sourcouf Restaurant in Marseille.

for 4 to 6 people

1 medium-sized eggplant, peeled and diced	2 1-pound cans tomatoes, drained
3 large yellow onions, peeled and diced	4 tablespoons olive oil, more if needed
2 large green peppers, sliced thinly	1 clove garlic, mashed
½ pound fresh mushrooms, sliced thinly	2 teaspoons Mixed Herbs (or basil and oregano)
	¼ pound cheddar cheese
	salt, pepper to taste

Preheat oven to 425°. Heat the olive oil in a large skillet, add the mashed garlic, and sauté the four vegetables separately, until soft but not brown. As each becomes tender, remove it to a large 3-quart casserole, placing one vegetable on top of another, in layers. Pour the tomatoes over the vegetables, sprinkle with the Mixed Herbs and seasonings. Dot the top with small pieces of cheese. Bake, uncovered, for 30 minutes.

PILAU (*India*)

Indian peas and rice

for 4 people

½ cup rice	1 package frozen peas
1 onion, sliced thin	¼ teaspoon ginger
4 tablespoons butter	1¼ cups chicken stock or
1 teaspoon turmeric	bouillon
½ teaspoon Mixed Herbs (or	¼ teaspoon cinnamon
thyme)	¼ cup slivered almonds
¼ teaspoon allspice	¼ cup golden raisins

In a pot large enough to cook the peas, melt 2 tablespoons of butter, add the onions, turmeric, herbs, allspice, ginger, cinnamon, and rice. Sauté this mixture until the rice and onions are golden. Add the chicken stock and the frozen peas, and cook, covered, over low heat until all the liquid is absorbed (about 15 minutes). Right before serving, sauté the almonds and raisins in the remaining butter, until slightly browned. Place the pilau in a heated serving dish, and garnish with the raisins and almonds.

EDIBLE SPINACH

For those, aged five to ninety-five, who ordinarily find spinach difficult to enjoy, we dedicate this recipe—with the thought that they will join us in saying, "This actually makes spinach fit to eat!"

for 2 or 3 people

1 package frozen chopped	1½ tablespoons vinegar
spinach	½ clove garlic, mashed
1 tablespoon olive oil	½ cup sour cream
1 teaspoon Mixed Herbs (or	
thyme and oregano)	

Cook spinach according to directions on package. Drain thoroughly. Blend balance of ingredients, and stir into the hot spinach. Place over a low flame, and reheat, stirring constantly.

BAKED SQUASH WITH ORANGE FILLING

for 4 people

2 large acorn squash	½ teaspoon rosemary
1 tablespoon melted butter	¼ teaspoon salt
1 large seedless orange	¼ teaspoon nutmeg
⅔ cup sour cream	chopped parsley
1 teaspoon sugar	

Preheat oven to 400°. Cut squash in half lengthwise, and remove seeds. Place squash, cut side down, on a baking sheet, and bake for 30 minutes. Turn halves cut side up, brush with melted butter, and continue baking for 20 minutes. Meanwhile, make the filling: grate the orange, getting about 1 tablespoon of grated rind. Blend the rind with the sour cream, sugar, rosemary, salt, and nutmeg. Mix well. Let the filling come to room temperature while squash is baking. Section the orange, if desired, to use as a garnish. When squash halves are baked, fill them with the orange filling, garnish with chopped parsley and orange sections.

PENNSYLVANIA DUTCH STRING BEANS

Just for a change, turn frozen string beans into a royal dish!

for 3 people

1 box frozen string beans (French or Italian style)	1 4-ounce can sliced mushrooms
2 tablespoons chopped onion	1 teaspoon Mixed Herbs (or savory)
1 tablespoon butter	⅛ teaspoon allspice
3 pimientos or roasted sweet peppers	¾ teaspoon salt
	1 hard-boiled egg

Cook beans according to package instructions. In a skillet or saucepan, melt the butter, and sauté the onion until soft; add the drained string beans, the pimientos, the mushrooms (plus their liquid), the herbs and seasonings, and cook for about 5 minutes or until well heated. Serve immediately, garnished with egg slices.

SUCCOTASH (*American Indian*)

This came from a friend in Tucson who is very interested in the Southwest and its lore.

for 4 to 6 people

1 10-ounce package frozen lima beans	4 tablespoons butter
	1 tablespoon chopped fresh dill
1 10-ounce package frozen kernel corn	(or pulverized dill seed)
	½ cup sweet peppers
1 onion, chopped	½ teaspoon chili powder
1 green pepper, chopped	

Cook the frozen vegetables according to package directions. Drain and set aside. Melt two tablespoons of the butter in a skillet, and sauté the onion and green pepper until soft but not brown. Add these sautéed vegetables to the corn and lima beans, together with the dill, sweet peppers, and chili powder. Add remaining butter, heat, and toss well before serving.

BANADOURA (*Lebanon*)

Baked tomatoes in herb sauce

We named this dish *banadoura,* the Arabic for "tomatoes." It came to us in a most flattering way—from the Arabian cook of a friend who lives in Beirut and who, she told us, "had never given out a recipe before." He wrote it for us on a small piece of paper after we had enthused at luncheon over "the marvelous tomatoes." (Knowing we were returning to the United States, the cook probably felt we would offer no competition to his cuisine.) Incidentally, the luncheon consisted of Quiche Lorraine, these baked tomatoes, a salad, fruit—a perfect luncheon menu, in our opinion.

for 4 people

4 peeled tomatoes, halved	1 tablespoon mustard
flour	1 large onion, cubed
2 tablespoons butter	2 cups light cream
1 tablespoon oil	salt, pepper to taste
2 teaspoons Mixed Herbs (or basil)	2 tablespoons chopped parsley

Preheat oven to 350°. Flour the tomato halves lightly. Heat butter and oil in a large skillet, and sauté the tomatoes until crust is a light brown. Set the tomatoes in a baking pan. Add the onion to the skillet, and sauté until soft. Add the cream, mustard, herbs, seasonings to the onion, and mix thoroughly. Pour this mixture over the tomatoes, and bake, uncovered, for 20 minutes. Garnish with chopped parsley.

PENNSYLVANIA DUTCH TOMATOES

for 2 or 3 people

3 or 4 large tomatoes, peeled and quartered	1 cup sour cream
1 large onion, chopped	1 teaspoon Mixed Herbs (or basil and thyme)
2 tablespoons butter	1 teaspoon chopped fresh dill
2 tablespoons flour	1 teaspoon salt

Sauté the onion in the butter until soft. Add the tomatoes, and cook for 5 minutes, stirring once or twice. Stir in the flour, simmer until thickened, then add the sour cream, herbs, and salt. Cook 1 minute longer until hot.

ZUCCHINI CREOLE

for 6 people

4 zucchini	1 1-pound can tomatoes
2 tablespoons butter	1 teaspoon Mixed Herbs (or oregano and thyme)
2 tablespoons bacon fat	1 garlic clove, mashed
1 large onion, chopped	1 8-ounce can whole kernel corn
2 green peppers, cubed	salt, pepper to taste
2 tablespoons chopped pimientos	

Remove stem ends of zucchini, and cut zucchini into ½-inch squares. Heat the butter and bacon fat in a skillet, and sauté the zucchini until light brown. Add the onion and peppers, cook until soft. Add the tomatoes, herbs, and seasonings, and simmer, uncovered, 30 minutes. (This may be done in advance.) Twenty minutes before serving, add the corn to the zucchini, and simmer until corn is heated.

AMBROSIAL ZUCCHINI

The name of this recipe describes how we feel about it!

for 2 or 3 people

3 or 4 small zucchini, peeled and sliced
½ cup of water, approximately
1 egg
1 cup milk
4 tablespoons butter

½ clove garlic, mashed
⅔ cup grated Parmesan cheese
1 teaspoon Mixed Herbs (or basil)
1 teaspoon salt

Preheat oven to 425°. Boil the zucchini, in just enough water to cover, until almost tender. Drain and put in a shallow baking dish. Beat the egg lightly, and add to it the milk, butter, garlic, herbs, salt, and ⅓ cup cheese. Stir well, and pour over the zucchini. Sprinkle the rest of the cheese over the top. Bake for ½ hour, or until mixture has thickened and top is slightly brown.

SALADS

SALATA DELPHI (Greece)

Greek salad

for 6 people

4 tomatoes, peeled
24 ripe black olives, pitted
3 pimientos, or sweet red peppers
3 tablespoons vinegar
⅓ cup olive oil

½ pound Feta cheese (or a mild Cheddar)
1 teaspoon Mixed Herbs (or basil and thyme)
1 teaspoon salt

Cut the tomatoes into bite-size pieces, slice the olives thinly, cut the pimientos into thin strips, and toss, together with the vinegar, herbs, and salt. Pour olive oil over the top, and allow to stand for ¼ hour. Right before serving, crumble the cheese, and add it, tossing the salad again lightly.

GUACAMOLE (*Mexico*)

There are many recipes for *guacamole,* and this is not the simplest. It is extra effort to remove the skins from the green peppers. However, the result of your diligence should be well worth it—you will have a superb dish, equally delectable as a salad or as a cocktail dip. (We usually serve our *guacamole* on lettuce, as a salad.)

for 4 people

3 large green peppers, peeled
2 small onions
1 large tomato, peeled
3 ripe avocados
1 teaspoon Mixed Herbs (or basil)

2 tablespoons mayonnaise
1 tablespoon herb French dressing
salt to taste

Preheat oven to 500°. Place the green peppers in a shallow baking pan, and leave them in the oven until the skins blister. Remove them, rinse them in cold water, and peel off the skins. Chop the peppers, onions, and tomatoes, and place them in a large bowl. Peel the avocados, and mash them well. Add them to the chopped vegetables, together with the mayonnaise, French dressing, herbs, and salt. Mix well. Chill thoroughly before serving.

FRIJOLES ENSALADA (*Mexico*)

Kidney bean salad

for 4 people

1 10-ounce can kidney beans and their juice
1 green pepper, chopped
½ red onion, chopped
½ cup sweet peppers, chopped
12 pitted black olives, sliced

1 tablespoon wild-garlic vinegar (or any vinegar, plus 1 clove of garlic put through a garlic press)
a pinch of chili powder
½ teaspoon oregano

Toss these ingredients until well mixed. Serve on lettuce leaves.

ANDERSON FARM CHICKEN SALAD

This is such a favorite of ours that, whenever we prepare chicken, we always fix an extra leg or breast or two to use the following day in this salad.

for 2 people

1 cup diced cooked chicken
1 stalk celery, chopped
4 scallions, chopped
¼ cup pimientos, or roasted sweet peppers

2 tablespoons mayonnaise
½ clove garlic, mashed
2 teaspoons Mixed Herbs (or basil, thyme, and oregano)

Toss it all together and serve any way you like—with hard-boiled egg, sliced tomatoes, pickles, potato chips, etc.

13

Twenty-seven Herb Hints

Note: If you make your own mixture of dried herbs, substitute it for the individual fresh minced herbs suggested in these hints, using half the quantities.

1. *Travel with mixed herbs.* If you don't dry your own mixture, buy a two-ounce bottle of Mixed Herbs and keep it handy when going into motel dining rooms, unknown American or foreign restaurants. You'll be surprised how almost unpalatable food can be made tasty with a sprinkling of a large pinch or two of herbs—on eggs, salads, vegetables, anything you like.

2. *Gourmet frozen vegetables.* Open a carton of frozen vegetables and let it stand at room temperature for about an hour. Then put 2 tablespoons of water, 1 tablespoon of butter, and 1 teaspoon of minced fresh herbs, with salt to taste, into the saucepan. Add the frozen vegetables, cover, and let come to a boil over medium heat. When vegetables are almost tender, remove cover and let them simmer until all liquid is evaporated.

3. *Herb butter, to use on steaks, fish, hot breads, toast, crackers.* To a softened and mashed ¼ pound of butter, add any of these combinations of minced fresh or dried herbs:

watercress, chervil, dill
chives, basil, burnet
savory, dill, basil
thyme, marjoram, chives
your own dried mixture

Lemon juice, salt, or a crushed clove of garlic can also be added if desired. Let the herb butter stand at room temperature for 2 hours to season thoroughly.

4. *Herbed cream cheese.* Soften the cheese, blend in any of the above combinations, add a little heavy cream to make spreading easy.

5. *Hot herb bread.* Cut a loaf of Italian or French bread (or long French rolls) into 1-inch slices, leaving about ½ inch uncut at the bottom of each slice. Spread herb butter thickly between the slices. Put loaf together again tightly, wrap in baking foil, and heat for 20 minutes in a 350° oven. (The foil-wrapped bread may be prepared in advance and refrigerated, but bring to room temperature before heating.)

6. *Herb toasts to serve with soups or salads.* Cut 2-inch rounds from slices of bread, and toast them on one side in a 450° oven. Remove the toasts, and spread the untoasted sides with herb butter. Return toasts to oven, and heat for 5 minutes.

7. *Herbed baked potatoes.* Before baking, cut a large baking potato in half, and rub each half with minced fresh or dried herbs. For extra flavor, insert a thick slice of onion between the halves. Put halves together tightly, wrap in baking foil, and bake.

8. *Herb summer drinks.* Steep ¾ cup lemon balm leaves in a quart of boiling water for about 20 minutes, then strain. To remaining liquid, add ½ cup mint leaves, 2 cups of any fresh or canned fruit juice, or strong tea, and, if necessary, sugar. Chill in refrigerator for 6 hours. Pour over ice, garnish with lemon balm leaves. (For a carbonated cooler, use ½ glass of ginger ale to ½ glass of the chilled liquid.)

9. *Herbed hollandaise sauce, for fish, asparagus, broccoli, etc.* Add minced parsley, chives, tarragon or dried mixed herbs to hot hollandaise sauce right before serving it.

10. *Herbed Russian dressing.* To your own recipe for Russian dressing, add some minced fresh or dried herbs. It gives a marvelous accent.

11. *Herbed poultry stuffing.* You can do better than just a sage accent! Try adding a combination of fresh minced or dried herbs, plus a crushed clove of garlic to your favorite poultry stuffing recipe. It's delicious.

12. *The h in hamburger should stand for Herbs.* It takes a second to mix 1 teaspoon of fresh minced herbs into ½ pound of ground beef, and the flavor difference is great.

13. *Gourmet soft-boiled eggs.* Yes, it can be done. Just sprinkle a large pinch of dried mixed herbs (or fresh minced) on soft-boiled eggs. Try it—you'll never eat them unherbed again!

14. *Zesty scrambled eggs.* Try mixing in ⅛ teaspoon dried mustard or curry powder, plus an equal amount of minced herbs, to 2 scrambled eggs. It's a delicious dish!

15. *Piquant deviled eggs.* Along with salt and pepper, always add generous pinches of dried or minced fresh herbs to your deviled egg mixture.

16. *Mayonnaise piquante.* Add 1 teaspoon of mustard and 1 teaspoon of minced fresh herbs to 1 cup of mayonnaise. An excellent accompaniment to seafood.

17. *Twelve hors d'oeuvres made in a jiffy.* Four different foods and three different sauces to dip them in does the trick! *The sauces:* To a cup of sour cream, add 2 teaspoons of minced fresh herbs, and mix well. Separate the sour cream into three small bowls. Add 2 tablespoons of mustard to one bowl; 1 teaspoon of curry powder to another bowl; ⅓ package of dried onion soup to the third bowl. *The foods:* Any four of the following—shrimp, baby frankfurters, cubes of cheese, tiny meatballs, potato chips, button mushrooms, celery hearts, etc.

18. *Quick dill sauce for fish or vegetables.* Heat ¾ cup of sour cream with 2 tablespoons of chopped dill and ¼ cup minced chives or scallions. For a quick herb sauce, substitute any herbs you like—let your palate be your guide.

19. *A non-fail rule for canned soups.* Open the can, add a pinch of herbs! Get in the habit of adding a pinch of dried herbs or a few minced fresh herbs to every saucepan of canned soup. You'll love the flavor.

20. *Marvelous mustard sauce.* Use 1 part bland mustard, 2 parts sour cream, and 1 teaspoon of any minced herb or herbs you fancy. Try it on asparagus, poached eggs, fish.

21. *Last-minute tomato rarebit.* Heat a can of condensed tomato soup. Add one cup of grated Cheddar cheese and 1 teaspoon minced herbs. Serve on toast.

22. *Piquant tomato juice or canned tomatoes.* Add a few minced leaves of basil, a few minced chives, or a blend of minced basil, thyme, and chives.

23. *Herbed coleslaw.* To your favorite coleslaw recipe, add some minced thyme and savory.

24. *Herbed baked apples.* Add a sprinkling of crushed dill seed or chopped dill to the sugar and cinnamon you use to make baked apples (also delicious in deep-dish apple pie).

25. *Gourmet canned meat stews.* Add ½ teaspoon of dried herbs, or 1 teaspoon of a fresh minced herb or herbs, and a tablespoon of sherry to any canned stew, while heating it. If you do this several hours before eating, the result is all the more delicious.

26. *A herb accent in aspics.* Add ½ teaspoon of minced chives, basil, or tarragon to poultry or vegetable aspics; crushed mint leaves in fruit aspics are delicious.

27. *Add herbs to marinades.* Marinating artichoke hearts—mushrooms? asparagus tips?—for hors d'oeuvres? Add ½ teaspoon of your favorite herb or herbs to your marinade. Better still, if you make your own herb salad dressing, it—by itself—makes a perfect marinade.

14

Some Menus Our Guests
Have Enjoyed

As you have noticed in most of our recipes, they can be prepared well ahead of dinnertime, with only a last-minute popping in the oven right before serving. The same is true of most of these menus. Also, the menus are simple and easy to serve. This is because, like most households, we have no cook or maid to assist in serving, and we both like to enjoy our guests from the minute they arrive, with no long sessions in the kitchen. We may sacrifice some fascinating gourmet dishes by living this way, but we feel good talk is far more important. Also, we have not specified desserts in most of these menus. We feel desserts are a very personal consideration; either the cook loves to make fancy desserts, or the guests watch their weight and prefer fruits or low-calorie desserts.

Recipes for the dishes marked with an asterisk (*) are given in Chapters Twelve and Thirteen.

A SUNDAY BRUNCH

fruit juice or herbed tomato juice
Pennsylvania Dutch egg casserole *
croissants
coffee cake   coffee

A DELICIOUS SUMMER LUNCHEON

Gazpacho *
herb toasts
shrimp salad with pineapple tidbits
tossed with Horcher sauce *
dessert
iced tea with mint or lemon balm leaves

AN ARABIAN NIGHTS COCKTAIL PARTY

Provide each guest with a fork (we use oyster forks, pickle forks, or small picnic forks) to sample the thirty-one delicacies in a typical Middle Eastern *mezze*. According to our notes, these are dishes served us in a little Arabian restaurant in Ramalla, a suburb of Jordanian Jerusalem. Each delicacy should be placed in its own saucer or on its own plate:

hummus *   carrot sticks   radishes   pistachio nuts
olives   canned chick peas   marinated sliced cucumbers
marinated sliced tomatoes   cucumbers in sour cream
deviled eggs   pickled turnips   three kinds of salami
pickled onions   four kinds of cheeses in cubes
pickled baby eggplants   celery hearts   mustard-sauce dip *
onion-soup dip *   curry dip *   tiny meatballs   anchovies
cooked shrimp   marinated kidney beans   sesame crackers
marinated mushrooms   sliced baloney

A SUMMER BUFFET DINNER

beef and fruit stew Horcher *
pickled watermelon rind   hot herb bread *
your own tossed green salad
dessert   coffee

A GOURMET OUTDOOR GRILL

herbed tomato juice
veal chops *en Papillote* *
herbed baked potatoes
hot herb bread *   celery hearts and radishes
your own green salad
dessert   coffee

A BUFFET DINNER FOR FIFTEEN OR TWENTY

picadillo *
Italian green beans
hot herb bread *
your own green salad
dessert   coffee

A DINNER FOR A MEAT-AND-POTATOES MAN

hamburgers
baked potatoes
Pennsylvania Dutch string beans *
hot herb bread *
Salata Delphi *
dessert   coffee

A DINNER WITH HAWAIIAN FLAVOR

watermelon and pineapple cut in finger-length sticks
Oahu chicken *
Pepitas rice *   peas with mint
hot herb bread *
sliced bananas and cream, sprinkled with coconut
coffee

A SPICE OF INDIA DINNER

Siem Reap chicken *
Pilau (Indian peas and rice) *
chutney   shredded coconut   crystallized ginger
hot herb bread *
your own green salad
pineapple ice
coffee

AN EVENING IN MEXICO DINNER

consommé
pollo en nogada (spiced chicken) *
rice
string beans Amandine
(toss sautéed slivered almonds into the beans before serving)
hot herb bread *
Guacamole *
dessert   coffee

AN EAT-AS-THE-ROMANS-DO DINNER

prosciutto and melon (or antipasto)
saltimbocca Romana (veal scallops with sage) *
zucchini
hot herb bread *
your own green salad
fresh fruit   cheese
caffè espresso

A BEST-OF-EUROPE DINNER

shrimp Horcher *
(served on sliced pineapple)
Ponte Vecchio chicken breasts *
ratatouille *
hot herb bread *
Salata Delphi *
fresh fruit   cheese
coffee

AN IRANIAN FAMILY DINNER

a small *mezze* of
hummus *   cucumbers   sesame crackers   cheese
chicken with cinnamon Teheran *
rice
batinjaan (baked eggplant) *
hot herb bread *
kidney bean salad *
stewed figs and apricots (or grapes in yogurt)
coffee

A GREEK TAVERNA DINNER

olives   radishes   cheese   salami
moussaka *
artichokes with hollandaise sauce *
hot herb bread *
Salata Delphi *
fresh fruit and cake
coffee

IN THE SHADOW OF THE ALHAMBRA

anchovies   sardines   pickled onions   olives
Granada beef soup *
paella Andalusia *
hot herb bread *
your own green salad
fresh fruit   or caramel custard
coffee

A FRENCH RIVIERA DINNER

your own choice of hors d'oeuvres
beef ragout Marseilles *
hot herb bread *
your own green salad
stewed fruit compote
coffee

UNDER A TAHITIAN MOON DINNER

Kalakaua oxtail soup (served without meat or peanuts) *
Tahitian pork stew *
baked sweet potatoes
hot herb bread *
avocado salad
sliced bananas with shredded coconut
coffee

A SIMPLE DINNER—I

Boeuf Luxembourg
noodles
cinnamon-flavored spiced apples slices
hot herb bread *
Salata Delphi *
dessert   coffee

A SIMPLE DINNER—II

fried chicken Anderson *
baked squash with orange filling *
hot herb bread *
your own green salad
dessert   coffee

Bibliography

The books listed below were consulted in the preparation of this book and are, for the most part, in the library of the author.

Apicius, The Roman Cookery Book, translated by Barbara Flower and Elizabeth Rosenbaum. London, George H. Harrap & Co., Ltd., 1958.

Banckes' Herbal. London, 1525; Boston, E. W. Hildreth, 1941.

Clarkson, Rosetta E., *Green Enchantment.* New York, The Macmillan Company, 1940.

—— *Magic Gardens.* New York, The Macmillan Company, 1939.

Coles, William, *The Art of Simpling.* London, 1657; Milford, Conn. (Mrs. R. E. Clarkson), 1938.

Coon, Nelson, *Using Plants for Healing.* New York, Hearthside Press, Inc., 1963.

Culpeper, Nicholas, *Complete Herbal.* London, 1684; London, Richard Evans, 1814.

Dawson, Thomas, *The Good Huswifes Jewell.* London, 1587.

Digby, Sir Kenelm, *Choice and Experimental Receipts in Physick and Chirurgery,* translated by George Hartman. London, 1668.

Dioscorides, *The Greek Herbal of Dioscorides,* translated by John Goodyer. London, 1655; New York, Hafner Publishing Co., 1959.

Doole, Louise Evans, *Herbs: How to Grow and Use Them.* New York, Sterling Publishing Co., Inc., 1962.

English Cookery Five Hundred Years Ago. London, 1849.

Estienne, Charles, *The Countrie Farme,* translated by Richard Surflet. London, 1600.

Evelyn, John, *Acetaria: A Discourse of Sallets.* London, 1699; New York, Brooklyn Botanic Garden, 1937.

Freeman, Margaret B., *Herbs for the Medieval Household.* New York, Metropolitan Museum of Art, 1943.

Gerard, John, *The Herbal.* London, 1597; London, Gerald Howe, Ltd., 1927.

Glasse, Hannah, *The Art of Cookery,* London, ca. 1750.

Grieve, Maud, *A Modern Herbal.* New York, Harcourt, Brace & Company, 1931.

Hemphill, Rosemary, *Fragrance and Flavour.* New York, Charles T. Branford Co., 1960.

Hewer, D. G., *Practical Herb Growing.* London, G. Bell & Sons, Ltd., 1941.

Hill, Sir John, *The British Herbal.* London, 1756.

Hogner, Dorothy Childs, *A Fresh Herb Platter.* New York, Doubleday & Co., 1961.

Hyll, Thomas, *The Gardener's Labyrinth.* London, 1577; Milford, Conn. (Mrs. R. E. Clarkson), 1939.

Jacob, Dorothy, *A Witch's Guide to Gardening.* New York, Taplinger Publishing Co., 1965.

Krutch, Joseph Wood, *Herbal.* New York, G. P. Putnam's Sons, 1965.

Langham, William, *The Garden of Health.* London, 1579.

Lawson, William, *The Countrie Houswifes Garden.* London, 1617; Herrin, Ill., Trovillion Private Press, 1948.

Leyel, Hilda Wauton (Mrs. C. F. Leyel), *Elixirs of Life.* London, Faber and Faber, Ltd., 1948.

——— *The Magic of Herbs.* New York, Harcourt, Brace & Co., 1926.

Loewenfeld, Claire, *Herb Gardening.* London, Charles T. Branford Co., 1965.

Markham, Gervase, *The English Hus-wife.* London, 1623.

Meager, Leonard, *The English Gardener.* London, 1699.

Meyer, Joseph E., *The Herbalist.* London, Charles Meyer, 1960.

Miloradovich, Milo, *The Home Garden Book of Herbs and Spices.* New York, Doubleday & Co., 1952.

Monardes, Nicholas, *De Simplicibus Medicamentis Ex Occidentali India Delatis Quorum in Medicina Usus Est.* Antwerp, 1574.

Muenscher, Walter C., and Rice, Myron A., *Garden Spice and Wild Pot-Herbs.* Ithaca, N.Y., Cornell University Press, 1955.

Murray, Margaret Alice, *The Witch-Cult in Western Europe.* London, Oxford University Press, 1921.

Parkinson, John, *Paradisi in sole paradisus terrestris,* or *A Garden of All Sorts of Pleasant Flowers.* London, 1629; London, Methuen & Co. Ltd., 1904.

Plat, Sir Hugh, *Delightes for Ladies.* London, 1609.

Ranson, Florence, *British Herbs.* Harmondsworth, England, Penguin Books, 1949.

Simmons, Adelma Grenier, *Herb Gardening in Five Seasons.* Princeton, N.J., D. Van Nostrand Co., Inc., 1964.

Smith, A. W., *A Gardener's Book of Plant Names*. New York, Harper & Row, 1963.

Sounin, Leonie de, *Magic in Herbs*. London, M. Barrows & Co., 1941.

Spencer, Edwin Rollin, *Just Weeds*. New York, Charles Scribner's Sons, 1940.

Street, Julian, *Wines*. New York, Alfred A. Knopf, Inc., 1933.

The Toilet of Flora. London, 1779; Milford, Conn. (Mrs. R. E. Clarkson), 1939.

Turner, William, *Turner's Herbal*. London, 1569.

Tusser, Thomas, *Five Hundreth Points of Good Husbandry*. London, 1573.

Walker, Winifred, *All the Plants of the Bible*. New York, Harper & Brothers, 1957.

Ward, Harold, *Herbal Manual*, London, L. N. Fowler & Co., Ltd., 1962.

Webster, Helen Noyes, *Herbs: How to Grow Them and How to Use Them*. New York, Ralph T. Hale & Co., 1939.

Index

277